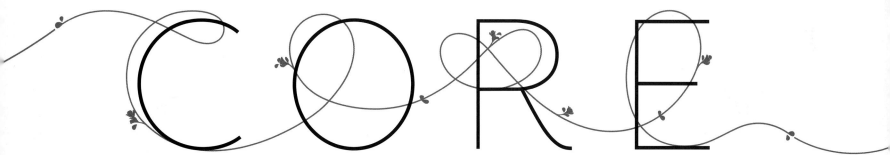

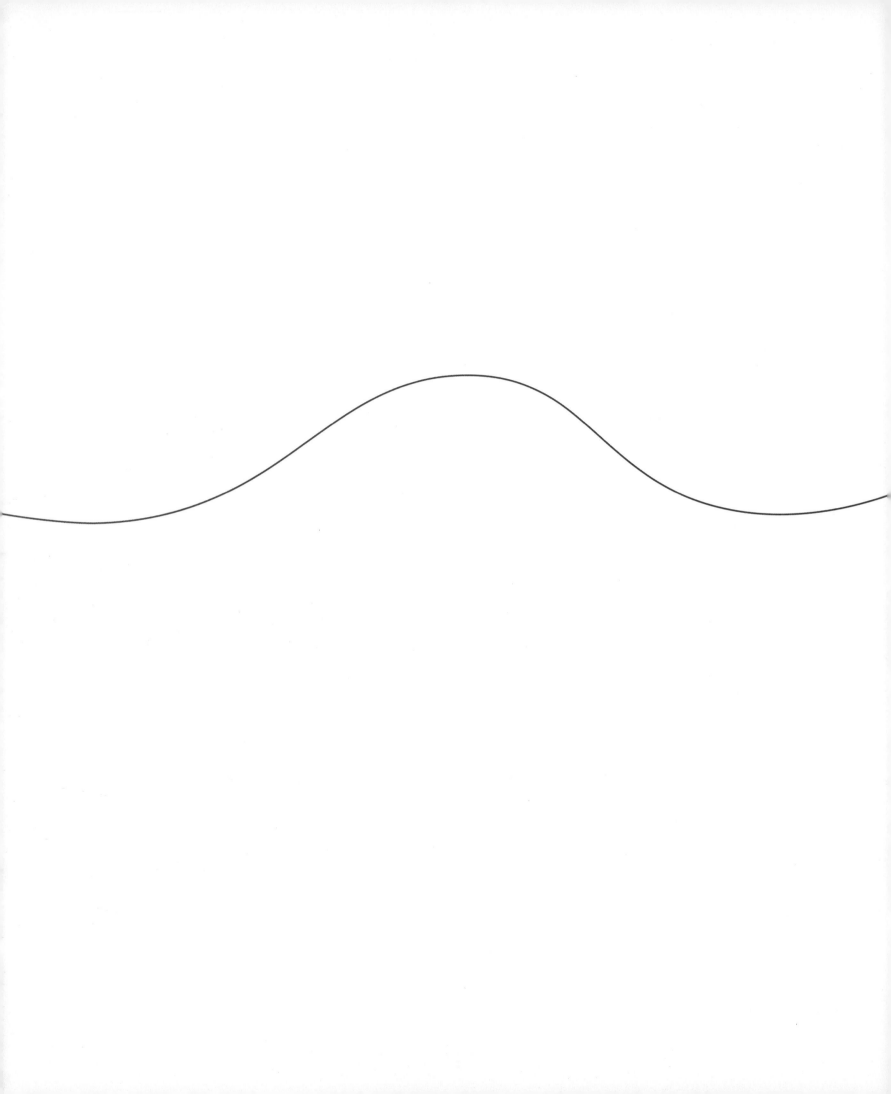

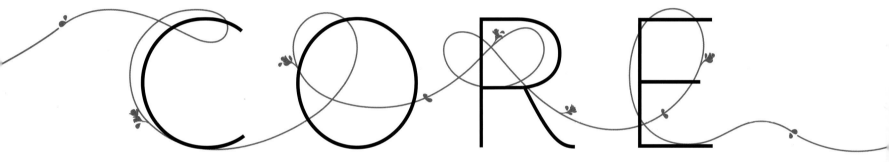

CORE

CLARE SMYTH

FOREWORD

In so many ways, Clare Smyth is one of the most talented chefs I have ever worked alongside. This woman is relentless, and in that pursuit of perfection, the exciting thing about Clare's demeanour is that she carries no passengers – she has a drive that cannot be bought or taught. But more than this, she has an understanding of finesse and style like few others; she cooks with attitude and personality, and that's rarer than you'd think.

When I was behind the pass at Restaurant Gordon Ramsay twenty years ago, we were the Manchester United of kitchens – we went to hell and back five days a week to keep our world-class standard. I loved raising the bar every single day, pushing my team to get better and better with each challenge. Clare was one of the very few chefs who not only met that bar, but soared right past it and came back asking for more. It was her hunger that set her apart: from joining us in 2002, to taking over the reins as head chef in 2007, to becoming chef-patron in 2012, right up to Core and beyond. As a lieutenant, I couldn't have asked for more: she was invaluable.

I'll never forget the first time I ate at Core. It was an emotional night. We'd brought some good friends with us, but I couldn't focus on entertaining them – all I had in my mind was the journey Clare had been on, which I could follow through her food. The flavours were rounded, the seasoning was on point and her dishes were so distinct and original. She has a near-unique ability to turn an idea into a plate of food without distorting her original vision, which is where I think her genius lies. To elevate a potato or a carrot in the way she does, with the critics circling you like sharks, takes serious skill and courage.

Restaurants spend ten, fifteen, twenty years chasing three Michelin stars. For Core to achieve that in under four years is remarkable, and totally deserved. I know she has our record at Royal Hospital Road – twenty-one years and counting – in her sights. But if there's one thing I want Clare to take from me, it's the value of passing on your knowledge and expertise. I want to see the next generation of young, homegrown chefs coming out of Core, trained and mentored by Clare, so that her restaurant becomes an epicentre of culinary talent. Core winning its third star brought my own career full-circle, like the seeds I'd sown had finally reached fruition; I'd love for Clare to experience the same with one of the chefs she has helped to succeed.

There are very few cooks in the world who'd be prepared to sacrifice themselves in order to achieve what Clare has, even though plenty will dream of her successes. She's the real deal. But let me assure you: behind the scenes, she sleeps with one eye open, and never, ever takes her foot off the gas.

GORDON RAMSAY

INTRODUCTION

If there is one single motivating power behind Clare Smyth, it is intensity. It's something she embodies, it's something she values and encourages in others; I don't think I have ever encountered someone, in a restaurant or elsewhere, so pursuant of perfection and exactitude. Over the last twenty years, Smyth has pursued the highest heights of *haute cuisine* with a single-mindedness that has stunned so many of the chefs she has worked alongside. Nothing but the best has ever been good enough. Not for her, not for her staff and not for the diners she has served.

Smyth is almost uniquely inured to the pressures of top-level restaurant cooking. Her CV forms a constellation of Michelin stars: a whole career spent in predominantly three-star kitchens, alongside some of the greatest luminaries to grace a stove. Long since accepting that there is no substitute for the value of hard work, Smyth took every opportunity to learn and improve, to work quicker and more precisely, with a spartan capacity for withstanding the pressure and perfectionism that drives elite kitchens. Every challenge was taken as a chance to strengthen and sharpen up; to work at the very pinnacle and excel.

Her restaurant, Core, set within an ornate townhouse in London's Notting Hill, opened in August 2017 and she has scarcely had a chance to look back since. Smyth's food is superlatively elegant, redefining modern British food in its own terms – a collection of stories about ingenuity, nostalgia, humour and craft, told across a series of courses. Core puts Britain's best foot forward, showcasing the country's most outstanding produce, all sourced from a tight-knit collective of trusted suppliers who, like the team in Smyth's restaurant, have spent their lives dedicated to excellence.

Front and back of house, Smyth has calibrated an extremely well-tuned gastronomic experience, led by colleagues she trusts and backs implicitly. Looking to bring a fresher, more welcoming, yet no less exacting approach to modern fine dining, Smyth instead places an emphasis on treating guests without pretension, making them feel as if they were sat in her home, with their every whim attended to. It is no surprise, in that case, that so many diners have fallen completely in love with Core – if the accolades do not speak for themselves, the dining room does, being packed out with as many regulars as new diners day and night.

Her list of personal achievements is a testament to the high esteem she is held in throughout the profession and beyond: Global Chef Ambassador of the Bocuse d'Or; World's Best Female Chef at the 2018 World's 50 Best awards; judge of both the Roux Scholarship and the National Chef of the Year awards; an MBE; and a doctorate from Queen's University Belfast for services to the hospitality industry. Not to mention, of course, being one of only twelve female chefs to have held three Michelin stars, and being just the second to hold them at two different restaurants – a record matched only by the mother of French gastronomy, Eugénie Brazier.

This relentless march to success has been a life's work for Smyth, whose dedication to showing instead of telling, working instead of boasting, has taken her to the pinnacle of the profession. It's intensity that drives you out of bed in the morning to get to the kitchen an hour before everyone else; it's intensity that takes you across the world, alone, to learn different ways of working and thinking; it's intensity, gnawing at you, that makes you bet on yourself, to trade a restaurant that you run for one that you own. If you want to get to the top, intensity can be a very good attribute indeed.

* * *

Picking up her first job at twelve at her neighbourhood restaurant in Bushmills, Northern Ireland – a coastal village more renowned for its whiskey distillery than for food – Clare Smyth was, initially, interested in other careers and pursuits. 'At first, I didn't think cooking was a great career to go into,' says Smyth. 'I was more interested in being a doctor or a lawyer or something.' Smyth continued working at local restaurants intermittently, through summer holidays and occasional weekends, until she was fifteen. It was then that she picked up a copy of Anton Mosimann's *Cuisine à la Carte*, being drawn in by the artfully presented plate on the cover; when she started to read its contents, her eyes were opened to the idea of food as creative expression, and an obsession began.

At first, she asked for more responsibility in the neighbourhood restaurant, until she turned sixteen and could dedicate herself fully to cooking. She left home and crossed the Irish Sea as quickly as she could to attend catering college in Portsmouth. By this point, her desire for learning – both from books and on the job – was so fevered that catering college became merely a formality: she whizzed through the course with total ease, and attended classes only when she needed to, often choosing to go and work in a kitchen instead.

After her apprenticeships, she moved to London, straight into a commis chef position at the impossibly stylish Bibendum in South Kensington. It was here that she received an education in the best products money could buy: Périgord truffles, San Marzano tomatoes, Bresse chickens, Whitstable oysters. 'Wherever the best produce was, we'd fly it in,' she says. 'I loved the restaurant, I loved the food – it was probably the best place I could've worked at the time.' Not too far away from the restaurant was Books for Cooks in Notting Hill, where Smyth spent the rest of her time devouring every cookbook she could get her hands on.

In the itinerant manner of a young chef, Smyth moved from South Kensington to Cornwall, to help open the St. Enodoc Hotel as its sous chef, then spent six months working for a catering company in Australia at the turn of the millennium, before returning to the Cornish hotel to take over as head chef. 'I wasn't any good as a head chef then, I was too young,' she says. 'I was comfortable, but I wasn't excelling as I wanted.' To reach that standard, Smyth used her days off to stage at some of Britain's best restaurants: with Michael Caines at Gidleigh Park; with Heston Blumenthal at The Fat Duck; with Michel Roux at The Waterside Inn.

Her biggest break came when she arrived at Restaurant Gordon Ramsay for the first time, six months after they had secured their third star, and at a time when Ramsay's media profile was skyrocketing. Ramsay didn't think she'd last a week – and to be fair, most of the staff didn't, with the kitchen being known for its rancorous, febrile atmosphere the world over. She survived the week, and the year, and the year after that, but it was hard. 'The entire brigade lived off nothing more than four hours' sleep a night and adrenaline. We were like the SAS of kitchens – an elite squadron able to handle any task that came our way.'

Despite the long hours and a bruising kitchen atmosphere, Smyth persevered, determined to show those around her that she could withstand anything thrown at her. When she had learned all that she could at Royal Hospital Road, she was held in such high regard that she could open any door she chose, armed with a glowing recommendation from Ramsay. Looking to broaden her gastronomic horizons, Smyth sought to learn under two of the world's greatest chefs, Thomas Keller and Alain Ducasse, before plotting the next move in her career.

First, she spent a week in both of Keller's restaurants: Per Se in New York, and The French Laundry in Yountville, California. 'Keller's restaurants worked in shifts, so some staff would work from 5.30 a.m. to midday; others would work midday to 6 p.m., and so on,' she says. 'I'd arrive for the first shift, and leave with the last, I was that eager to take all that I could from it.'

With Ramsay's encouragement, Smyth turned towards an education in the classical French style; the foundations of *haute cuisine* that underpinned Western fine-dining for over a century. And to learn this, there was no greater establishment than Le Louis XV in Monaco, Ducasse's flagship, which has held its three Michelin stars since 1990. When she first applied, they sent her away to learn French before she could work in their kitchen; naturally, she took a private chef's job on the French Riviera, earned the money for intensive schooling, and returned to the restaurant suitably fluent for kitchen life.

Ducasse's kitchen was, in its organisation, as rigid and military as one of Escoffier's kitchens a century prior. All dishes were cooked *à la minute* – that is, to order, every single time, with minimal cooked prep-work prior. As such, the brigade needed everything to hand at a moment's notice. Cooking was a constant, and timings were extremely delicate: one overcooked fillet could knock the entire kitchen equilibrium out of balance. The produce was truly the finest that money could buy – an honour to cook with, but equally a genuine travesty to waste. As such, Le Louis XV's kitchen had its own unique form of pressure; every aspect of it was elite. And yet, despite arriving in the kitchen as a 25-year-old with a rudimentary grasp of the French language, Smyth soon established herself as one of the old master's brightest and most enthusiastic pupils.

* * *

Watching Clare Smyth in the kitchen at Core (as you can do with ease, through the restaurant's glass partition) you see her personality and values on display. Staying calm, respectful, but absolutely in command, she stands practically fixed to the spot by the corner of the pass; the final barrier between kitchen and dining room. As plates arrive in front of her, she checks and sends on, checks and sends on, checks and sends on. If there's anything that needs fixing, she points it out politely but firmly, and the kitchen gets to work on correcting it.

This is a demonstration of the quiet, efficient style that she cultivated at Royal Hospital Road, after Gordon Ramsay asked her to return from Monaco to be his head chef in 2007. At first, feeling under pressure to perform from the media, her peers, and the kitchen team she was returning to, she returned as – in her words – 'too single-minded'. 'That wasn't who I was, but it was how I was trained,' she says. 'I had to go back in and put a marker down, or others wouldn't think I was strong enough to be in charge.' Gradually, however, with Ramsay's encouragement, Smyth grew into the role and made it her own. Her first task was to change the kitchen culture, moving away from the hire-and-fire cycles that typified life at the top level for so long by developing a far more attentive way with her staff.

Along with evolving the kitchen culture, Smyth was also able to hone her own style and imprint it on the menu at Royal Hospital Road, although not abruptly. 'Restaurants like that have a strong DNA that you need to respect,' she says. 'After all, that's why they held their stars, and that's why diners waited months to eat there. Change has to be gentle, taking the guests with you bit by bit.' Ramsay staples like his trademark lobster ravioli dish remained, but found company alongside some of Smyth's signatures, which were developed upon her return.

Influenced by the gentle, natural cooking of Alain Ducasse, Smyth brought to the menu delicate poached fish fillets and sea vegetable nages; leeks layered with thick slices of truffle and wrapped in on themselves like a roly-poly. She revived and reinvented classics from her first spell at the restaurant, too, like the decadent foie gras and duck confit terrine. Perhaps her most iconic signature dish, however, was the restaurant's trademark dessert, the Lemonade parfait: an artful balance of confit lemon, yogurt and honey that delighted her diners again and again.

It did, however, take leaving Restaurant Gordon Ramsay and opening Core for Smyth to fully realize her culinary identity – not least for the fact that she had to leave a lot of her signature dishes on her old restaurant's menu. While this was frustrating in some senses (it was particularly hard to leave the Lemonade parfait behind, so she was moved to reinvent it for Core), it was also immensely liberating, and allowed Smyth to cultivate a far more personal style, which spoke to her heritage and her passion for British produce.

With full control over her own space, Smyth was also able to translate her more personal style into the restaurant's design and layout. Core is full of little touches and nods to Clare's loves or Britain's past: copies of Fernand Point's *Ma Gastronomie*; carafes full of fine Cognac or Somerset brandy; flowers cut and arranged just so. Her exacting eye and uncompromising attitude to quality

can be felt across every glance. It is an approach built from thoughtfulness and consideration – her aim is to make guests feel totally at ease, able to enjoy great food, great wine and great company in equal measure.

* * *

To a guest, the attention to detail succeeds as intended. Smyth is a rare chef at her level, who truly wants her food to be approachable to every guest; there's little in the way of pushing the envelope for its own sake, or putting out a course that may divide the dining room. From the first amuse-bouche to the dregs of your digestif, a dinner at Core impresses you over and over again. The food is delicate, elegant, smart, funny, luxurious and addictive – you return your plate after each course with an implacable sense that you have one more bite left in you, if the kitchen would be kind enough to give you it. More often than not, you'll have to return to try those dishes again, as many do.

It takes an extraordinary amount of effort to deliver a dinner as calm and accommodating as Core's. Every eventuality needs to be prepared for, from a coconut allergy to a guest's preference for cold milk in their Earl Grey tea. Before every service is a staff meeting, led by Smyth and her restaurant director, Rob Rose, where the team talks about the service before, what they could improve and how they're going to do so.

None of this would be possible without extremely thorough training, but if staff can make it at Core, Smyth argues, they can make it anywhere. 'We try to teach all of our team how to actually run a restaurant like a business, rather than just training them in their one specific field,' she says. 'We want them to master as many aspects as they can, so that if they leave us to open something of their own, they'll have the tools to do so.'

Many of Smyth's team have been at Core since opening night, or at the very least the first year – a testament to the loyalty and hard work that she commands. It's hard to get in, but those that do are offered jobs because Smyth and her senior team are confident that the new hire will fit into their team dynamic. 'We're a collection of individuals. We have the jokers in the team, the sensitive souls who listen to people's problems, the trailblazers who set the benchmark for their stations. Everybody plays a role.'

Core's story is still only emerging. So, too, is Clare Smyth's: she has moved from prodigy to protégé, and now to the rarefied tier of bona fide culinary giants. Core's first sister restaurant, Oncore, opened in November 2021 on the other side of the world, in Sydney, on the same harbour where Smyth saw in the millennium. As much as anything else, Smyth viewed Oncore as an opportunity to reward staff who were ready, after years of training, to step up and lead. 'I couldn't just give these guys away to another restaurant, that'd be giving away the gift of a lifetime,' she says. 'But if we can help one set of staff move up with Oncore, that frees up another set of staff to take their next step here in London.'

Both Smyth and Ramsay take pleasure from the fact that Core earned its three Michelin stars for the first time in the same year that Restaurant Gordon Ramsay maintained them for their twentieth year. Smyth wants twenty years, and more. 'I run four times a week to stay fit, on top of everything else, because I want to stay focused on this restaurant,' she says. 'I don't ever want to burn out, or step aside, or find myself too far away from here. In forty years' time, I still want to be here, running the pass from time to time, with three stars on the door outside, because this restaurant is who I am, and everything I have worked towards.' There is nothing to suggest that Clare Smyth will be slowing down any time soon.

KIERAN MORRIS

THE THREE-STAR KITCHEN

For the better part of two decades, I've worked in three-Michelin-star kitchens – half of that time spent in a senior position. From Restaurant Gordon Ramsay and Le Louis XV, to stages in some of the world's most daring and celebrated restaurants, I would say that, at this point in my career, I understand what it takes to earn three Michelin stars, and what it means to maintain them. In five words: everything perfect, all the time.

My first real exposure to the three-star kitchen came at Restaurant Gordon Ramsay, which I joined in 2002 – its legendary full-throttle heyday, when Gordon was still at the pass. It was the hardest, hottest, fastest and most turbulent kitchen on the planet. Shifts were merciless. We stood for military discipline and surgical precision in everything that we did, and if you slipped from those standards, you were gone – and somebody else would be waiting to take your job. Kitchen life was testosterone-fuelled, with dozens of chefs jostling for Gordon's attention. It wasn't for everyone, but I knew it was for me, because I wanted to be the best, and I refused to let anything distract me from that aim.

Gordon was, and still is, a brilliant mentor. He was always fair, even if he was very blunt about it – he just wanted perfection. My first aim had been to survive one year. When that was over, I challenged myself to survive another. One night, at the start of service, Gordon told the kitchen that he wouldn't be looking after the pass tonight because he was taking the head chef out for a meeting. He nominated me to take his place, and I was stunned. 'Really?' I asked, in disbelief. 'Yes, really,' he replied. 'If you can't do it now, you'll never be able to.' And he was right: after all that training, I did know how, and I needed to step up when it was asked of me.

When I wanted to develop myself further, I left Restaurant Gordon Ramsay for Alain Ducasse's flagship restaurant in Monte Carlo, Le Louis XV – a restaurant so luxurious that it practically ran without a budget. I have, to this day, never seen a kitchen so precise and meticulous. From the moment I first looked over their pass to watch the team at work, I knew I had found the perfect place to improve myself. They worked in total harmony, cooking everything *à la minute* without a single misstep – you couldn't misstep, or you'd knock everybody out of place. It was a new kind of pressure with which to refine my style and strengthen my stamina, with the highest-quality produce I had ever experienced. For as much as it was a challenge, it was equally a privilege.

After two years in Monaco, Gordon asked me to come back to London and head up the brigade at Royal Hospital Road, entrusting me with his three Michelin stars. The papers were quick to note that I was the first female chef in Britain to hold those stars – I was more preoccupied with not being the first female chef to lose them. But it was a case of coming back with confidence, and rallying the kitchen around my direction. Once that was secured, we started the process of evolving: changing the kitchen culture, modernizing the menu, refining things further so we didn't grow stagnant. When you're at this level, standing still is as good as moving backwards. You can't just defend your three stars and hope to cling on to them; every year, you have to justify keeping them over and over again, and for that, you need to keep improving.

Leaving that world to open Core was a bit of a culture shock. I had only five staff who had worked with me before and the other thirty-five were new, so only a small percentage of the starting team knew the standards that I expected. The first few months were rough; to me, it felt like I'd plummeted from the top to the very bottom. One night, at the end of a bad service, I sat six of them down around a table and told them honestly: 'This isn't good enough. I haven't worked my whole life for this to be the end result. We need to think about who we are and where we want to be.' They knew the names of the chefs who had trained through the kitchen at Royal Hospital Road and who had gone on to better things, restaurants of their own. They knew the level we aspired to, and I told them in no uncertain terms that now was the time to bed in and get this right. If they wanted to turn our kitchen into a three-star kitchen, just like all the other famous restaurants they had read about and idolized, they would have to reach that standard: everything perfect, all the time. After three years, we got there.

CORE

TEAM &

VALUES

A restaurant lives and dies on the strength of its brigade. To be at the top level – where we aspire to stay – you need a team of all-stars, each of whom are dedicated, trustworthy and talented. Building this team takes time; it takes leadership and reflection; it takes training; and it takes failing and recovering. Beyond all else, it takes hard work and an attitude that's fixed on succeeding and improving, never content with standing still or doing just enough.

To work at Core, you need to hold yourself and your profession to the highest of standards. Restaurants of our calibre can't have off-nights, not when diners have waited and waited for a seat at our table. We simultaneously offer two tasting menus and à la carte options. As a result, our kitchen is a busy place. Your station stays active until closing time, every time. You're relying on everyone around you to stay at the same pace you're working at, and that's a lot easier to do when you have real trust in those working around you.

It's no less challenging for the front-of-house team; the fate of service is as much in their hands as the kitchen's, and as the smiling face of the restaurant to our diners, they need to work with a greater sense of calmness and ease. Thankfully, we're blessed to have an incredibly well-drilled and professional team in charge of the dining room, all of whom have the charm and personality to keep things ticking over smoothly.

Sommeliers are a breed of their own. They study, work hard and never stop looking to improve – they're serious professionals, every bit as integral to our team as front or back of house. You can see the results of their work in our wine list, which is held to the same standards as everything else in the restaurant. We love fine wines, but they have to be approachable, fun and there for anyone to pick from – that's where our sommeliers step in and deliver. Our sommeliers take great care in making sure that all tastes and preferences are catered for with truly special bottles. To be great, you need great food, great wine and great service, all as dedicated as each another.

Core's foundation began as me, our restaurant director, Rob Rose, and our head chef, Jonny Bone: we started the restaurant together, and to this day they are as important to me as my left and right arms. I trust them implicitly. For ten years Rob was part of the front-of-house team at Restaurant Gordon Ramsay – he joined specifically to work with the legendary maître d', Jean-Claude Breton, and learned almost everything there is to know about hospitality in the process.

Jonny worked with me at Royal Hospital Road, and his rise through the kitchen was similar to mine. He started off as a commis chef and climbed up the ladder before leaving for France after three and a half years. Much like me, he took so much from his time in France, falling in love with the produce and the artisans behind it. When it came to planning Core, I knew Jonny would be ready for the head chef role.

I'm in near-constant dialogue with Rob and Jonny each and every day, talking about services past, services ahead of us, dish ideas, staff performance, supplier updates. Our other two 'heads' – Gareth Ferreira, our head sommelier, and Antonio Acquaviva, our head of development – are equally integral, pushing themselves and the restaurant forward with relentless creativity. Gareth is a fount of knowledge when it comes to wine, and yet he never, ever stops studying, working tirelessly to keep our wine list exciting and engaging to all.

Antonio serves two very important functions in our kitchen: for service, he's executive sous chef, responsible for patrolling and coordinating the kitchen sections on Jonny's behalf. Alongside this role, Antonio is the point-man when it comes to turning a dish idea into a reality, something that his palate and his patience make him suited for.

Handling the dining room alongside Rob, we have our restaurant manager, Tiago Correia, and our assistant manager, Marion Pépin – two of the most loyal individuals I have ever encountered in our profession.

Taking care of nearly everything else is our operations manager, Michal Jankowski – or, as we call him, Mikey. Mikey started off at Restaurant Gordon Ramsay as a commis waiter, and I've watched him work his way up to where he is today with remarkable tenacity. He's an amazing character, incredibly intelligent, and he has an unstinting can-do attitude towards just about anything.

We are so lucky to have this senior team, and luckier still to have an entire generation of staff being mentored and trained by them, ready to step up when the moment calls for them to do so. Through this, we can make sure that our restaurant, and the values we stand for within our profession, can be maintained for years to come.

24 CORE

BRITISH

FINE

DINING

Developing a personal style takes years and years of preparation and self-analysis. When I first began to plan out what Core would be, I had to ask myself who I was, what my style really is, and why it's distinct. In short, I'm a British chef who is passionate about offering the very best of hospitality, and has trained and been moulded by classical French *haute cuisine*. For fifteen years, I'd cooked in that style, but I wanted Core to embody our country's *haute cuisine*, where we are in the world and what we identify with: British fine dining.

The first test, for me, was to demonstrate that this style could be achieved without an excessive reliance on imported luxury ingredients. Over the course of my career, I have been so lucky to work with some of the rarest, purest, most expensive products money can buy. As a result, I can appreciate a foie gras torchon or a Breton lobster as much as anyone. But those items can be found on menus all across the world. We don't disavow those amazing products, of course, but we don't prioritize them above all else. Treated with skill and attention by both producer and chef, we believe that an onion or an artichoke can be every bit as satisfying and luxurious as a piece of A5 beef.

If you search hard enough, and look for people who care about what they do, you can find world-class produce up and down the British Isles. The fact that we ship our Scottish langoustines all over the world without taking the time to enjoy them ourselves is saddening – they're on our doorstep! Core's conception of British Fine Dining is one that champions what our country has to offer.

More than this, however, we want British Fine Dining to relate to our country's rich and diverse culinary history; our sense of nostalgia, cultural memory and shared experiences. A great many of our dishes are explicit plays towards those warm feelings of remembrance: the salt and vinegar crisps atop the 'Potato and roe' (p. 86); the 'Beef and oyster' (p. 120) steeped in centuries of tradition; the indulgent 'Core-teser' (p. 140). Our menu should be more than a succession of

delicious dishes – we want to tell a story of Britain that should feel both familiar and original. Whether you've flown across continents to eat here or walked five minutes from your home, we want to leave you with a greater appreciation of what British produce can be.

Beyond that, we want to work imaginatively within the British food system, collaborating with our suppliers to find new uses for what they grow and produce. By maintaining strong, trusting relationships with the suppliers, producers and farmers we work with, we are able to support them through harder times, and in turn, they allow us to improve our own working methods, as we adapt to nature's bounty through what they're able to offer us. Whether it's using shrimp bycatch to enrich a butter sauce, pickling mini cucumbers that had originally been grown for their flowers, or using undersized egg yolks to top our tartlets, we feel the benefit of this dynamic and empathetic approach to nature, and our suppliers are better for it, too.

Central to our style and philosophy – and, in fact, our entire way of working – is a constant process of improvement and refinement. We're proud of the fact that we have classic dishes that we served on opening night and still serve today. We know those dishes intimately, and we've improved them with every service. You cannot jump straight to perfection, no matter how good a chef or a cook you are. You need to tweak, tweak and tweak again, until that dish is flawless night after night with no exceptions, even as nature changes what you work with each and every day.

We put the work in because we want to be, and to offer our guests, the very best; only through total dedication can we know that we have paid the proper respect to the produce we use and the diners we serve. We believe that British food and produce, treated with care and skill, can stand alongside any of the great cuisines of the world, and we want to celebrate it with pride.

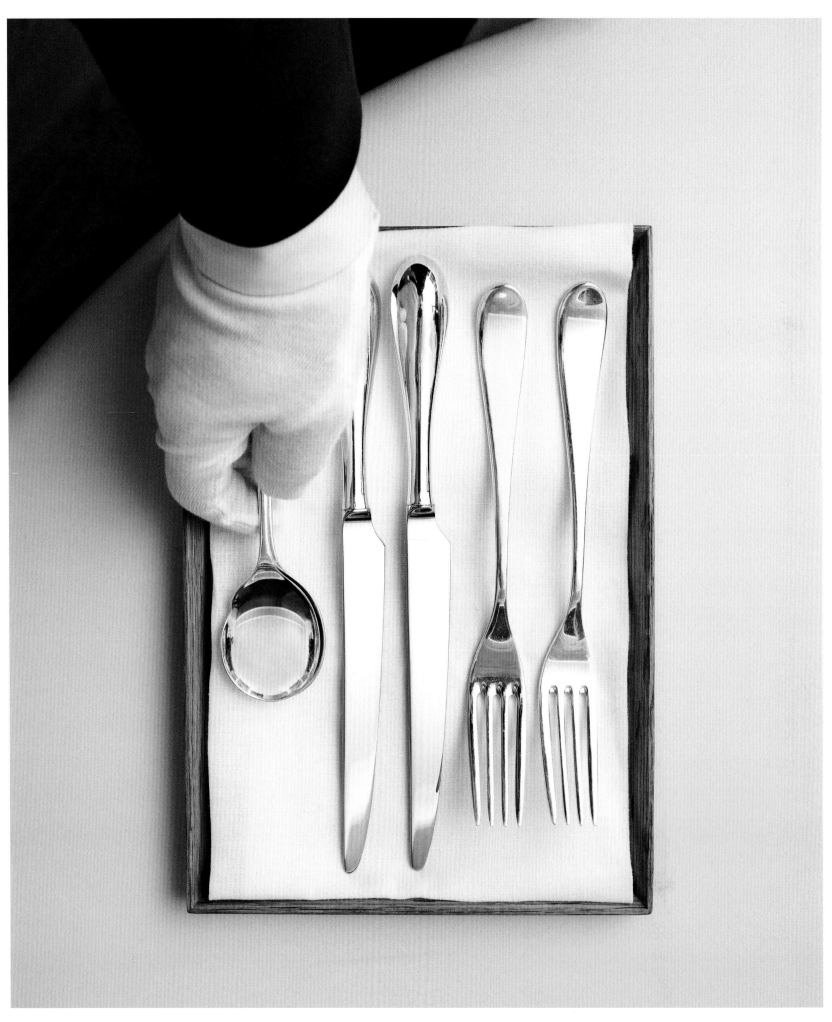

OUR PRODUCERS, SUPPLIERS & GROWERS

In the life cycle of, say, a Charlotte potato or a Herdwick lamb, we arrive at the end. Our products have spent their lives under soil, growing from seedlings; or on mountaintops, grazing; or clung to reefs at the mercy of the tide. Above ground, they have custodians – those who know every last detail of their short but eventful lives. When those ingredients reach a certain point where they can grow and develop no further, those same custodians remove them from nature's grasp and provide them to us. Our role as chefs is solely to provide the finishing touches.

Since we have these experts to hand, we make sure that every member of our restaurant team, front and back of house, is educated in what makes our produce so special. Every Wednesday afternoon is dedicated to training and we'll often either have suppliers teaching our team, or we'll head on down to the farms ourselves so we can get to know their operations first-hand. These products are themselves a lifetime's work for our suppliers – they know all there is to know about what they grow. We are lucky to learn from their experiences, and as we do so, we become not only better chefs, but more sensitive and appreciative individuals.

In turn, we can be of benefit to our team of suppliers in unexpected ways. As a kitchen, we have a militant contempt for waste: waste is the greatest insult to Mother Nature, and we have a responsibility to eliminate it everywhere we can. When we visit our suppliers, we are often able to use our chefs' perspective on the waste they would otherwise dispose of. A shrimper in Morecambe has no use for a bucket full of shells after a day spent peeling – but we do, and we'll buy them. We get a new product to enhance our dishes, the fisherman profits from what he'd otherwise throw away and nothing is then left to waste.

We believe that this tight-knit, collaborative dynamic has the power to drive change in our profession. We are so lucky in this country to still have small producers forming the patchwork of our national food system – they are the foundation of our culinary culture. The trust and support goes both ways: they want to offer up the very best ingredients they can produce and we want to see their businesses thrive, and their hard work given the respect that it's owed. It's this lifelong friendship, synergy and respect that serves as the platform for all that we do.

INFORMAL

LUXURY

At Core, we have very consciously developed a style that's designed to welcome and embrace our guests. We call it 'informal luxury', and it's this ethos that guides our diners' experience from the second they walk up our steps to the moment they depart. Firstly, we want people to feel welcome and comfortable: there's no dress code, no pretension and certainly no exclusion. In turn, we won't hide from you, or stand apart from you – we will always take the time to greet you as you pass the kitchen and wave goodbye as you leave.

We define ourselves by our openness. The only thing separating the kitchen from the dining room is a wall of glass, through which you can see our service and the way we treat one another. Our colour scheme symbolizes the two forces that have shaped my life: the green of nature and the copper of traditional French cookware. The books on our shelves are the ones I learned from as I trained; the art on our walls, all produced by British artists, are the pieces that resonated most with me. Our name, Core, came to me in the middle of the night like all of my best ideas, and fits the aim of our restaurant perfectly: to begin as a planted seed, full of potential, and to grow and grow into something new, with the values we began with still at our heart.

We're a British restaurant, and we're proud of it. This is on display in our food, of course, but there are so many more craftspeople in this country that deserve to be celebrated and championed. Our china comes from Royal Crown Derby, who have produced chinaware in the British Midlands for nearly 300 years. All of our silverware comes from a family business called Carrs – based in the UK's Steel City, Sheffield – which originally started its life as an outlet for a factory worker to craft silver jewellery in his garage. We source our woodware from County Tyrone, back home in Northern Ireland, from a virtuoso carpenter named Patrick Walsh – he taught himself the craft of wood carving while working in construction, and now dedicates himself to creating beautiful pieces of all shapes and sizes, carved from the trees he finds around him.

Our relationship with these craftspeople helps enable them to keep producing things in the traditional way, and passing those methods to the next generation, so that their products aren't superseded by ones made by cheaper, lower-quality manufacturers.

It is through this that we can make our ethos of informal luxury something that's felt and experienced by our diners – our chinaware, silverware, tables and chairs form part of the story that we're trying to tell through our food. Not only that, but they are all beautiful objects in themselves, which you engage with time and again through your meal. Great wine is greater in the right glass; a dish can be so much more exciting and enjoyable on a plate that was designed with it in mind.

Things haven't always been this way, although it has always been our intention. When we opened, we put the majority of our focus into the kitchen, to create a world-class working space where our chefs could thrive and our food could excel. We didn't have the biggest budget, so we had to be patient; our waiter stations were made of MDF and our tables were bare and bought in. But over time, whenever we had the money, we invested it in ourselves. We were able to replace the old wooden tables with bespoke British leather ones, with chairs to match. We've installed a bakery for our bread, and switched out nearly every piece of furniture so that every item speaks to our identity, and the message of craft and care that we want to convey to our diners.

We are Core, and when you enter our restaurant, you can see us for who we are and what we care about. We celebrate our individuality, and yours.

RECIPES

JELLIED EEL
TOASTED SEAWEED
AND MALT VINEGAR

Some of our guests have travelled from all over the world to visit London, and so we like to open their meal at Core with one of the city's most storied dishes: the East End classic, jellied eels. Of course, jellied eels are a bit of a historical curio nowadays, but they're an indivisible part of the capital's culinary heritage, and a rite of passage for anyone looking to experience a bite of 'old London'. For years, eels swam in the River Thames, and were snatched up in the hundreds and thousands to feed hungry city-dwellers in the nineteenth and early-twentieth centuries. Eel consumption was so popular in the capital that one of the islands on the Thames, which housed a tavern famous for selling them, became known as Eel Pie Island – a name it holds to this day.

We start with a tartlet case made with toasted seaweed, for that opening hit of salinity, and fill it with the smoked eel cream, cubes of parsley jelly and a meaty chunk of Devonshire eel on top. At the table, we spray the tart with malt vinegar that we've infused with the eel bones, so you get both the flavour and the aroma of a proper East End eel shop.

'CAVIAR SANDWICH'

Caviar is the archetype of luxury, and a staple in high-end restaurants like ours. I love caviar, and I love it with all of its traditional garnishes: chopped egg yolks, chopped egg whites, crème fraîche, minced shallot, all on top of a featherlight blini. It really doesn't get any better. But it can be a messy affair, and it's hard to achieve the right balance of everything – if you've got good caviar, you don't want to drown it out, and you certainly don't want to spill it. I wanted to create the perfect effortless bite, with everything balanced just so, and from this quest we came up with the 'caviar sandwich'. Between layers of buckwheat crêpe, we build up each component tier by tier, with an extra touch of puffed buckwheat for a note of nuttiness, before spooning over a generous helping of caviar.

'CFC'
CORE FRIED CHICKEN AND CAVIAR

There's a fine balance to developing new dishes. Sometimes, your focus can be too squarely set on refinement, polishing things up and smoothing rough edges. Over time, we've learned that if we want to connect with our sense of nostalgia, we need to meet it where it is – and in the case of our 'CFC', this meant harking back to the spicy, juicy, so-wrong-it's-right fried chicken that so many of us know.

We originally developed this as a canapé for a very special event, and the response was so overwhelming that we felt we should put it on our menu, too. What makes our fried chicken so good is the quality of our spices, sourced from our supplier, Ren Patel, who imports them in their rawest, purest state. We kept adjusting our mix, over and over again, until we got close to another famous 'proprietary spice blend', and at Core, we serve it with an extra measure of caviar.

'TFC'
TRUFFLE FRIED CHICKEN

In the autumn, we switch our fried chicken up a little bit to fit with the season, toning down the paprika and cayenne pepper for Parmesan, oregano and heaps of fresh black truffle. It's decadent, comforting and yet still familiar.

CORE 'CAESAR SALAD'

We'd been growing these beautiful, minuscule Little Gem lettuces in our courtyard herb garden, and they looked so delicate that we thought to serve them whole; as a salad course, yet still in their natural form. We make a Caesar 'soil' from crumbled bacon, anchovies and Parmesan, and compress the lettuce heads in vinaigrette so that they absorb its flavours without going limp. To serve, we 'plant' the head, root attached, into the soil, and dot it with flowers, chives and a pinch of the crumb. When it arrives at the table, we snip it from the root and pull it from the soil, presented like it came straight from the earth – an elegant, fresh and natural mouthful.

A lot of people wonder how the team at Core really eat on a day-to-day basis. For us, it's salads like these: we're big fans of salad. Jonny, our head chef, can't go a day without one. So we wanted to capture, in one bite, the ideal palate cleanser that celebrates the salads we turn towards time after time.

CRISPY SMOKED CHICKEN WING
BEER, HONEY, LEMON AND THYME

For our wings, we make use of a little-known yet very traditional cut from our birds: the manchon, the fatty drumette from the first part of the wing that is usually sacrificed or ignored in pursuit of the breast or leg, but that holds so much flavour and tenderness in just a couple of bites.

CRISPY SMOKED DUCK WING
BURNT ORANGE AND SPICES

We switch our wings around seasonally: lighter, sweeter chicken in the warmer months, and the richer duck when winter creeps in and the season calls for a deeper, darker flavour profile. Sticky, sweet, herbaceous and savoury – they're unforgettably good, and you'll want more than one.

CHICKEN LIVER PARFAIT
SMOKED DUCK AND MADEIRA

When I first started working at Restaurant Gordon Ramsay in 2002, they had a version of this on the menu: a terrine layered with duck confit, foie gras and air-dried smoked duck ham. I'd never experienced food so luxurious, and I just found it so beautiful – I adored it. When I came back from Le Louis XV to be Gordon's head chef in 2007, I put a version of it back on the menu, and it's been part of my repertoire since then. I've always loved it, and I feel a sense of connection to it. Now, at Core, we just serve it as a sumptuous one-biter.

SAUSAGE IN BRIOCHE

The traditional sausage in brioche is a Lyonnaise classic; something you'd eat on the cobbly terrace of an old-school *bouchon* on a sunny afternoon. But I wanted to do a version that called two familiar British classics to mind – the sausage roll and the picnic-in-the-park hot dog. For the meat itself, we sourced a smoked summer sausage from a farmer and sausage-maker from Wales who has spent years breeding the ultimate pig for charcuterie: the result is a sausage with a pleasing bite and firmness – almost approaching a frankfurter. We dot the sliced sausage roll with finely diced cornichons and a few sprigs of dill to reinforce the gherkin flavour. Encased in the sweet, buttery brioche, it becomes something really comforting and familiar.

CORE GOUGÈRES

To me, nothing says hospitality like a warm gougère. When I was working for Alain Ducasse in Monte Carlo, our kitchen brigade was invited to attend the Bocuse d'Or in Lyon – fine dining's most prestigious competition. For a group of young chefs like us, it was a thrilling, overwhelming experience; giants of international gastronomy, whose cookbooks we had studied and studied, strolling past us so casually in France's culinary capital. It was hard not to be starstruck.

On a freezing lunchtime, we took a trip out of the city to visit Restaurant Paul Bocuse – not even to eat, just to take pictures, because we couldn't afford to go in. A staff member noticed us outside just before the beginning of service, and asked where we had come from. When we told them that we were with Alain Ducasse, they invited us in to the bar for a glass of champagne and a warm gougère, and it was perfect. In that moment, from that temple of *haute cuisine*, I learned a fundamental lesson about hospitality and what it should stand for: at its purest and best, it's an act of giving; it should be selfless.

We've listed eight filled gougères here, but the possibilities are endless. They're the perfect vessel for any combination in any season.

ASPARAGUS GOUGÈRES
CAVIAR GOUGÈRES

CHEESE AND ONION GOUGÈRES
PUMPKIN GOUGÈRES

BLACK TRUFFLE GOUGÈRES
PEA AND MINT GOUGÈRES

BLACK OLIVE GOUGÈRES
TOMATO AND BASIL GOUGÈRES

ISLE OF HARRIS SCALLOP TARTARE
SEA VEGETABLE CONSOMMÉ

While other dishes may have more intricate components or methods, this one adheres to one guiding principle: buy something beautiful and leave it alone. We're lucky to serve this ingredient, and treat it with that respect.

Our scallops come from the Isle of Harris, way up in the Outer Hebrides on the western Scottish coast. We work with divers from Keltic Seafare, some of whom have been diving for scallops in these waters for well over thirty years: they have explored every reef and seabed hundreds of times over, and know exactly where to look. These divers work by scuba come rain, wind or shine, seeking out the very finest scallops to bring to the surface – they never pick ones younger than four years old, but we ask for the largest ones, which can be anything from eight to ten years old or upwards. We have enormous respect for the work of these divers and the efforts they go to in order to provide us with this amazing product. It is that respect that informs our approach to the final dish.

We couldn't talk about scallops without talking about Bernie, Keltic's delivery man. He's an unsung hero of the London restaurant trade, a born and bred Londoner, and a familiar face to countless kitchens all over the capital. I've worked with Bernie since the beginning of my time at Royal Hospital Road, and he's been a constant figure ever since, always on hand with a smile and a joke – always a new joke every day! It's hard to overstate the importance of characters like Bernie; he plays such a vital role in making sure that we have what we need, when we need it, at its very freshest and best. We couldn't do what we do without his hard work, and the work of so many others.

SCOTTISH LANGOUSTINE AND WASABI PEA
ROSE GERANIUM, ALMOND

We have beautiful langoustines in Britain – we ship them all over the world from the Scottish coasts, and don't keep enough of them for ourselves. But the story of this dish is in the English wasabi we use. It's a product I'm completely enamoured with; to me, it represents the very best of British entrepreneurial spirit.

Our wasabi, the quintessentially Japanese horseradish, is grown in Dorset by our supplier, Tom Amery – his crops were the first wasabi rootstalks to be grown and sold in Europe. Better yet, Amery grows his wasabi in the abandoned watercress beds of southern England; beds that had long since fallen into disrepair.

These beds were once integral to Victorian life and culture, at a time when the peppery salad leaf was one of the staple greens in the British diet. Watercress was found in high-society sandwiches, school dinners, and curative winter soups – it was, in many senses, Britain's first 'superfood', celebrated for its extraordinary nutritional value, and called upon as medicine in the time before there was a public health system.

Demand was once so high for watercress that a dedicated train line between London and Southampton would bring tons and tons of it into the city's markets, where it would be sold by street-sellers or distributed all the way through the rest of the country. After the war, as imports opened up and the British larder was flooded with new crops from all over the world, watercress fell out of favour, coming to be seen as little more than a garnish. Amery's business has been responsible in no small part for the crop's resurgence in the UK, but his exploits in growing wasabi are even more groundbreaking.

The fresh product itself is a far cry from the root's fearsome, fiery reputation: when grated, it has a pleasing floral elegance to it. We pair it with peas in homage to the famous pub snack, and the combination works perfectly alongside langoustine and almond. It's Britain past and present, driven by suppliers who care about doing something daring and moving things forward, and that's what Core's all about.

COLCHESTER CRAB
SABAYON, CONSOMMÉ, CAVIAR

One lesson I have learned as my style has matured is that sometimes, the best thing you can do with an exceptional product is to serve it at its freshest with as little intervention as possible. This occurred to me, as lessons often do, while tasting the crab meat I was picking and prepping for service. It had been steamed just enough to cook it, and we were pulling it from its shell to chop, season and incorporate it into something else. But in those moments immediately after cooking, I thought it was perfect; sweet, succulent, stunning. So, with that in mind, why turn it into something else when it has already reached its perfect state?

That's the moment we chase at Core. We take Colchester crabs – which are some of the best in the world, if you ask me – and steam them until they just about reach doneness. The giant crab claw is the star – shelled, intact, and still at its meatiest – but we incorporate the rest of the crab into all other aspects of the dish, hiding the pulled leg meat underneath the sabayon, and turning the shells into both consommé and crab butter to douse the claw in.

LOBSTER AND SPELT
FENLAND CELERY, CAVIAR
AND SELIM PEPPER

We always have spelt on the menu. Not only is it delicious and incredibly good for you, it's also one of Britain's staple grains, and we've eaten it on these isles for millennia.

We get our spelt from a man named Roger Saul: in another life, he founded the iconic fashion brand Mulberry, then he sold it and bought the beautiful, 300-acre Sharpham Park estate in Somerset. After buying the land, he researched the history of his estate, and discovered that spelt was grown on his land well over 4,000 years ago.

The grain was used to feed the friars and abbots of nearby monasteries, not to mention the surrounding villagers and workers who tilled the land. It was one of Britain's first cash crops, enabling the growth and spread of towns and markets – it helped, in some part, to build the country we know today.

With all of this in mind, Saul revived the tradition of the crop being grown at Sharpham Park, milling and processing it on site to exceptional quality. He's on a mission to repopularize the grain – he's an evangelist for it – and we're proud to play our part. It's an amazing product, with a rich history and a connection to this country, grown by someone whose values we share.

'COLD SLAW'

If you were in London for the summer of 2018, you'll remember just how hot it was. It was one of those heatwaves – rare though they are in this country – in which all you wanted to eat were cool, refreshing salads. For those few scorching days when guests are coming in to dine, we have our 'Cold slaw': shredded cabbage tossed in smoked buttermilk and flavoured with tarragon, thyme and mint – three herbs that, when eaten together, give off a cooling sensation. If the herbs aren't enough to cool you down, we serve it with a frozen green tomato gazpacho, which should do the trick.

NETTLE AND NASTURTIUM VELOUTÉ
CELTUCE, VOATSIPERIFERY PEPPER AND ARGAN OIL

This dish was created as a way to make use of what grows abundantly around us: young, spring nettles, one of the most sustainable plants you can use; and nasturtiums, which, aside from looking beautiful, have such a wonderful peppery bite to them. We use this velouté to showcase another amazing and underused vegetable – the celtuce. It's not something we make use of very much in the UK, although in France it's more popular. It has a distinctive crispness, almost like a kohlrabi, and the flavour is a cross between cucumber and celery. It's brilliant enough raw, but the strangest thing happens when you roast it – it tastes almost like beef.

'POTATO AND ROE'
TROUT AND HERRING ROE
AND DULSE BEURRE BLANC

This is one of Core's most celebrated dishes, and one of my most personal.

Growing up by the coast in Northern Ireland, I would eat potatoes every day. Potatoes are the taste of home – my aunt and uncle were, and still are, potato farmers on the North Antrim coast, where the soil holds onto all that minerality from the ocean. When I was younger, I would help them with seeding and harvesting, working against the creeping frost to make sure the crops avoided damage. Afterwards, we'd eat a few – boiled and served only with salt, pepper and butter. Seaweed was another taste of childhood for me; dulse grew plentifully along the shoreline, and we'd buy little paper bags of it for five pence, to snack on as we walked along. Those flavours are foundational for me.

My potato habit is a lifelong one. At the start of all my services, practically without fail, I would always snatch a boiled potato from the station making pomme purée, season it a touch, and eat it. Our head chef, Jonny, watched me indulge this habit for years, and when it came to opening Core, he suggested we put together a dish that illustrated the centrality of the potato to my life. So, we got to work on developing just that.

I should say, the potato we use isn't just any potato. We have a grower, who would prefer to remain nameless, who grows potatoes and only potatoes, and they're the best you've ever had. I've worked with him now for fifteen years, and he's completely obsessed with what he does – he wants to produce the finest potato possible, and we believe he does. This dish has become a calling card of our restaurant: a case study in our culinary style, with the humble potato unashamedly front and centre, punctuated with briny bursts of trout and herring roe. More than this, however – the dulse, the roe, the potato, even the salt and vinegar crisps on top (my favourite snack) – it's an expression of my identity and history on a plate. Where I came from, and where I am now.

'LAMB CARROT'
BRAISED LAMB, SHEEP'S MILK YOGURT

At Royal Hospital Road, we used to make a navarin of lamb, where the meat would be braised for hours with vegetables and aromatics. Once we'd got what we needed from the braising, we'd discard the vegetables, but I always stepped in to steal the carrots, which had spent all that time absorbing the fat and the flavour and the seasoning. They were soft and sweet, almost fondant – they were the best bit. So I wanted to celebrate the carrot, push it all the way to the front, and have the lamb stand aside for it.

This, to me, demonstrates the importance of greediness. You should always be a little bit greedy when you can be – if there's something to hand that you could eat, try it. Every stolen bite or spare trimming is another chance to train your palate, to register a memory of a sensation or a flavour. Through this, you can discover so much more about yourself and what you enjoy. And sometimes, you might discover, like me, that the best part of a meal has been hiding from you in plain sight, waiting to be uncovered by your greedy curiosity.

'CHEESE AND ONION'

Cheese and onion crisps, cheese and onion pasties, cheese and onion sandwiches – if you were to poll the British public on their favourite flavour combination, you'd likely find cheese and onion right at the top. We wanted to take that flavour combination to the furthest point it could go, and this is what we came up with.

Our onions are from Lancaster, and we use them in every imaginable way: an onion purée, a consommé, an onion reduction that is twenty-four hours in the making, crispy shallot rings, spring onions, leek-top oil, onion and allium flowers, pickled onion. And that's before we factor in the onion as the centrepiece, which is layered with a cheese royale made from five-year-old Cheddar. We reinforce the cheesiness, and counteract all that onion, with puffed cheese rind and dots of cheese purée. And to mop up what's left, we serve it with an onion brioche bun (p. 169), to ensure that nothing is left behind.

JERUSALEM ARTICHOKE
MUSHROOM, TRUFFLE, MALT AND CHEDDAR

In wartime, Jerusalem artichokes were so nutritious and easy to grow that they eclipsed the potato for a little while as Britain's carb staple, although nowadays you'd be hard-pressed to find them at the supermarket. We play on their earthiness and richness by pairing them with classic autumnal flavours: mushroom, truffle, malt, Cheddar – flavours for darkening nights and shrivelling leaves. Beyond that, we do everything we can with the artichokes themselves, so we can demonstrate just how versatile and compelling this knobbly tuber can be.

'BEANS ON TOAST'

This dish came about from a challenge I was set on-air by the host of a famous TV show here in the UK. I was tasked to think of a three-Michelin-star version of Britain's most basic, no-frills meal: beans on toast. It was a challenge I accepted with gusto; I thought I could take that humble concept and turn it into a plate of luxury. The end result worked so well that we felt compelled to serve it as a special in truffle season.

Replacing the typical bread, we take a slice of brioche, fry it like French toast, and top it with beautiful, pearlescent coco beans, which I fell in love with while working for Alain Ducasse in Monte Carlo. We build it up further with a fried egg, before going even more luxurious with some shaved black truffle and a Parmesan velouté.

CELERIAC
ROASTED OVER WOOD WITH
BLACK TRUFFLE AND HAZELNUT

This is one of our seasonal vegetarian dishes, and is very much in keeping with
our theme of making stars out of the more unheralded, yet incredibly versatile,
vegetables. We marinate and bake our celeriac in barley miso, before roasting
it over wood so it softens and sweetens while taking in those smoky notes from
the fire. Truffles, mushrooms and hazelnuts harmonize beautifully with the rich,
yielding celeriac we're left with after roasting, and so we incorporate them into
a crumble that sits beneath. To ensure those brooding elements don't come to
dominate the dish, we reinforce the celeriac flavour with a powder made from
the root tops, a faux 'risotto' made with the flesh, crisps made with the skin and
a self-clarifying consommé.

 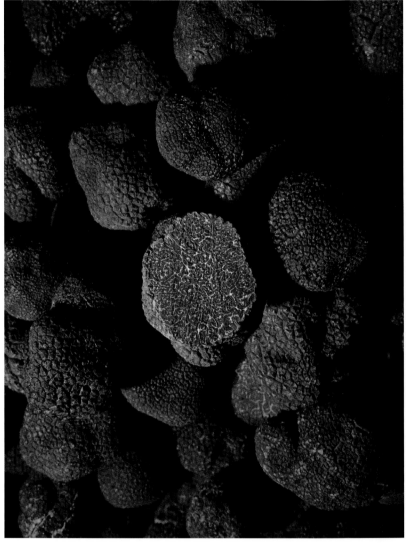

TARTLETS

I first became enamoured with tartlets through my first job in London in 1998. Every lunch service, we'd make these stunning seasonal tarts and serve them fresh from the oven, by the slice. Once they were gone, they were gone, so you had to order them early, which regulars understood. Should you have been lucky enough to get a slice, you would find yourself blown away by its elegance and delicacy.

Our tartlets carry everything, from plump morels and wild garlic, to wisps of shaved ceps strewn amongst Alba white truffle and tiny, tart-sized pullet egg yolks (something we rescue from our egg suppliers who would otherwise dispose of them for being undersized). They're another one of those things we like to keep on the menu throughout the year.

MOREL TART
WITH WILD GARLIC
AND VIN JAUNE

GIROLLE AND TOASTED BUCKWHEAT TART
WITH FRESH ALMONDS

JERUSALEM ARTICHOKE TART
PÉRIGORD BLACK TRUFFLE,
MUSHROOM AND THYME

CEP TART
FLUFFETTS FARM EGG YOLK
AND WHITE TRUFFLE

POACHED SEA BASS
COCKLES, CLAMS, COASTAL HERBS AND LOVAGE

This is one of my favourite dishes: a celebration of Cornish sea bass and the incredible shellfish our island waters have to offer. Poaching sea bass is such a gentle way of treating it, and when it is paired with briny cockles and unctuous clams in a delicate broth, you're placing it back in its natural environment, ending up with something so harmonious and clean.

After breaking our bass down into fillets, we separate the bones and trimmings, and put them to work for the rest of the dish. The bones go straight into our broth, to give it depth and body, and with the trimmings we make beautiful little fish quenelles, which mingle amongst the minestrone of cockles and sea vegetables underneath the poached fillet.

ROASTED MONKFISH
MORECAMBE BAY SHRIMPS, SWISS CHARD AND BROWN BUTTER

With this dish, we wanted to explore one of Britain's last great shellfish traditions: the potted shrimpers of Morecambe Bay, off the country's north-west coast. Precious few trawlers still wade out for these small, succulent shrimp, which for centuries have been caught, peeled, cooked and preserved by Morecambe fishermen. With the tradition dying out, we felt a responsibility to find a supplier, work with them for the best of their product, and support them so that this regional speciality isn't lost to the sands of time. To do so, we buy not only their shrimp, but also the bags and bags of leftover shrimp shells, which we can turn into oils and butters and sauces.

We wanted to make the Morecambe shrimp tradition the real story of this dish, and to achieve that, we chose to commemorate their most famous application: the quintessential British appetizer, potted shrimp on toast – one of Her Majesty's favourite snacks. Rather than replicate it directly, we evoke its spirit in the sauce for our roasted monkfish, infusing it with potted shrimp, brown butter, kelp and slices of our own toasted sourdough.

CORNISH TURBOT
SMOKED MUSSELS, RED APPLE, CABBAGE AND CIDER

We get the majority of our fish and shellfish from the coast of Cornwall; a region of Britain with a rich cultural and culinary heritage, and incredible produce from land and sea. Much like their Breton counterparts in Normandy on the other side of the English Channel, Cornish cooks have paired mussels with local cider for years and years, typically serving it with stewed cabbage and red apple for a hearty, warming maritime meal. We wanted to take this classic dish and intensify the mussel flavour in every way we could.

To do this, we use one of our favourite kitchen techniques: steaming our shellfish patiently in its own liquor until the very moment the shells pop open, then using every last drop of the steaming liquid to lend depth and intensity to our sauce. With this, we are able to retain far more flavour, before smoking the mussels for additional complexity, giving this dish a homely warmth that transports you to the rugged edge of South West England.

CORNISH BRILL
OYSTERS, CUCUMBER AND CAVIAR

Nothing, for me, is quite as good as oysters, cucumber and caviar. I love them enough individually, but adore them in combination – it's like something magical happens when you pair them alongside one another. We use a simple, classical oyster velouté to give the dish body and minerality; nothing more than a classic *haute* fish stock velouté, blended with raw oysters and their juice. The poached brill almost acts as the canvas for these three distinctive flavours, giving way just enough so they can come through in their brilliance. When a combination works this well, all that's left for you to do is to balance them correctly.

DOVER SOLE
BLACK TRUFFLE, LEEKS AND CHAMPAGNE SAUCE

When I worked at Le Louis XV in Monaco, I would find myself looking over people's shoulders to learn more about the techniques and combinations that other chefs worked on. One time, while working on the meat section, I was able to watch a couple of chefs wrapping leek ballotines with slices of black truffle, and immediately thought of a way I could do it differently. I told the chef de partie about it afterwards, and he said, 'Sounds like a great idea – keep hold of it until you open a restaurant.'

And so I did: our leeks are wrapped with black truffle, just as Alain Ducasse's were, but also a Dover sole mousse made from the leftover trimmings, so it comes out in a beautiful spiral of black, white and green.

DUCK AND NECTARINE
THYME, HONEY AND TIMUT PEPPER

Here in Britain, we've been rapidly catching up with our friends across the Channel when it comes to our poultry. French poultry has a well-earned reputation as the best in the world, owing to centuries of tradition and quality control that very often set it apart quite comfortably from the rest. But in the last few years, farmers all over the UK have been able to produce birds that are every bit as taut and flavourful as their French counterparts, and we take no greater pride than in celebrating British producers of that calibre.

We keep it simple with these ducks, cooking them with honey and thyme, and a few cracks of Timut pepper – a wonderfully aromatic peppercorn that brings a grapefruit note to the dish. For the tart alongside it, we confit and shred the duck legs, and combine them with the liver and heart to enrich it all further. To dial back the richness, we top the tart with slices of pert nectarine, which cuts through the fattiness and brings a balance of sweetness and freshness.

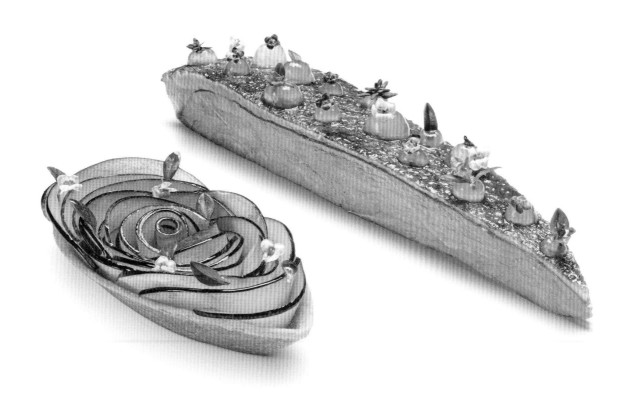

'BEEF AND OYSTER'

Far from their modern status as a symbol of decadence and luxury, oysters were once the lowliest, cheapest form of protein that money could buy in Britain, and as such, became a staple of the Victorian working-class diet. When you needed to bulk out a pie, you'd use oysters, and the less meat you could afford, the more oysters you would use. Oysters were Britain's first fast food, and consumption was so vast in London that mountains of calcified oyster shells can still be found on the shores of the River Thames. And yet, out of necessity came a delicious British combination: beef and oyster, often washed down with stout.

Paying tribute to this Victorian phenomenon, we pair two of this country's greatest ingredients; one from its ancient past, and one from its modern, enterprising future. First, we use Porthilly oysters, harvested on the Cornish coast from an area that's very close to my heart. I love Cornwall — I had my first head chef role there at the St. Enodoc Hotel, and made some of my dearest friends in the process. I even got married in the church beside the oyster farm! But these oysters aren't on the menu for sentiment: they're substantial enough to work with the strong, meaty flavours running through this dish without fading into the background.

With the oysters, we use beef from our friends at Highland Wagyu — a husband-and-wife team with an incredible passion for fine food, and an aim to produce some of the best beef in the world. As well as having purebred Wagyu on their farm, they also set about on a plan to crossbreed Aberdeen Angus and Wagyu cattle, to produce meat that really is the best of both worlds, possessing exquisite flavour and sumptuous marbling. Ten years after they began, we can say that they have succeeded in their efforts; theirs is a truly special cut of beef, brought about by the kind of entrepreneurial spirit that typifies the best of Britain.

LAMB, HOGGET AND MUTTON
CELTUCE, SAVORY
AND BLACK CARDAMOM

We source our lamb from perhaps the most idyllic farm in the UK. Picture the rolling hills, craggy valleys and verdant plains of the Beatrix Potter books and you'd be right on the money, as our farm was quite literally Beatrix Potter's farm in the Lake District. Nowadays, it is owned and run by a farmer named Eric Telford, who doesn't so much shepherd as supervise his flock of Herdwick sheep. These sheep, native to the Cumbrian fells, are so hardy that they all but look after themselves, getting all the food, herbs and medicine they need from their natural grazing environment.

We use this course to tell the story of his sheep, in all their stages – lamb, hogget and mutton – because to eat the first, we need to produce, and make more use of, the older two. Making use of the entirety of Eric's flock allows us to support his farm further, and we like to think that you will come away from the dish feeling a little bit more open to the hogget and mutton that's available to you.

DEXTER SHORT RIB
OXTAIL, ONION AND BONE MARROW

Here we're taking another classic British pairing, beef and onion, with the onion as the centrepiece and the short rib stepping to the side just a touch. In terms of flavour, however, there's no doubt that this is about beefiness in all its guises, and making all we can from some of the most savoury cuts – braised oxtail, short rib, bone marrow – to deliver on maximum flavour.

We use Dexter beef from a Lake District farmer co-operative – the same one we met Eric Telford through – and we know how vital these co-ops are to the survival of traditional livestock farming in this country. Co-operatives allow us to work with and support our farmers directly, as well as meet new suppliers who share our values and standards of excellence. Through paying not just for quality but for the diversity of what they are able to provide, we aim to ensure that these farmers, and their methods, continue to shine in our country's food system.

ROAST GROUSE
RED CABBAGE AND BELL HEATHER

We're so lucky to still be eating grouse in the UK – it has all but disappeared across the continent, much like pheasant and woodcock and other game birds. Thankfully, the tradition of grouse-shooting has held true in Britain, primarily as a means of land management and conservation, but also because of grouse's role in our gastronomic history (not to mention, of course, just how good it tastes). Shooting season begins on 12 August each year: the so-called Glorious Twelfth, as ordained by the British Parliament's Game Act of 1831, and adhered to by gamekeepers ever since.

We treat our grouse with respect when we receive them, smoking them in the bell heather they grazed on, to return them to the land they came from. When we can serve it at Core, we do; when stocks are too low, and our serving it risks damaging the long-term survival of the grouse flock, we simply skip a year. We only work with what nature gives us.

RHUG ESTATE VENISON
'HAGGIS', PEARL BARLEY
AND LAGAVULIN WHISKY

Venison is another meat we don't eat anything close to enough of. It's sustainable, it's available all year round – not just in winter – and it's remarkably good for you. It even has more omega-3s than mackerel, if brain food is what you're after.

We source our venison from a supplier called Robert Wynn of the Rhug Estate in Wales – better known by his honorific title, Lord Newborough. Having inherited the farm from his father, Wynn has spent the last twenty years transforming the estate into a permacultural paradise; everything they need is grown on-site, with minimal waste or impact to the environment. He does everything on that estate, from making his own silage to working in the farm shop. Not only is his product excellent, we know he treats nature with respect and reverence.

This dish is woodsy, warm and as Scottish as we can make our little corner of Notting Hill – even if the venison is Welsh! We want it to feel like a night in a Highland cabin, sat beside a crackling fire, eating venison and haggis and pearl barley, with a snifter of Lagavulin whisky to warm you all the way through. We try to make use of venison in other seasons, too, to demonstrate its versatility, but there's a real joy in presenting it in this festive, wintry way when the year draws to a close.

'CHERRY BAKEWELL'

Cherries and almonds are natural bedfellows, even down to the molecular level; both ingredients share many of the same flavour and aroma compounds. We're not sure if the bakers of Bakewell, in Derbyshire, were aware of that fact when they first dropped a glacé cherry on top of one of their frangipane tarts, but they certainly had the right instincts. Cherry Bakewells have the power to evoke nostalgia, and we wanted to recreate the tart as a dessert, making use of the glut of cherries we get from Kent every summer. Alongside the cherry filled with almond mousse, we serve a cherry cola cocktail made with kirsch, to reinforce memories of the childhood sweetshop.

'CORE APPLE'

We had to do this dish. Opening with a name like Core, we were always going to have an expectation of an apple course, and we're pretty happy with what we came up with. When we first sketched out our ideas for the 'Core apple', we wanted to make it quite autumnal, like the toffee apples you'd get on Bonfire Night, but still tart enough to work as a dessert. To create a sense of warmth running through the dish, we use mead and ten-year-old Somerset cider brandy, two of the country's oldest-produced forms of alcohol.

'CORE-TESER'

Maltesers were my favourite chocolate growing up, and they still hold on to that spot. I attack them in the same way each time, systematically: one by one, I scrape off the outer layer of chocolate with as delicate a bite as I can, trying my hardest to keep the malt centre intact, before eating that separately. Nostalgia, comfort and connection are three values we pursue through our food at Core – particularly our desserts – and this dish brings about those emotions for so many people.

This is as unctuous and childish as desserts get: it's fun, indulgent and seriously addictive. Aerated chocolate and featherlight puffs of malt, stacked on top of each other, only kept from floating off into the sky by an anchor of hazelnut ice cream. We source our chocolate from Udzungwa Park in Tanzania – a light, approachable 70% chocolate that fits with the sweet and nostalgic flavour profile of this dessert. What's more, through buying their chocolate, we are able to support the farmers and producers of Udzungwa Park in their efforts to conserve the biodiversity of their region.

LEMONADE PARFAIT
HONEY AND SHEEP'S MILK YOGURT

After spending so long at Restaurant Gordon Ramsay, first as head chef and then chef-patron, the restaurant's cuisine was so suffused with my own that many of my signature dishes were cornerstones of the menu. I couldn't just take them with me to Core – to do so would harm both restaurants – so I had to bid a few of my classics farewell. The Lemonade parfait was perhaps the hardest to leave behind. People adored it at Royal Hospital Road. They may not have come for dinner just to have it, but they certainly expected it at the end of their meal.

So, we tried to rework the concept at Core, turning it into more of a honey dessert to differentiate it from the original. In doing so, I learned a lot about myself; I had to look inward, at how the chef I was in that moment would approach a signature dish like this. My tastes and techniques had changed in the years since I first put it together, just as everyone's palate changes over time. Once I had a second version I was happy with, I tweaked it and challenged it. I adjusted the acidity, the creaminess, the sense of fizz; its layout on the plate, its texture. Over time, that second version evolved into what it is today, the 'Lemonade parfait 3.0' – it has come a long way since Restaurant Gordon Ramsay, but so have I.

ETON MESS

This is our take on the British summertime classic, Eton mess: cream, meringue and ripe summer fruit. We switch out the fillings from season to season: when we're in the peak of summer, juicy wild strawberries take the lead; in the hardier months, heritage pears from the National Fruit Collection at Kent's Brogdale Farm; and, occasionally, we switch in a pink grapefruit version – there's no limits to the variations we can make when we work with what's in season. All three fruits work perfectly with the floral, herbaceous lemon verbena running through the meringue, and the sorbets round out the dish with a satisfying cleanness.

PEAR AND VERBENA
WITH POIRE WILLIAMS SORBET

WILD STRAWBERRY
MERINGUE AND LEMON VERBENA

'THE OTHER CARROT'

Over the last few centuries, whenever sugar has been scarce or a luxury, people have often turned to the humble carrot to bring sweetness back to their lives, falling in love with it at the same time. Carrot puddings and cakes have been on British and European tables since the 1500s, often combined with woody spices and dried fruits just as they are today. During the Second World War, with the rationing of sweeteners, carrot cake exploded in popularity among thrifty British households, being touted not only as a delicious dessert, but a superfood that could help you see in the dark; a handy skill in the time of blackouts.

Just as we serve our 'Lamb carrot' (p. 90) as the best bit of lamb, we serve our 'Other carrot' as the best bit of carrot cake – which is, in our opinion, the cream cheese icing. We make a cream cheese mousse, set it in a carrot gel, and place it onto a spiced cake crumb, before topping it with a mix of candied ginger and walnut in the same manner as the lamb in the original dish.

'MONT BLANC PAIN PERDU'

This might be one of my favourite desserts, not just of ours but of anywhere. I love a Mont Blanc, and I love a *pain perdu*, and this dessert couldn't be simpler in its ethos: take two amazing desserts and bring them together into one dessert, with chestnuts, pine, vanilla, cream, brioche and a tiny touch of gold leaf.

'NOTTING HILL FOREST'
CHESTNUT, HAZELNUT, PINE AND WOODRUFF

We wanted to create something that would capture the essence of the forest floor, inspired by the mounds and mounds of fallen leaves we wade through on our way to the restaurant every autumn and winter. We'd paired chestnut and prune together years before as a warming winter eggnog to serve as a seasonal cocktail and wanted to re-explore this combination. At first, the balance was off: we'd made it almost too foresty, and not familiar enough. But, bit by bit, we refined and lightened it, incorporating more of the sticky-sweet prune flavour, the richness and nuttiness of chestnut and chocolate in harmony. As a finishing touch, we dot the leaves with a couple of drops of woodruff oil – the woodruff harvested in the summer by one of our cooks, Nick, and preserved for the winter months just as foragers have always done. This brings a welcome note of vegetal grassiness, and brings our forest floor to life.

'SNOWBALL'
RUM, PRUNE AND PINE

In our first winter at Core, it snowed and snowed all day and night. As we saw it, you can let snow get you down, or you can lighten up, pack a snowball between your palms and have some fun with it. There was no amount of snow that could bring us down after our first year, and after months in the heat of the kitchen, we enjoyed the cold snap, and took the time to have snowball fights in the courtyard between services.

For our New Year's Eve dinner that year, we decided to celebrate the season's weather with a snowball dessert: a chestnut crémeux sphere with a warming eggnog centre, dusted with pine snow and meringue snowflakes. Thankfully, none of our guests took to throwing them across the dining room at one another!

WINE GUMS

We'd been cooking dishes over discarded grapevines in our wood-fired oven, and one day, the bundles of vines just caught my eye – they were absolutely stunning. We had to make use of them. We sent them to Patrick, our wood guy in Northern Ireland, and he polished the vines into these gorgeous table centrepieces.

We were left with something beautiful to place on our tables, but no clear idea of what to actually do with them. Given that they were once grapevines, we thought that a pair of perfect grapes might be the best option. We decided to turn two of our favourite dessert wines, Sauternes and Banyuls, into wine gums, another classic British sweet. They're a digestif and petit four wrapped up into one, and for added effect, we mould each wine gum into the shape of the grape that would've gone into the wines. There's beauty everywhere, if you know where to look.

WARM CHOCOLATE TART

In Paris, there's a magnificent restaurant by the name of L'Ambroisie, just around the corner from the capital's oldest square, the legendary Place des Vosges. L'Ambroisie has held onto its three Michelin stars since 1986, and has always served a slice of chocolate tart, dusted with cocoa, at the end of every meal. That tart is one of the most exceptional things I have ever eaten – it's mind-blowingly good, and yet so simple.

Our tarts are a homage to the L'Ambroisie classic, and we've served a miniature chocolate tart at the end of the meal since our very first night's service. Our tarts move with the seasons, too; sometimes we flavour them with lavender, other times with clementine, both of which pair beautifully with the rich chocolate filling. When you can share a simple, beautiful pleasure like a warm chocolate tart, one of the very best things in life, you should always do so.

MALTED SOURDOUGH

Our Core bread is something of a passion project. We wanted to offer one bread, baked in-house, composed with the same skill as the rest of our menu, and made from ingredients that accord with our values – an awesome loaf, with depth and complexity. We've approached our recipe like chefs, rather than bakers, but to give us the foundation, our head chef Jonny spent time with the master Breton baker Richard Bertinet, who kindly donated his seventeen-year-old sourdough starter to get us going.

Our flour comes from Wessex Mill in Oxford, which is run by the Munsey family: a family of millers now entering their fifth generation in the trade. All of their wheat is gathered from the fields of Oxfordshire, and everything they collect is rigorously tested before it enters their milling process. Theirs is a slow milling process, operated on a smaller scale, which allows them to be far more selective with the wheats they choose for milling, as well as maintaining more of the nutritional benefits of wheat bran, which would be removed in the processing of hulling in commercial milling.

They care enormously about what they do, and work with a level of confidence and accuracy that comes with generations of collective knowledge. As such, they know everything there is to know about their flour. If we ever have a problem with our bakes that we can't diagnose, we can contact them to discover why one day's bread might be different to another's: they check our flour's gluten and protein levels, establish the optimal temperature for the flour to be stored at, and get back to us on what we should do. We make our bread not just with their flour, but with their support and expertise.

Jonny looks after our bread the most, alongside our head of development, Antonio. It's their baby – and in many ways, they have to treat it like one, feeding the starters every day at the exact same time, and making sure they're kept in comfortable conditions. We use two starters for our dough: one with Wessex Mill white flour, and another with rye flour, to deepen the bread's flavour. We make the dough with a treacle and malt 'bread stock' in place of water, and then reinforce the maltiness further with the spent grains from our specially brewed Core beer.

We have to adapt every single day to the bread; it requires understanding and rhythm and technique. As much as we can try to standardize our processes, it's a living thing. Sometimes it reacts to a change in humidity, or it rises energetically, or tightens up a little bit more out of the oven. It's a labour of love to keep it at the standard that we do, but the end result is absolutely worth it.

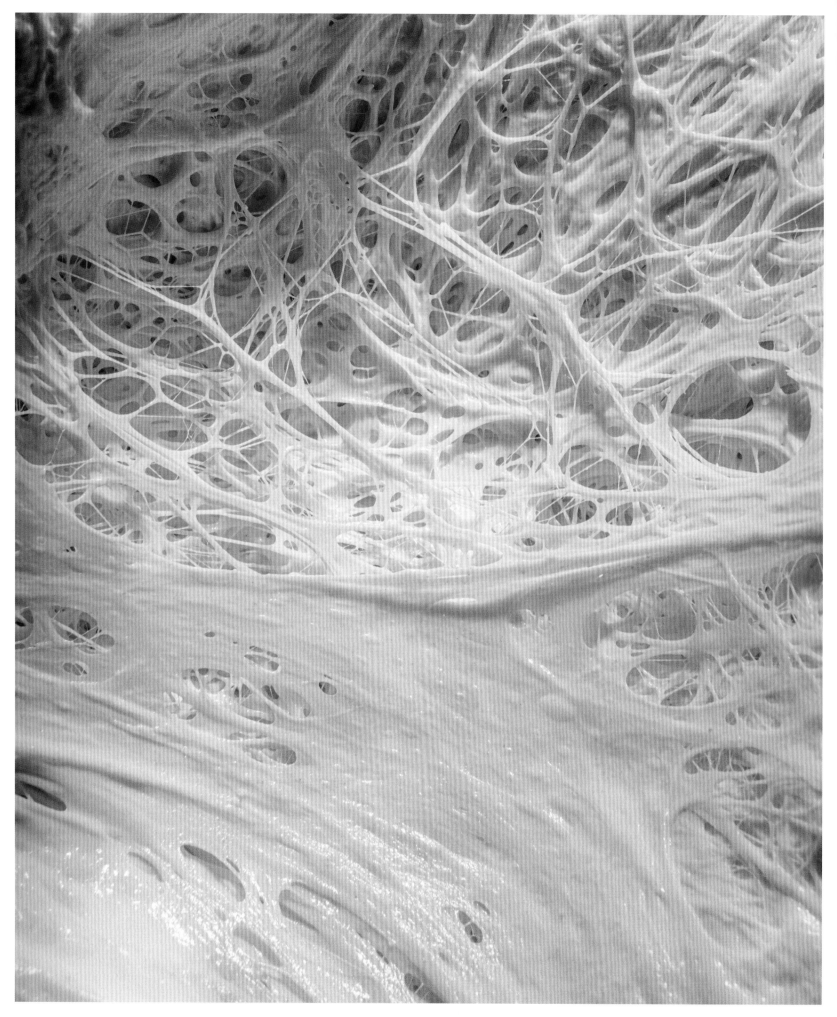

BUNS

A spotless plate is the ultimate compliment you can give to a chef, and we love to see our guests mopping up the sauce from their plates with our sourdough. For some courses, however, we like to encourage the practice by providing buns that are specially tailored to the dish at hand, helping our guests to a few extra flavourful mouthfuls as they finish their meals. Using an enriched brioche dough for one and laminated dough for the other, we offer Lamb buns for the 'Lamb carrot' (p. 90) and Onion buns for the 'Cheese and onion' (p. 92), stuffing the first with crispy lamb fat lardons, and the second with sticky onion jam.

LAMB BUNS

ONION BUNS

CHEESE AND CRACKERS

Our cheese supplier, Davidstow Creamery, takes its name from the village in North Cornwall where it's located and sells its Cheddar across the country. As a seventy-year-old company that works mostly with family run farms, they've learned, in their words, that 'taste takes time'. This holds true in their five-year-old extra mature Cheddar, which is used in our 'Cheese and onion' dish (p. 92). Lesser known, is Davidstow Creamery's clandestine side-operation, away from their more commercial production, where they age batches of their cheese for far longer than many cheesemakers would dare.

We tried a sample of their craggy, crystalline seven-year-old Cheddar when we visited their creamery and fell in love with it. Somehow, we convinced them to let us serve it on our cheese board, alongside creamy Colton Bassett Stilton carved straight from the wheel, and a seasonal third cheese we rotate through the year. People ask us for an extra block to take home and we have to turn them down, because we don't have enough to give away!

To complement these strong cheeses, we serve a number of accompaniments: home-baked crackers, honey, pickled onions, and our take on the classic British childhood biscuit, the fig roll. Typically, fig rolls are dense sticks of crumbly shortbread filled with a sweet fig jam. We trade pastry for soft, sweet dough, and swirl fig compote throughout our rolls, before baking them in fig leaves and dusting them with fig leaf powder. If you ask me, there's no better companion for a chunk of Stilton than a warm fig roll – that balance of sweet and savoury is something we do very well in this country.

FIG ROLLS

OAT AND PUMPKIN SEED CRACKERS
MULTIGRAIN CRACKERS

TREACLE YOGURT BUNS

These buns are a delight to make and even better to eat. We alternate them with the Fig rolls through the year as an accompaniment to our cheeses, but they're great as dinner rolls, sandwich rolls, or simply smothered with good butter. They have the right balance of rich, dark molasses and yogurty tang, with a lovely toasty note from the beurre noisette and brown ale enriching the dough.

JELLIED EEL
BEER TOASTED SEAWEED AND MALT VINEGAR

Serves: 20

EEL BONE VINEGAR
250 g eel bones
250 g malt vinegar

NORI TART CASE
12 sheets toasted nori
100 g Stock syrup (p. 249)
salt, to taste

EEL CREAM
250 g double cream
125 g Chicken stock (p. 244)
125 g water

250 g smoked eel bones (no skin)
½ onion, cut into large dice
2 celery sticks, cut into large dice
1 garlic clove
Gellan F (1% of the weight of the
  liquid at the end of the cooking
  process)
salt, to taste

EEL CONSOMMÉ JELLY
1 kg Chicken stock (p. 144)
1 kg water
1 kg eel bones

300 g dried kombu sheets
200 g dry white wine
8 sheets bronze gelatine
salt, to taste

PARSLEY NAGE
450 g Vegetable nage (p. 243)
150 g flat-leaf parsley

PARSLEY JELLY
8 sheets bronze gelatine
400 g Parsley nage (above)

PARSLEY PURÉE
1 kg flat-leaf parsley, leaves picked
salt, to taste

TO ASSEMBLE
20 x 1-cm (½-inch) diamonds
  of skinless smoked eel
parsley tips

EEL BONE VINEGAR
Preheat the oven to 180°C/350°F (fan). Roast the eel bones in the oven for about 20 minutes, until nice and golden, then put the bones and vinegar into a sous vide bag, seal and infuse in the fridge for 24 hours. Strain through a chinois, then store in a spray bottle.

NORI TART CASE
Preheat the oven to 120°C/250°F (fan). Brush each sheet of toasted nori with stock syrup and sprinkle with salt to season, then stack in piles of three. Cut each stack into five 4 x 4-cm (1½ x 1½-inch) squares (to make a total of 20 squares), press between two 2.5 x 1-cm (1 x ½-inch) tart moulds (you will need 40 moulds), then trim with scissors. With the moulds pressed together, cook in the oven for 20 minutes, then check – the tart cases should be crisp. Remove the moulds and reserve the tart cases in a dehydrator at 65°C/150°F until needed.

EEL CREAM
Put all the ingredients (except the gellan gum and salt) into a sous vide bag, seal and cook in a steam oven at 100°C/210°F for 1 hour. Strain the liquid through a chinois and season to taste with salt. Measure the liquid. Pour the strained liquid into a temperature-controlled high-speed blender and bring to 90°C/200°F on medium speed. Add the Gellan F (1% of the weight of the liquid at the end of the cooking process) and bring the mixture back up to 90°C/200°F, then blend for 2 minutes. Remove the lid, scrape down the sides and bottom of the jug, then blend on full power for 1 minute. Pour the mixture into a tray and place in the fridge to set for at least 1 hour. Remove from the fridge and blend the mixture again until smooth, then transfer to a piping bag fitted with a 5-mm (¼-inch) nozzle and reserve in the fridge.

EEL CONSOMMÉ JELLY
Put the stock, water, bones, kombu and 100 g of the white wine into a sous vide bag, seal and cook in a steam oven at 100°C/210°F for 1 hour. Strain the liquid through a chinois. Skim the fat from the stock and pour the liquid into a 3-litre rectangular container. Freeze until it becomes an ice block in order to start the ice filtration process. Place the ice block in a clean muslin cloth and onto a steamer

tray with holes in it with a larger tray underneath. Allow the stock to defrost in the fridge for 24 hours. (Clarification is ready once half the stock has melted, and impurities are left remaining in the jelly in the cloth.) Season the clarified eel stock with the remaining white wine and salt. Discard the jelly (this contains the impurities). Soften the gelatine sheets in ice water for 10 minutes. In a small pan, add the gelatine (drained and squeezed of excess water) to 400 g of the clarified stock and gently heat to dissolve, then pour into a small rectangular tray (about 25 x 15 x 2 cm/10 x 6 x ¾ inch) with the remaining stock and place in the fridge until set. Once set, brunoise the jelly and reserve in the fridge.

PARSLEY NAGE
Put the nage and parsley into a blender and blend at high speed for 2 minutes. Strain through a chinois and reserve.

PARSLEY JELLY
Soften the gelatine sheets in ice water for 10 minutes. Bring the parsley nage to the boil in a saucepan, then drain the gelatine, squeeze out the excess water and add it to the nage. Mix well, remove the liquid from the heat, pour into a small rectangular tray (about 25 x 15 x 2 cm/10 x 6 x ¾ inch) and place in the fridge to set. Once set, dice the jelly into brunoise and reserve in the fridge.

PARSLEY PURÉE
Wash the picked parsley leaves in cold water to remove any dirt. Drain the leaves using a salad spinner to remove any excess water, then blanch them for 5 minutes in boiling water. Drain thoroughly and squeeze out the excess water. Transfer the leaves to a blender and blend on full speed until completely smooth. Transfer to a piping bag fitted with a 2-mm (¹⁄₁₆-inch) nozzle.

TO ASSEMBLE
In a mixing bowl, combine the diced parsley jelly and eel jelly. Pipe a dot of parsley purée in the middle of the nori tart case, then, to the left side, pipe a thin layer of the eel cream, and on the right side place the jellies. Place a smoked eel diamond in the middle and top with a parsley tip. Spray with eel vinegar before serving.

'CAVIAR SANDWICH'

Serves: 24

BUCKWHEAT CRÊPES
80 g buckwheat flour
2 g salt
250 g whole milk
I egg
25 g butter

EGG WHITE
6 hard-boiled egg whites
30 g Mayonnaise (p. 248)
2 g salt
10 g flat-leaf parsley, finely chopped

EGG YOLK
6 hard-boiled egg yolks
30 g Mayonnaise (p. 248)
2 g salt

CRÈME FRAÎCHE
200 g crème fraîche
I small shallot (brunoised, rinsed
   and dried using a clean dish towel)
salt, to taste

TO ASSEMBLE
20 g puffed buckwheat
caviar
2 sheets gold leaf

BUCKWHEAT CRÊPES
Combine the buckwheat flour, salt, 100 g of the milk and the egg in a medium bowl and mix until it forms a smooth paste. Add the remaining 150 g milk and whisk to combine. To make the crêpes, heat a 25-cm (10-inch) non-stick frying pan, add a small piece of the butter, and once it's melted, pour a ladle of crêpe batter into the pan. Rotate the pan until the mix covers the base. Place it back over the heat and cook until golden brown, then turn the crêpe over and cook the other side until lightly browned. Remove from the pan. Repeat this process until you have four crêpes. (You may have some mixture left over.)

EGG WHITE
Pass the egg whites twice through a fine chinois into a bowl. Add the remaining ingredients and mix.

EGG YOLK
Pass the egg yolks twice through a sieve into a bowl. Add the remaining ingredients and mix.

CRÈME FRAÎCHE
Combine the ingredients in a small bowl and mix, making sure the shallots are well drained so that they do not dilute the mix.

TO ASSEMBLE
Trim the edges of each crêpe to create 16 x 12-cm (6½ x 4¾-inch) rectangles. Spread the egg white mixture over one trimmed crêpe, then layer with another crêpe and spread over the egg yolk mixture. Layer this with another crêpe and evenly spread with the crème fraîche mix, then sprinkle over the puffed buckwheat and top with the final crêpe. Place the sandwich in the freezer for 20 minutes to set. Cut the sandwich lengthwise to create 3 rectangles, then take each rectangle and cut into 4 squares. Cut each square in half on the diagonal to form the sandwich shape. Top each sandwich with caviar and gold leaf.

'CFC'
CORE FRIED CHICKEN AND CAVIAR

Serves: 20

MARINATE THE CHICKEN
5 boneless chicken thighs
200 g buttermilk
40 g sour cream
15 g Dijon mustard
2 g cracked black pepper
0.5 g Garlic powder (p. 242)
5 g salt

SPICE FLOUR MIX
4 g dried sage
4 g dried marjoram
4 g dried basil
2 g celery salt
6 g salt
4 g Onion powder (p. 242)
2 g Garlic powder (p. 242)
12.5 g paprika

11 g sweet smoked paprika
5 g cayenne pepper
4 g ground oregano
4 g chilli powder
1.5 g ground allspice
225 g plain flour
75 g cornflour
75 g tapioca starch

CHICKEN PREPARATION
2.5 kg grapeseed oil
5 Marinated chicken thighs (left)
flaky sea salt, to taste

TO ASSEMBLE
caviar

MARINATE THE CHICKEN
Remove the skin and cut the chicken thighs into quarters. Combine all the ingredients in a bowl with the chicken thigh pieces and marinate in the fridge for a minimum of 12 hours.

SPICE FLOUR MIX
Combine all the dried herbs, salts, powders and spices and blend with a hand blender until it forms a powder. Add the flour, cornflour and tapioca starch and mix well.

CHICKEN PREPARATION
Heat the grapeseed oil in a medium saucepan to 180°C/350°F. Drain the chicken thigh pieces from the marinade and coat with the spice flour mix. Fry the chicken for 2–3 minutes until the internal temperature reaches 75°C/165°F and the thighs are nicely golden. Drain on paper towels and season lightly with flaky sea salt.

TO ASSEMBLE
Skewer the chicken thigh pieces with a small cocktail stick and add a quenelle of caviar on top.

'TFC'
TRUFFLE FRIED CHICKEN

Serves: 20

MARINATE THE CHICKEN
5 boneless chicken thighs
200 g buttermilk
40 g sour cream
15 g Dijon mustard
2 g cracked black pepper
0.5 g Garlic powder (p. 242)
5 g salt
5 g black truffle oil

SPICE FLOUR MIX
3 g ground oregano
3 g dried sage
3 g dried marjoram
5 g salt
3 g Onion powder (p. 242)
2 g Garlic powder (p. 242)
5 g Parmesan powder (p. 242)
5 g vinegar powder
3 g chilli powder
180 g plain flour
60 g cornflour
60 g tapioca starch

PARMESAN AND VINEGAR POWDER
50 g Parmesan powder (p. 242)
35 g vinegar powder

TRUFFLE PARMESAN PURÉE
250 g whole milk
60 g Parmesan, grated
15 g mascarpone
5 g Gellan F
5 g chives, finely chopped
2.5 g flat-leaf parsley, finely chopped
2.5 g chervil, finely chopped

5 g black truffle, finely chopped
5 g Barolo vinegar

CHICKEN PREPARATION
2.5 kg grapeseed oil
5 Marinated chicken thighs (left)
flaky sea salt, to taste

TO ASSEMBLE
white spring onion rondelles
triangle shavings of Parmesan
shaved black truffle

MARINATE THE CHICKEN
Remove the skin and cut the chicken thighs into quarters. Combine all the ingredients in a bowl with the chicken thigh pieces and marinate in the fridge for a minimum of 12 hours.

SPICE FLOUR MIX
Combine all the dried herbs, salt, powders and chilli powder and blend using a hand blender until it forms a powder. Add the flour, cornflour and tapioca starch and mix well.

PARMESAN AND VINEGAR POWDER
Combine both the ingredients in a bowl and mix.

TRUFFLE PARMESAN PURÉE
Pour the milk into a temperature-controlled blender set to speed 2 and heat to 90°C/200°F. Stir in the Parmesan and mascarpone and bring the temperature back up to 90°C/200°F. Add the Gellan F and bring the mixture back up to 90°C/200°F,

then blend on speed 3 for 2 minutes. Remove the lid, scrape the mixture down from the sides of the bowl, put the lid back on and blend on full power for another 30 seconds. Pour into a tray and place in the fridge to set for at least 1 hour. Once it's set, blend in a blender until smooth. Transfer the mixture to a bowl, add the herbs, black truffle and vinegar and mix well. Place into a piping bag fitted with a 5-mm (¼-inch) nozzle and reserve in the fridge.

CHICKEN PREPARATION
Heat the grapeseed oil in a medium saucepan to 180°C/350°F. Drain the chicken thigh pieces from the marinade and coat with the spice flour mix. Fry the chicken for 2–3 minutes until the internal temperature reaches 75°C/165°F and the thighs are nicely golden. Drain on paper towels and lightly season with flaky sea salt.

TO ASSEMBLE
Sprinkle the Parmesan and vinegar powder on top of the crispy chicken thigh pieces. Add a small dot of truffle Parmesan purée on top, followed by a Parmesan triangle and spring onion rondelle. Finally, cover with shaved truffle.

CORE 'CAESAR SALAD'

Serves: 4

CAESAR DRESSING
4 hard-boiled egg yolks
100 g Mayonnaise (p. 248)
50 g Parmesan, grated
5 g anchovy fillets in oil, finely chopped
1 g garlic purée
lemon juice, to taste
salt, to taste

CAESAR CRUMBLE
30 g smoked streaky bacon
100 g clarified butter
6 garlic cloves, crushed
6 sprigs thyme
100 g white sourdough,
   cut into 2-cm (¾-inch) cubes
2 g Parmesan powder (p. 242)
1 g Onion powder (p. 242)

1 g Garlic powder (p. 242)
0.1 g vinegar powder
salt, to taste

SMOKED BACON
10 g grapeseed oil
50 g smoked streaky bacon,
   cut into 5-mm (¼-inch) dice

LITTLE GEM LETTUCE
4 Little Gem lettuces, including
   the root

TO ASSEMBLE
Parmesan shavings
chive tips
alyssum flowers

CAESAR DRESSING
Pass the cooked egg yolks through a sieve into a bowl. Add all the remaining ingredients and mix. Season and transfer to a small piping bag fitted with a 5-mm (¼-inch) nozzle and reserve in the fridge until required.

CAESAR CRUMBLE
Preheat the oven to 180°C/350°F. Grill the bacon until golden and crispy, transfer to paper towels to remove any excess fat, then chop finely. Melt the butter in a medium saucepan over a medium heat and add the garlic and thyme. Add the cubed sourdough and let it colour on all sides, then remove from the pan (discarding the garlic and thyme) and cook in the oven for 8 minutes until crispy. Drain on paper towels to remove any excess fat, then chop finely. Combine the bacon and bread in a bowl with the remaining ingredients, season if needed and reserve.

SMOKED BACON
Heat a non-stick frying pan over a high heat, add the oil and diced bacon and fry until crispy, then remove from the pan and drain on paper towels.

LITTLE GEM LETTUCE
Remove two layers of the external leaves of each lettuce. With your hand, open up the lettuce. Using a paring knife, trim the stem of the lettuce, leaving the root attached at the bottom. Wash the lettuce hearts three times to completely remove any dirt.

TO ASSEMBLE
Dress the lettuce with dots of the Caesar dressing, diced bacon, Parmesan shavings, chive tips and alyssum flowers. Place the lettuce in a bowl and surround with most of the crumble so that it stands up ready to be cut and dipped. Sprinkle the remaining crumble on the top before serving.

CRISPY SMOKED CHICKEN WING
BEER, HONEY, LEMON AND THYME

Serves: 20

**DEHYDRATED LEMON
AND THYME**
60 g grated lemon zest
40 g picked thyme leaves

BRINED CHICKEN WINGS
20 chicken wings
1 kg 10% Herb brine (p. 247)

**CHICKEN WINGS
PREPARATION**
20 Brined chicken wings (left)
2 kg grapeseed oil
8 sprigs thyme
1 garlic clove

LEMON THYME SPICE MIX
10 g coriander seeds
dehydrated lemon and thyme (left)
10 g salt

HONEY BEER GLAZE
318 g honey
32 g Chardonnay vinegar
93 g mead

43 g pale ale
43 g mirin

TO FINISH AND ASSEMBLE
1 kg grapeseed oil
grated lemon zest
thyme leaves
flaky sea salt, to taste

DEHYDRATED LEMON AND THYME
Place the lemon zest and thyme onto a dehydrator tray and dehydrate at 70°C/160°F for 24 hours until fully dried.

BRINED CHICKEN WINGS
Put the chicken wings and brine into a sous vide bag, seal and reserve in the fridge for 1 hour. Drain the chicken wings in a colander.

CHICKEN WINGS PREPARATION
Preheat the oven to 98°C/208°F (fan). To prepare the chicken wings, dislocate the joints between the tip, wingette and drumette and cut through both joints. Reserve the drumettes and tips for later use in stocks and place the wingettes in a deep tray, cover with the grapeseed oil, thyme and garlic and cook in the oven for

about 2 hours. Once the wingettes are cooked, leave to cool in the oil until they reach room temperature, then gently slide out the bones, being careful to keep the wing intact. Place a long piece of cling film on the table and position eight wings one next to the other in a line – keeping them flat – then tightly roll the wings in the cling film. Repeat the process for the remaining wings, rolling another eight wings, then another four in a shorter length of cling film. Lightly press the chicken wings between two flat trays and leave to rest in the fridge for 6 hours. Remove the chicken from the cling film. Cut each wing at a 45° angle at both ends, from left to right, to create a diamond shape, and reserve for later.

LEMON THYME SPICE MIX
Toast the coriander seeds, then set aside and cool. Blend the dehydrated lemon and thyme with the coriander in a blender.

Transfer the resulting powder to a bowl, add the salt and mix well. Store in a sealed sous vide bag or airtight container.

HONEY BEER GLAZE
Combine all the ingredients in a medium saucepan, bring to the boil, then reduce the heat and simmer until the liquid reduces to 135 g in weight or has a thick, glossy consistency. Pour into a container and reserve at room temperature.

TO FINISH AND ASSEMBLE
Heat the grapeseed oil in a small pan to 180°C/350°F and add four chicken wings. Fry for 1½ minutes, then flip and cook on the other side until golden brown. Fry the remaining wings, four at a time.

Drain the chicken wings on paper towels to remove the excess oil. Using a brush, glaze the wings with the honey beer glaze. Sprinkle with the lemon thyme spice mix and lightly season with flaky sea salt. Garnish with thyme leaves and lemon zest. Skewer the chicken wings with a small cocktail stick, place under a cloche and add smoke using a smoking gun (food smoker).

CRISPY SMOKED DUCK WING
BURNT ORANGE AND SPICES

Serves: 20

BURNT ORANGE SPICE MIX	BRINED DUCK WINGS	HONEY GLAZE	TO FINISH AND ASSEMBLE
6 g orange peel	20 duck wings	300 g honey	1 kg grapeseed oil
50 g coriander seeds	1 kg 10% Herb brine (p. 247)	15 g soy sauce	thyme leaves
40 g fennel seeds		45 g red wine vinegar	grated orange zest
35 g Tasmanian mountain pepper	DUCK WINGS PREPARATION	5 g salt	flaky sea salt, to taste
35 g salt	20 Brined duck wings (above)		
120 g caster sugar	2 kg duck fat		
	10 g thyme		
	1 garlic clove		

BURNT ORANGE SPICE MIX
Burn the orange peel on the grill, or in the oven, until charred. Place it onto a dehydrator tray and dehydrate at 70°C/160°F for 24 hours until fully dried.

Toast the coriander and fennel seeds, then set aside and cool. Blend the dried orange peel and spices together with a hand blender. Transfer the powder to a bowl, add the salt and sugar and mix well. Store in a sealed sous vide bag or airtight container.

BRINED DUCK WINGS
Put the duck wings and brine into a sous vide bag, seal and reserve in the fridge for 1 hour. Drain the duck wings in a colander.

DUCK WINGS PREPARATION
Preheat the oven to 98°C/208°F (fan). To prepare the duck wings, dislocate the joint between the tip, wingette and drumette and cut through both joints. Reserve the drumettes and tips for later use in stocks and place the wingettes in a deep tray, cover with the duck fat, thyme and garlic and cook in the oven for about 2 hours. Once the wingettes are cooked, leave to cool in the fat until they reach room temperature, then gently slide out the bones being careful to keep the wing intact. Place a long piece of cling film on the table and position eight wings one next to the other in a line – keeping them flat – then tightly roll the wings in the cling film. Repeat the process for the remaining wings, rolling another eight wings, then another four in a shorter length of cling film. Lightly press the duck wings between two flat trays and leave to rest in the fridge for 6 hours. Remove the duck from the cling film. Cut each wing at a 45° angle at both ends to create a diamond shape and reserve for later.

HONEY GLAZE
Combine all the ingredients in a medium saucepan, bring to the boil, then reduce the heat and simmer until the liquid reduces to 250 g in weight or has a thick, glossy consistency. Pour into a container and reserve at room temperature.

TO FINISH AND ASSEMBLE
Heat the grapeseed oil in a small saucepan to 180°C/350°F and add four duck wings. Fry for 1½ minutes, then flip and cook on the other side until golden brown. Fry the remaining wings, four at a time.

Drain the duck wings on paper towels to remove the excess oil. Using a brush, glaze the wings with the honey glaze. Sprinkle with the burnt orange spice mix and lightly season with flaky sea salt. Garnish with thyme leaves and orange zest. Skewer the duck wings with a small cocktail stick, place under a cloche and add smoke using a smoking gun (food smoker).

CHICKEN LIVER PARFAIT, SMOKED DUCK AND MADEIRA

Makes: 20 tarts

SHALLOT INFUSION
100 g shallots, thinly sliced
3 g garlic cloves, peeled
10 sprigs thyme, bound in muslin cloth
190 g Madeira
190 g port
88 g white port
55 g brandy

CHICKEN LIVER PARFAIT
125 g cleaned and trimmed
   chicken livers
125 g foie gras
1 g pink salt
4 g caster sugar
7 g salt
Shallot infusion (left)
3 g gelatine sheet
100 g double cream

MADEIRA JELLY
1 kg Duck stock (p. 246)
300 g Madeira
3 sheets bronze gelatine
salt, to taste

PARMESAN SHORTCRUST
350 g plain flour
6 g salt
3 g baking powder
180 g butter

150 g whole eggs
30 g egg yolks
15 g Parmesan, grated

TO ASSEMBLE
100 g smoked duck ham, cut into slices
   5 mm (¼ inch) thick
chive tips
red oxalis leaves
20 sorrel flowers

SHALLOT INFUSION
Combine all the ingredients in a small saucepan, set aside and allow to infuse for 12 hours. After 12 hours, place over a medium heat, stirring occasionally, and let it reduce to a glaze. Discard the thyme and garlic and reserve the shallot mixture for later.

CHICKEN LIVER PARFAIT
Preheat a water bath to 60°C/140°F. Cut the livers and foie gras into 2-cm (¾-inch) dice and add to a bowl. Add the pink salt, sugar and salt and mix well, then add the infused shallots and transfer the mixture to a sous vide bag. Seal and cook in the water bath for 35 minutes.

Soften the gelatine in ice water for 10 minutes. Gently heat the cream in a saucepan over a low heat, drain the gelatine and squeeze out the excess water, then add it to the cream and stir until dissolved. Transfer the cream mixture to a temperature-controlled blender and bring it to 50°C/120°F. Add the cooked chicken livers and foie gras and blend at full speed for 1 minute. Pass the mixture through a chinois and place everything into a tray over ice, so it cools quickly. Once it is cold, transfer to a piping bag fitted with a 5-mm (¼-inch) nozzle and reserve in the fridge.

MADEIRA JELLY
Pour the duck stock into a large saucepan, bring to the boil and boil until it reduces to 150 g. In a separate pan, bring the Madeira to the boil and boil until it reduces to 50 g. Soak the gelatine sheets in a bowl of cold water for 10 minutes. Once both liquids are reduced, combine in one container, season with salt and add the soaked gelatine (drained and squeezed of excess water) to the warm liquid. Stir well to ensure the gelatine has dissolved, then pour 200 g of it into a 50 x 36 x 2-cm

(20 x 14 x ¾-inch) tray and place in the fridge to set. Once the jelly is set, cut out twenty 4-cm (1½-inch) discs and reserve for later.

PARMESAN SHORTCRUST
Put the flour, salt, baking powder and butter into the bowl of a stand mixer fitted with the paddle attachment. Mix on low speed for about 2 minutes. While the paddle is still turning, gradually add the whole eggs, egg yolk and Parmesan and mix for another 2 minutes until everything is fully incorporated. Remove the dough from the bowl and lightly work it by hand into a ball. Cover with cling film and leave to rest in the fridge for 1½ hours.

Preheat the oven to 160°C/325°F (fan). Remove the dough from the fridge and roll it out to a thickness of 4 mm (⅛ inch). Use a 4-cm (1½-inch) round cutter to cut twenty discs from the dough and position the discs between two round tart moulds 3.5 cm (1½ inch) in diameter and 1.5 cm (¾ inch) deep (you will need 40 moulds) and press down. Trim any excess dough with a small knife. Bake at fan speed 3 for 8 minutes until golden brown. Remove the shortcrust tart cases from the moulds and reserve in an airtight container.

TO ASSEMBLE
Pipe chicken liver parfait in the middle of the tart case to reach the top of the case and cover with a Madeira jelly disc. Pinch each side of the disc, bringing them slightly closer to the centre and creating four subtle folds. On two opposite sides of the folds, place two duck ham pieces. On the remaining opposite sides, add some chive tips and red oxalis leaves (side by side). Finish with a sorrel flower in the middle of the tart.

SAUSAGE IN BRIOCHE

Serves: 40

BRIOCHE
500 g strong white flour
16 g salt
25 g caster sugar

25 g inverted sugar
25 g fresh yeast
260 g whole eggs
90 g water

280 g butter, cubed, at room
 temperature
1 smoked summer sausage
 (2.5 cm/1 inch in diameter)

TO ASSEMBLE
Pickle gel (p. 248)
dill tips

BRIOCHE
Put all the ingredients, except the butter and summer sausage, into the bowl of a stand mixer fitted with the paddle attachment and mix for 4 minutes to form a dough, then replace the paddle with a dough hook, reduce the speed to low and continue mixing. Gradually start adding the butter a few pieces at a time, allowing them to be fully incorporated into the dough before adding more. Once all the butter is mixed in, transfer the dough to a large tray, cover with cling film and allow to rest in the fridge for 12 hours.

In the meantime, wrap four 20 x 2.5-cm (8 x 1-inch) wooden dowels with greaseproof paper and spray with non-stick spray all around. Set aside. Spray four 25 x 4-cm (10 x 1½-inch) cylinder (lidded) bread moulds with non-stick spray.

Remove the dough from the fridge and portion it into four 300-g balls. Roll each ball out into a 30 x 21-cm (12 x 8 inch) sheet, 5-mm (¼ inch) thick. Wrap the dough around the greased dowels so that the ends are only just overlapping, then place the dowels and dough into the four bread moulds, with the lids open. Place cling film over the dough and leave to prove at room temperature for 30 minutes or until it has doubled in size. Preheat the oven to 180°C/350°F (fan). Once the dough has fully proved, remove the cling film and close the lids. Bake for 8 minutes, then rotate the moulds 90 degrees and bake for another 8 minutes. Check if the brioche is golden. If not, cook for another 2 minutes. Once it's cooked, remove the brioche from the moulds and place on a wire rack to completely cool. Gently cut one side and remove the wooden dowels, then gently push and twist the sausage through the hole left by the wooden dowel. Be careful not to break the brioche shape. Reserve for later.

TO ASSEMBLE
Preheat the oven to 180°C/350°F (fan). Place the sausage rolls onto a baking tray and bake in the oven for 5 minutes, then cut into slices 1 cm (½ inch) thick and lay them out on a tray. Dress each one with three dots of pickle gel and finish with a dill tip over each dot.

CORE GOUGÈRES
MASTER RECIPE

Makes: 20 gougères

SAVOURY CRAQUELIN
50 g butter, at room temperature
50 g T45 flour
2 g baking powder
50 g Parmesan, finely grated

GOUGÈRE MIX
200 g water
80 g butter
4 g fresh yeast
160 g T45 flour
50 g Parmesan, finely grated
50 g Cheddar, finely grated
7.5 g salt
140 g whole eggs

MORNAY SAUCE
 (makes about 250 g)
15 g butter
15 g T45 flour
150 g whole milk
80 g Cheddar, finely grated
40 g Gruyère, finely grated
salt, to taste

SAVOURY CRAQUELIN
Put all the ingredients into a mixing bowl and beat until smooth, being careful not to overwork the dough. Roll out the dough to a thickness of 2 mm (1/16 inch) between two sheets of greaseproof paper, then cut out twenty discs with a 3-cm (1¼-inch) ring cutter. Reserve in the freezer.

GOUGÈRE MIX
Preheat the oven to 165°C/330°F (30% humidity, no fan). Put the water and butter into a saucepan and bring to the boil, then crumble in the yeast and whisk to dissolve. While mixing with a spoon, tip in the flour and cook for about 5 minutes, stirring, until the mixture comes away from the sides of the pan. Transfer the mix to the bowl of a stand mixer fitted with the paddle attachment and beat for 1 minute. Add the cheese and beat again until melted, then add the salt. Gradually add the eggs, beating, until everything is incorporated, meanwhile scraping down the sides of the bowl. If the mixture is not glossy around the edges, add an extra egg. Transfer to a piping bag fitted with a round size-8 nozzle.

GOUGÈRE PREPARATION
Pipe twenty 2-cm (¾-inch) rounds of gougère mixture onto a silicone mat. Place a disc of craquelin on top of each gougère and bake for 1 minute. Put the fan setting to level 3 and bake for another 12 minutes, then remove the gougères from the oven and allow to cool on the tray.

MORNAY SAUCE
Melt the butter in a large saucepan over a medium heat, then stir in the flour. Continue stirring for about 7 minutes until the mixture is smooth and the flour becomes a light, golden colour, then increase the heat to medium-high and slowly whisk in the milk until thickened. Bring to a gentle simmer, reduce the heat and continue to simmer for 10–20 minutes, until the flour has softened and cooked out. Add the Cheddar and Gruyère, season to taste and mix well. Set aside and reserve.

ASPARAGUS GOUGÈRES

Serves: 20

ASPARAGUS PURÉE
12 g butter
200 g asparagus, thinly sliced
  (reserve the tips)
50 g Chicken stock (p. 244)
45 g spinach
salt, to taste

ASPARAGUS FILLING
75 g Mornay sauce (p. 183),
  at room temperature
125 g Asparagus purée (left)
50 g blanched asparagus, brunoised
salt, to taste

TO ASSEMBLE
Gougères (p. 183)
Parmesan powder (p. 242)
Asparagus powder (p. 242)
asparagus tips, blanched
brassica flowers

ASPARAGUS PURÉE
Melt the butter in a medium saucepan over a medium heat, add the asparagus and sweat until tender (with no colour), then season with salt. Once the asparagus is tender, add the chicken stock and cook for another 4 minutes until fully softened. Remove from the heat, add the spinach and transfer straight away to a blender and blend on full power until smooth. Pass through a chinois onto a metal tray set over ice to cool it instantly. Reserve in the fridge.

ASPARAGUS FILLING
Combine all the ingredients in a bowl and mix until completely smooth. Transfer to a piping bag fitted with a 5-mm (¼-inch) nozzle and reserve in the fridge.

TO ASSEMBLE
Preheat the oven to 180°C/350°F (½ fan). Insert the tip of the piping bag into the bottom of a gougère and pipe in the asparagus filling, being careful not to overfill. Repeat with the remaining gougères and filling. Reheat the gougères in the oven for 3 minutes. Dust the Parmesan and asparagus powders on top, followed by a small dot of asparagus filling and, finally, the asparagus tip and brassica flower.

CAVIAR GOUGÈRES

Serves: 20 *Note: the craquelin on this recipe is different to the others.

SAVOURY CRAQUELIN
63 g butter
63 g T45 flour
32 g buckwheat flour
2.2 g baking powder
63 g Parmesan, finely grated

GOUGÈRE FILLING
150 g Mornay sauce (p. 183)
50 g crème fraîche
1 cooked egg white, finely chopped
1 cooked egg yolk, finely chopped
8 g chives, finely chopped

8 g flat-leaf parsley, finely chopped
5 g lemon juice

TO ASSEMBLE
Gougères (p. 183)
Parmesan powder (p. 242)

Buckwheat powder (p. 242)
100 g crème fraîche
120 g caviar
20 pieces gold leaf

SAVOURY CRAQUELIN
Put all the ingredients into a mixing bowl and beat until smooth, being careful not to overwork the dough. Roll out the dough to a thickness of 2 mm (¹⁄₁₆ inch) between two sheets of greaseproof paper, then cut out twenty discs with a 3-cm (1¼-inch) ring cutter. Reserve in the freezer.

GOUGÈRE FILLING
Mix the mornay sauce with the crème fraîche in a medium bowl to make a creamy-textured mixture. Add and combine all the remaining ingredients using a spatula. Transfer to a piping (pastry) bag fitted with a 5-mm (¼-inch) nozzle and reserve in the fridge.

TO ASSEMBLE
Preheat the oven to 180°C/350°F (½ fan). Insert the tip of the piping bag into the bottom of a gougère and pipe in the filling, being careful not to overfill. Repeat with the remaining gougères and filling. Reheat the gougères in the oven for 3 minutes. Dust the Parmesan and buckwheat powders on top, followed by a small dot of the crème fraîche. Finish with 6 g caviar and a small piece of gold leaf.

CHEESE AND ONION GOUGÈRES

Serves: 20

CHEESE AND ONION FILLING
25 g butter
25 g green spring onion tops,
    thinly sliced
25 g shallots, brunoised, rinsed and
    drained well using a muslin cloth
100 g Onion purée (p. 246)
75 g Mornay sauce (p. 183)
salt, to taste

TO ASSEMBLE
Gougères (p. 183)
Parmesan powder (p. 242)
Onion powder (p. 242)
spring onion rondelles
onion flowers

CHEESE AND ONION FILLING
Melt the butter in a small saucepan over a medium heat, add the spring onion tops and sweat until tender, then remove from the heat and chill.

Combine all the ingredients, including the cooked, chilled spring onion tops, in a mixing bowl. Season to taste. Transfer to a piping bag fitted with a 5-mm (¼-inch) nozzle and reserve in the fridge.

TO ASSEMBLE
Preheat the oven to 180°C/350°F (½ fan). Insert the tip of the piping bag into the bottom of a gougère and pipe in the cheese and onion filling, being careful not to overfill. Repeat with the remaining gougères and filling. Reheat the gougères in the oven for 3 minutes. Dust the Parmesan and onion powders on top, followed by a small dot of cheese and onion filling on top, and finish with a spring onion rondelle and an onion flower.

PUMPKIN GOUGÈRES

Serves: 20

PUMPKIN PURÉE
500 g iron bark pumpkin, washed,
    peeled and cut into 1-cm (½-inch)
    dice
50 g butter
salt, to taste

PUMPKIN FILLING
100 g Mornay sauce (p. 183)
150 g Pumpkin purée (left)
20 g pumpkin oil
10 g Barolo vinegar
salt, to taste

TO ASSEMBLE
Gougères (p. 183)
Parmesan powder (p. 242)
Pumpkin powder (p. 242)
toasted pumpkin seeds

PUMPKIN PURÉE
Line a tray with paper towels and lay out the diced pumpkin in an even layer. Allow the pumpkin to dry out in the fridge overnight.

Put the diced pumpkin and butter in a large saucepan over a medium heat, season lightly and stir. Cover and cook for 5 minutes to release the moisture from the pumpkin, stirring regularly so that the pumpkin does not catch on the bottom of the pan, then reduce the heat and cook for 1 hour or until the pumpkin has cooked and softened but not taken on any colour. Transfer the pumpkin to a blender and blend on full speed until smooth. Store in a container and reserve in the fridge.

PUMPKIN FILLING
Combine all the ingredients in a bowl and mix until smooth. Transfer to a piping bag fitted with a 5-mm (¼-inch) nozzle and reserve in the fridge.

TO ASSEMBLE
Preheat the oven to 180°C/350°F (½ fan). Insert the tip of the piping bag into the bottom of a gougère and pipe in the pumpkin filling, being careful not to overfill. Repeat with the remaining gougères and filling. Reheat the gougères in the oven for 3 minutes. Dust the Parmesan and pumpkin powders on top, followed by a small dot of pumpkin filling, and finish with a pumpkin seed.

BLACK TRUFFLE GOUGÈRES

Serves: 20

TRUFFLE FILLING	TO ASSEMBLE
200 g Mornay sauce (p. 183)	Gougères (p. 183)
50 g Black truffle purée (p. 198)	Parmesan powder (p. 242)
5 g black truffle oil	finely shaved black truffle
10 g Barolo vinegar	
salt, to taste	

TRUFFLE FILLING
Combine all the ingredients in a bowl and mix well. Transfer to a piping bag fitted with a 5-mm (¼-inch) nozzle and reserve in the fridge.

TO ASSEMBLE
Preheat the oven to 180°C/350°F (½ fan). Insert the tip of the piping bag into the bottom of a gougère and pipe in the truffle filling, being careful not to overfill. Repeat with the remaining gougères and filling. Reheat the gougères in the oven for 3 minutes. Dust the Parmesan powder on the top, add a small dot of the truffle filling, and finish with shaved truffle.

PEA AND MINT GOUGÈRES

Serves: 20

PEA AND MINT PURÉE	PEA AND GOAT'S CURD FILLING	TO ASSEMBLE
150 g frozen peas	100 g Pea and mint purèe (left)	Gougères (p. 183)
7.5 g mint leaves	75 g goat's curd	Parmesan powder (p. 242)
salt, to taste	75 g Mornay sauce (p. 183)	Pea powder (p. 242)
	salt, to taste	pea shoots
		mint tips

PEA AND MINT PURÉE
Bring a large pan of salted water to the boil and blanch the peas with the mint for 3 minutes. Transfer the peas and mint (reserving the cooking liquid) to a blender with three ice cubes and blend for 2–3 minutes, gradually adding a little of the cooking liquid until the purée is smooth. Strain the purée through a fine chinois, using the back of a ladle to push it through. Check the seasoning and add salt, if needed. Place over an ice bath to cool the purée as quickly as possible, to retain the bright green colour. Reserve in the fridge.

PEA AND GOAT'S CURD FILLING
Combine all the ingredients in a bowl and mix until completely smooth. Transfer to a piping bag fitted with a 5-mm (¼-inch) nozzle and reserve in the fridge.

TO ASSEMBLE
Preheat the oven to 180°C/350°F (½ fan). Insert the tip of the piping bag into the bottom of a gougère and pipe in the pea and goat's curd filling, being careful not to overfill. Repeat with the remaining gougères and filling. Reheat the gougères in the oven for 3 minutes. Dust the Parmesan and pea powders on top, followed by a small dot of pea and goat's curd filling. Finish with a pea shoot and a mint tip.

BLACK OLIVE GOUGÈRES

Serves: 20

BLACK OLIVE TAPENADE		TAPENADE FILLING	TO ASSEMBLE
75 g pitted black olives, finely chopped	2 g grated lemon zest	175 g Mornay sauce (p. 183)	Gougères (p. 183)
10 g capers, finely chopped	salt, to taste	75 g Black olive tapenade (left)	Parmesan powder (p. 242)
1 tinned anchovy (in oil)	lemon juice, to taste	salt, to taste	Black olive powder (p. 242)
2 g flat-leaf parsley, chopped			black olive rondelles

BLACK OLIVE TAPENADE

Combine all the ingredients in a mortar and pound with a pestle until smooth. Season to taste and reserve in the fridge.

TAPENADE FILLING

Combine all the ingredients in a bowl and mix until completely smooth. Transfer to a piping bag fitted with a 5-mm (¼-inch) nozzle and reserve in the fridge.

TO ASSEMBLE

Preheat the oven to 180°C/350°F (½ fan). Insert the tip of the piping bag into the bottom of a gougère and pipe in the tapenade filling, being careful not to overfill. Repeat with the remaining gougères and filling. Reheat the gougères in the oven for 3 minutes. Dust the Parmesan and black olive powders on top, followed by a small dot of tapenade filling, and finish with a slice of black olive.

TOMATO AND BASIL GOUGÈRES

Serves: 20

CONFIT TOMATO	DRIED TOMATO FONDUE	TO ASSEMBLE
100 g Tomberry Red cherry tomatoes, halved	300 g Tomato fondue (p. 247)	Gougères (p. 183)
3 g picked thyme leaves		Parmesan powder (p. 242)
5 g salt	TOMATO FILLING	Tomato powder (p. 242)
2 g caster sugar	100 g Mornay sauce (p. 183)	Basil powder (p. 242)
60 g olive oil	150 g Dried tomato fondue (above)	baby basil leaves
	salt, to taste	

CONFIT TOMATO

Combine all the ingredients in a medium bowl and mix until fully incorporated. Leave to macerate for 5 minutes, then remove the tomato halves from the bowl and place them onto a dehydrator tray lined with parchment paper, ensuring the tomatoes are cut side up. Insert the tray into the dehydrator and dehydrate at 65°C/150°F for 5 hours. Check the tomatoes are semi-dried. If so, remove them and place into a container. Reserve in the fridge.

DRIED TOMATO FONDUE

Put the tomato fondue into a small saucepan over a low heat and cook it for about 30 minutes until it has dried out and is deep red in colour, with an intense taste. Reserve in the fridge.

TOMATO FILLING

Combine all the ingredients in a bowl and mix until completely smooth. Transfer to a piping bag fitted with a 5-mm (¼-inch) nozzle and reserve in the fridge.

TO ASSEMBLE

Preheat the oven to 180°C/350°F (½ fan). Insert the tip of the piping bag into the bottom of a gougère and pipe in the tomato filling, being careful not to overfill. Repeat with the remaining gougères and filling. Reheat the gougères in the oven for 3 minutes. Dust the Parmesan, tomato and basil powders on top, followed by a small dot of tomato filling and a confit tomato, and finish with a basil leaf.

ISLE OF HARRIS SCALLOP TARTARE
SEA VEGETABLE CONSOMMÉ

Serves: 4

NASTURTIUM OIL
100 g nasturtium leaves
100 g grapeseed oil
2 g salt
2 g caster sugar

SCALLOP TARTARE
4 extra-large scallops
  (320 g scallop meat), shells reserved
4 g lime juice
4 g chives, finely chopped
4 g mascarpone
salt, to taste

SEA VEGETABLE CONSOMMÉ
200 g Vegetable nage (p. 242)
25 g sea lettuce
25 g sea rosemary
25 g sea fennel
25 g sea purslane
lime juice, to taste
salt, to taste

TO ASSEMBLE
baby nasturtium leaves
dill tips
chive tips
oyster leaves
wasabi flowers
baby wasabi leaves

NASTURTIUM OIL
Put all the ingredients into a blender and blend to a smooth purée. Prepare a bowl over ice. Pass the purée through a fine muslin cloth into the bowl, leaving it to hang overnight in the fridge. The next day, pour the oil into a sous vide bag, seal and hang it at an angle in the fridge for 24 hours, allowing the water and the oil to separate. Once the water has drained to the bottom corner of the bag, cut a small hole to allow the water to slowly escape, leaving only the oil. Reserve the oil until required.

SCALLOP TARTARE
Cut the scallop meat into 5-mm (¼-inch) cubes on a cold chopping board. In a bowl set over an ice bath, combine the scallops, lime juice, chives and mascarpone. Mix gently and add salt to taste. Reserve in the fridge until required.

SEA VEGETABLE CONSOMMÉ
Bring the nage to the boil in a medium saucepan, then remove from the heat. Add the coastal herbs and leave to infuse for 15 minutes, then pass through a fine chinois into a bowl set over ice. Add lime juice and salt to taste.

TO ASSEMBLE
Place some scallop tartare in the centre of a reserved scallop shell. Add some of the herbs, leaves and flowers on top. Pour some sea vegetable consommé into the shell around the scallop and add droplets of nasturtium oil onto the consommé.

SCOTTISH LANGOUSTINE AND WASABI PEA
ROSE GERANIUM, ALMOND

Serves: 4

INFUSED ROSE GERANIUM BASE
30 g butter
250 g onions, thinly sliced
30 g garlic cloves, thinly sliced
400 g whole milk
100 g double cream
10 g ginger, grated
8 g wasabi root, grated
10 g rose geranium leaves
10 g marjoram
50 g toasted almonds
wasabi paste, to taste

TO PREP THE LANGOUSTINES
4 x 250-g langoustines

LANGOUSTINE BUTTER
langoustine heads and shells (reserved
  from above)

50 g grapeseed oil
50 g carrots, diced
50 g white onions, diced
50 g celery, diced
½ garlic clove, crushed
5 coriander seeds
5 fennel seeds
1 star anise
5 white peppercorns
250 g butter
25 g tomato purée (paste)
salt, to taste

ALMOND PURÉE
250 g Infused rose geranium base (left)
5 g wasabi paste
20 g almond syrup
25 g toasted ground almonds
1 g Gellan F
salt, to taste

ROSE GERANIUM SAUCE
300 g Infused rose geranium base (left)
20 g wasabi paste
40 g almond syrup
5 drops of geranium extract
salt, to taste

PEA PURÉE
50 g butter
100 g onions, thinly sliced
200 g frozen peas
50 g Chicken stock (p. 244)
100 g double cream
20 g wasabi leaves
15 g wasabi root, grated
salt, to taste

PEA STOCK
150 g water
250 g pea pods
salt, to taste
lemon juice, to taste

WASABI VINAIGRETTE
15 g lemon juice
40 g wasabi paste
25 g olive oil
salt, to taste

TO ASSEMBLE
25 g fresh baby peas
pea shoots
rose geranium petals
baby wasabi leaves
wasabi flowers
chive tips

INFUSED ROSE GERANIUM BASE

Melt the butter in a medium saucepan over a medium heat, add the onions and garlic and sweat until translucent, then transfer to a tray to cool. Combine the onions and garlic with the remaining ingredients in a container, seal and reserve in the fridge to infuse for at least 12 hours. Strain through a chinois into a container.

TO PREP THE LANGOUSTINES

Bring a medium saucepan of water to the boil. Separate the langoustine heads from the tails, reserving the heads for later use. Place the tails flat on a chopping board, then carefully remove the intestinal tract from the langoustine by pulling on the central tail fin. If it breaks as you're doing it, a pair of tweezers can be used to remove the tract. Once all the tracts are removed, tie the langoustines together, top to tail, using butchers' string. Blanch the langoustines in the boiling water for 10 seconds, then immediately place in ice water. As soon as they are cooled, untie them and carefully peel the shell off the flesh. Combine the shells with the heads and reserve. Place the langoustines on a flat tray.

LANGOUSTINE BUTTER

Preheat the oven to 180°C/350°F (fan). Roast the langoustine heads and shells in the oven for 10 minutes.

Heat the oil in a medium saucepan over a medium heat, add all the vegetables and the garlic and cook until lightly browned. Season with salt, then add the spices and sweat down. Add the roasted langoustine heads and shells and crush them with a rolling pin, then add the butter and allow it to foam and roast. Reduce the heat, add the tomato purée and cook for 2 minutes, then transfer the pan to a warm area for 30 minutes and allow the butter to clarify. Pass through a fine chinois lined with muslin cloth into a container.

ALMOND PURÉE

Place the infused rose geranium base, wasabi paste, almond syrup and ground almonds in a temperature-controlled blender, season to taste, then mix on a medium speed until it reaches 90°C/195°F. Add the Gellan F and bring the temperature back up to 90°C/195°F while mixing (still on medium speed). Once the mixture has reached 90°C/195°F, remove the lid and scrape down the sides and around the bottom of the jug with a spatula. Blend on medium speed for 2 minutes, then on full power for 30 seconds. Pour onto a tray set over ice to chill the mixture as quickly as possible. Once the mixture has fully set, cut into small pieces, add to a blender and blend on full speed until smooth. Pass through a chinois and transfer to a squeeze bottle.

ROSE GERANIUM SAUCE

Put the infused rose geranium base in a medium saucepan and bring to the boil, then remove from the heat, whisk in the remaining ingredients and allow to cool. Blend the liquid using a hand blender, then transfer to a container.

PEA PURÉE

Melt the butter in a medium saucepan over a medium heat, add the onions and sweat (with no colour) until fully cooked, then season with salt. Add the peas and cook for 2 minutes, then add the chicken stock and cream. Bring to the boil, then remove from the heat and add the remaining ingredients. Pass through a chinois and reserve the liquid. Add the ingredients to a blender and blend on full power, gradually adding the reserved liquid to create a smooth purée. Pass through a chinois once more and chill as quickly as possible over ice. Transfer to a squeeze bottle.

PEA STOCK

Place all the ingredients in a blender and blend on full power. Pass through a sieve and season to taste.

WASABI VINAIGRETTE

In a small mixing bowl, combine all the ingredients except the salt, then whisk to emulsify. Once its fully emulsified, add the salt and whisk again.

TO ASSEMBLE

Create a circle of dots with the almond purée, 5 cm (2 inches) from the middle of the plate, using a circular template, leaving gaps to be filled with the pea purée. Fill the gaps with the pea purée, then repeat the process for the outer ring, creating two rings of alternating purées. Combine the pea stock and fresh baby peas in a small saucepan over a medium heat and cook for 1 minute. Drain the peas into a small bowl and add the wasabi vinaigrette.

Melt the langoustine butter in a non-stick frying pan over a medium-high heat, then add the langoustine (flesh side down). Gently sear the langoustine for 45 seconds–1 minute, then remove from the pan and set aside to rest in a warm place. Using a 5-cm (2-inch) ring, spoon the peas and wasabi vinaigrette at the centre of the plate. Glaze the langoustine with the remaining langoustine butter, then gently place it on top of the peas. Arrange the pea shoots, herbs and flowers on each side of the langoustine. In a small saucepan, gently warm the rose geranium sauce. Using a hand blender, blend the rose geranium sauce in the corner of the pan to create a mousse. To finish the dish, add a spoonful of the rose geranium mousse on top of the langoustine.

COLCHESTER CRAB
SABAYON, CONSOMMÉ, CAVIAR

Serves: 4

COLCHESTER CRAB
PREPARATION
1 x 2-kg live cock crab

FOR THE CRAB SABAYON
CRAB BUTTER
15 g grapeseed oil
150 g crab shells (above), crushed
100 g butter, cut into 2-cm (¾-inch)
  dice

EGG YOLK
150 g egg yolks

BROWN CRAB MEAT
300 g brown crab meat (from
  Colchester crab preparation, left)
2.5% Gellan F
salt, to taste

FINISHING THE CRAB SABAYON
75 g Crab butter (left)
150 g Brown crab meat (above)
150 g Cooked egg yolk (left)
lemon juice, to taste
salt, to taste

CRAB JELLY
250 g Crab consommé (p. 243)

0.5 g Gellan F
0.4 g Gellan LT100

CRAB SALAD PREPARATION
picked white crab meat (from
  Colchester crab preparation, left)
20 g apple, diced
10 g celery, diced
lemon juice, to taste
2 g chives, chopped
salt, to taste

HERB BOUQUET
4 chives, blanched
sprig parsley

sprig chervil
2-cm (¾-inch) lemongrass baton
2-cm (¾-inch) lemon peel baton

TO ASSEMBLE
lava stone
zest from 1 lemon
kelp seaweed
Crab consommé (p. 243)
sea fennel
baby nasturtium leaves
marsh samphire
Crab butter, melted (left)
caviar

COLCHESTER CRAB PREPARATION
Preheat the steam oven to 75°C/167°F (fan). Kill the crab by putting a sharp spike through the main nerve centres on the underside of the body. Remove the crab claws and legs from the body. Place the crab claws in the steam oven and cook for 2 minutes, then add the legs and cook for 8 minutes. Increase the heat of the steam to 100°C/210°F (fan) and cook the bodies for 15 minutes. Remove all the crab from the oven and transfer to a new tray to cool over ice.

Gently crack the shells and slide out the cartilage, keeping the claw meat intact, then set aside in the fridge. Scrape out the brown meat from the head and body of the crab, and reserve in the fridge. Pick out the remaining white crab meat from the body, and sift through to remove any small remaining shell or cartilage pieces.

FOR THE CRAB SABAYON
CRAB BUTTER
Heat the grapeseed oil in a roasting tin over a medium heat, add the crab shells and roast until golden brown, then reduce the heat and add the diced butter. Once the butter has melted, gently heat to 85°C/185°F, then remove from the heat, cover the pan and set aside to infuse for 1 hour. Pass the crab butter through a fine chinois and muslin cloth and discard the shells. Allow the butter to cool, then transfer to a container.

EGG YOLK
Preheat a water bath to 70°C/160°F, place the egg yolks in a small sous vide bag, seal and cook for 30 minutes, then cool down as quickly as possible in an ice bath.

BROWN CRAB MEAT
Combine the brown crab meat and some salt in a bowl and blend using a hand blender. Strain through a fine chinois. Weigh the liquid, then place into a temperature-controlled blender and heat to 90°C/200°F on speed 2. Measure 2.5% of Gellan F for the amount of liquid you weighed. Once the liquid reaches 90°C/200°F, add the Gellan F and mix on a medium speed for 2 more minutes, maintaining the temperature at 90°C/200°F. Pour the liquid into a tray and chill over ice. Once set and completely cool, cut into small pieces, transfer to a blender and blend on full speed for 5 minutes or until smooth.

FINISHING THE CRAB SABAYON
Combine all the ingredients in a bowl and blend until smooth and emulsified using a hand blender, then season to taste.

Transfer the mix to a siphon and charge with 1 cartridge. Keep the siphon in a water bath, maintaining the temperature at 55°C/130°F.

CRAB JELLY
Add the consommé to a temperature-controlled blender and set to 90°C/200°F on a medium speed. Once it reaches the temperature, add both the Gellan F and LT100. Blend on the highest speed for 10 seconds, then for 2 minutes on a medium speed, while maintaining the temperature at 90°C/200°F. Transfer the liquid to a warm chinois piston and pour over a flat cling-filmed surface, creating a thin, even layer. Cut out four 6-cm (2½-inch) rounds and place on a tray.

CRAB SALAD PREPARATION
Lay the picked crab meat onto a paper towel to absorb any excess moisture. Combine the picked crab meat, apple, celery and lemon juice in a bowl and mix gently. Add the chives and season to taste.

HERB BOUQUET
Using the chives, tie the parsley, chervil, lemongrass and lemon peel baton together into a bouquet.

TO ASSEMBLE
Heat the small lava stone in the oven. Heat a medium saucepan of water with some lemon zest and kelp seaweed and cover with a steamer. Add a crab claw to a tray, sprinkle with lemon zest and lay the crab jelly disc on top, then gently steam for 2 minutes.

Gently reheat the crab consommé in a small saucepan.

To prepare the crab presentation, fill the steam chamber of the brass plate that the crab will be presented on with the lemon and seaweed-infused water. Remove the crab claw from the steamer and decorate it with herbs, then place onto the brass steamer plate. Lay the lava stone inside the steam chamber, then top with the crab claw on the brass steamer plate and cover with a glass cloche.

Dress the crab salad with the melted crab butter and place into a marble bowl. Fully cover the salad with the crab sabayon and finish with a quenelle of caviar.

Fill a small glass teapot with the herb bouquet and hot crab consommé. To serve, pour the crab consommé into a small glass cup alongside the sabayon and crab claw.

LOBSTER AND SPELT
FENLAND CELERY, CAVIAR AND SELIM PEPPER

Serves: 4

LOBSTER PREPARATION
2 x 450–500-g live native lobsters

LOBSTER CONSOMMÉ INFUSION
400 g Lobster consommé (p. 243)
200 g puffed buckwheat, toasted
5 g lapsang souchong tea

SPELT
200 g pearled spelt
50 g grapeseed oil
100 g shallots, brunoised
50 g white wine
500 g Lobster stock (p. 243)
salt, to taste

FENLAND CELERY
2 Fenland celery sticks, washed, peeled, and cut into 5-mm (¼-inch) dice
salt, to taste

CELTUCE DISC
1 celtuce stick, washed, peeled and cut into slices 5 mm (¼ inch) thick
salt, to taste

SMOKED CRÈME FRAÎCHE
100 g crème fraîche
20 g maple wood chips
salt, to taste

ACIDULATED BUTTER
80 g onions, cut into slices 4 mm (⅛ inch) thick
150 g white wine
150 g white wine vinegar
200 g unsalted butter, cut into 2-cm (¾-inch) dice

TO FINISH AND ASSEMBLE
Lobster butter (p. 247), melted, for brushing
Lobster stock (p. 243)
Parmesan, grated
ground selim pepper
2 g chervil, chopped
grapeseed oil, for frying

15 g caviar
celery leaves
chive tips
spring onion rondelles, green and white
chervil tips
onion flowers
baby lettuce leaves
salt, to taste

LOBSTER PREPARATION
Preheat the oven steamer to 90°C/195°F (fan). With a large, heavy knife, cut along the natural crease on the lobsters' heads through the centre of the eyes and straight down to the board. Twist the claws and the tail from the head. Put the claws, tails and heads on a steamer tray and allow to drain. Cut the lobster heads in half lengthways and remove everything inside. Reserve the heads to make lobster stock and lobster butter (pages 243 and 247). Remove the digestive tube from the tail and discard. Tie the lobster tails together, top to tail, as straight as possible. Cook the lobster tails in the oven steamer for 4 minutes. Remove and chill in an ice bath, then cook the lobster claws in the oven steamer for 7 minutes. Remove and chill in an ice bath. Remove the lobster meat from the shells, keeping the tail and claw meat separate. Dice the claw meat into 5-mm (¼-inch) cubes and keep the tails whole.

LOBSTER CONSOMMÉ INFUSION
Bring the consommé to the boil in a saucepan and remove from the heat. Add the toasted buckwheat and infuse for 2 minutes, then strain. Add the tea and infuse for another 4 minutes, then strain and leave to cool.

SPELT
Place the spelt into a container and cover with water, allowing any spelt husks to float to the surface and be removed, then transfer to a sieve and rinse under cold running water for 5 minutes until the water runs clear. Heat the oil in a large pan over a medium heat, add the shallots and sweat until soft and translucent. Increase the temperature, add the spelt, and toast for 2–3 minutes until a nutty odour is produced. Add the wine and cook until the alcohol has evaporated, then add 200 g of the lobster stock, season lightly and reduce the heat, allowing the liquid to reduce while stirring continuously. Add the remaining 300 g stock, allow it to reduce until the spelt is tender. The spelt should take 15 minutes to cook. Season to taste and place the cooked spelt on a large tray to cool.

FENLAND CELERY
Bring a small saucepan of salted water to the boil and blanch the diced celery until tender. Cool in an ice bath, then drain.

CELTUCE DISC
Using a 2-cm (¾-inch) cutter, punch-cut each slice and lightly season. Blanch in a pan of salted boiling water until tender. Cool in an ice bath then drain.

SMOKED CRÈME FRAÎCHE
Place the crème fraîche in an airtight container. Fill the smoking gun (food smoker) with the wood chips. Start the machine and light the chips. Insert the pipe into the airtight container and fill with smoke. Seal the lid of the container and leave for 20 minutes. Remove the lid, season to taste and transfer to a squeeze bottle.

ACIDULATED BUTTER
Combine the onions, white wine and vinegar in a medium saucepan over a medium heat and cook until it reduces by three-quarters. Remove from the heat and gradually whisk in the butter until it is thoroughly emulsified. Leave to infuse for 20 minutes, then pass through a fine chinois.

TO FINISH AND ASSEMBLE
Cut each lobster tail into six slices (three pieces per portion), season and brush with lobster butter. Gently heat under the grill or in an oven just until warm. Reheat the spelt in a medium saucepan with a dash of lobster stock. Add a piece of acidulated butter, grated Parmesan and selim pepper, then add the chervil and remove from the heat.

Gently heat the diced celery and lobster claws in a pan and season to taste. Heat a dash of grapeseed oil in a non-stick frying pan over a medium heat, and cook the celtuce discs until lightly coloured on both sides. Warm the consommé infusion in a saucepan.

Add the spelt to a crescent-shaped mould. Add the celery and lobster on top. Altinate the lobster and celtuce discs from the top of the crescent to the bottom. Remove the mould. Add dots of crème fraîche on top, then three domes of caviar.

Place the herbs and flowers on top. Finally, add the consommé infusion to a sauce jug and pour it into the centre of the crescent.

'COLD SLAW'

Serves: 4

PICKLE
50 g white wine vinegar
60 g water
25 g caster sugar
1 g fennel seeds
1 g white peppercorns
1 g coriander seeds
salt, to taste

PICKLED VEGETABLES
1 carrot, peeled
1 cucumber, peeled
1 red cabbage
1 white cabbage
Pickle (above), passed through
 a chinois

GAZPACHO INFUSION
250 g green tomatoes, diced
150 g cucumber, diced
35 g shallots, diced
35 g olive oil
30 g Chardonnay vinegar
50 g celery, diced
60 g green peppers, diced
5 g mint
6 sprigs thyme
5 g tarragon
salt and pepper, to taste

GAZPACHO GRANITA
200 g Gazpacho infusion (above)
liquid nitrogen

VINAIGRETTE DRESSING
5 g Dijon mustard
30 g Chardonnay vinegar
100 g olive oil
salt, to taste

LETTUCE PREPARATION
2 iceberg lettuces

SMOKED BUTTERMILK
150 g thick buttermilk
20 g maple wood chips
salt, to taste

VEGETABLE SLAW
100 g white cabbage, sliced
100 g red cabbage, sliced

30 g Gazpacho infusion (left)
salt, to taste

TO ASSEMBLE
nasturtium leaves
rocket flowers
sweet rocket flowers
salad burnet
celery cress
sorrel flowers
tarragon cress
mint cress
cucumber flowers
chive tips
chive flowers

PICKLE
Combine all the ingredients in a saucepan over a medium heat, stir and bring to the boil, then transfer to a container.

PICKLED VEGETABLES
After peeling the carrot and cucumber, cut four 5-cm (2-inch) triangles 2 cm (¾ inches) thick. Do the same with the leaves of the red and white cabbage. Place each vegetable in a separate container and divide the pickle juice among them. Marinate for a minimum of 12 hours.

GAZPACHO INFUSION
Put all the ingredients, except the herbs, into a medium container and mix together. Leave to marinate for 30 minutes, then place into a blender and blend until smooth. Transfer to a container, add the herbs and allow to infuse for a minimum of 12 hours. Pass through a chinois into a container.

GAZPACHO GRANITA
Put the gazpacho infusion (reserving the rest for the slaw and for plating) into a medium metal bowl and whisk while pouring liquid nitrogen onto the mixture, until it becomes frozen and looks like a crumble. Transfer the granita to a container and freeze until needed.

VINAIGRETTE DRESSING
Combine the mustard and vinegar in a bowl, season with salt and whisk to emulsify. Slowly add the olive oil, whisking continuously.

LETTUCE PREPARATION
Remove the hard stem end at the bottom of the lettuce and remove the layers of external leaves. With your hand, open up the lettuce to expose the core. Without tearing or damaging the leaves, separate the lettuce into single leaves. Wash the lettuce three times, completely removing any dirt.

SMOKED BUTTERMILK
Put the buttermilk into an airtight container. Fill the smoking gun (food smoker) with the wood chips. Start the machine and light the chips. Insert the pipe into the airtight container and fill with the smoke. Remove the pipe and seal the lid of the container. Leave for 20 minutes, then remove the lid and season to taste.

VEGETABLE SLAW
Mix all the ingredients in a medium bowl and season with salt.

TO ASSEMBLE
In a small tray, lay down the smaller lettuce leaves, dress them with the vinaigrette, then place a small amount of vegetable slaw in the middle. Dress with the remaining gazpacho infusion and position the pickled vegetable triangles around the mix. Place a second centre lettuce leaf around the first to enclose the slaw and create a ball. Season the lettuce on the outside with the vinaigrette and place all the herbs and flowers on top. In the centre of a plate, add a large dot of smoked buttermilk. Position the ball of cold slaw on top. To finish, sprinkle the gazpacho granita all around the salad.

NETTLE AND NASTURTIUM VELOUTÉ
CELTUCE, VOATSIPERIFERY PEPPER AND ARGAN OIL

Serves: 4

NETTLE VELOUTÉ
500 g Chicken stock (p. 244)
2 medium shallots, sliced
2 sprigs thyme
I garlic clove
100 g dry white vermouth
250 g double cream
200 g nettle leaves
200 g nasturtium leaves
100 g spinach
salt, to taste

NETTLE PESTO
20 g nettle leaves
20 g nasturtium leaves
20 g chervil leaves
20 g turnip tops
20 g spinach
20 g rocket
150 g grapeseed oil
Barolo vinegar, to taste
salt, to taste

CELERY
8 large celery sticks, peeled and
   cut into 20-cm (8-inch) lengths
   that are 3 mm (⅛ inch) thick

CELTUCE
2 large celtuce, cut into 20-cm (8-inch)
   lengths that are 3 mm (⅛ inch) thick

TURNIP
I turnip, peeled
salt, to taste

NUTMEG EMULSION
20 g nutmeg, grated
50 g Chicken stock (p. 244)
50 g butter
grated lemon zest, to taste
freshly ground Voatsiperifery
   pepper, to taste
salt, to taste

TO ASSEMBLE
blue nasturtium leaves
green nasturtium leaves
variegated nasturtium leaves
chive tips
baby nettles
wild garlic flowers
argan oil
goat's curd
salt, to taste

NETTLE VELOUTÉ
Put the chicken stock, shallots, thyme and garlic into a saucepan along with a good pinch of salt and bring to the boil, then reduce by three-quarters. In a second pan, bring the dry white vermouth to the boil, then remove from the heat. Once the stock has reduced, pour in the vermouth, add the cream and let it reduce by half. Strain the liquid through a chinois into a clean pan.

Prepare a metal tray over an ice bath. Add the nettle, nasturtium and spinach to the liquid, then transfer the mixture directly to a blender and blend on full power until smooth. Pass the liquid through a chinois into the tray to chill, then reserve in the fridge.

NETTLE PESTO
Wash all the greens and dry in a salad spinner. Add to a blender with the oil and pulse for 30 seconds at a time until smooth, then season with vinegar and salt. Reserve the pesto in a squeeze bottle.

CELERY
Bring a medium saucepan of water to the boil and season for blanching. Blanch the celery batons until tender. Chill in an ice bath, then drain.

CELTUCE
Bring a medium saucepan of water to the boil and season for blanching. Blanch the celtuce batons until tender. Chill in an ice bath, then drain.

TURNIP
Using a vegetable sheeter, slice the turnip into sheets 3 mm (⅛ inch) thick. Cut the turnip sheets into slices 3 mm (⅛ inch) wide, 20 cm (8 inches) in length, to give you strands. Lay the turnip strands on a tray, season with salt and leave for 4 minutes, then rinse well.

NUTMEG EMULSION
Reduce the chicken stock by half in a small saucepan over a high heat. Remove from the heat and add the butter, then use a hand blender to emulsify. Add the lemon zest, Voatsiperifery pepper, nutmeg and salt to taste. Reserve in a warm place.

TO ASSEMBLE
Put the nutmeg emulsion into a medium saucepan over a medium heat and bring to the boil. Add the strands of celery, celtuce and turnip to heat through. Bring the velouté to a simmer in a small saucepan over a medium heat and season to taste. Using a large carving fork, mix the strands of vegetables, then wind them around the fork until you have a tight bundle. Turn this vertically so the bundle is upright and place in the centre of a bowl. Pipe a small amount of pesto into the centre of the bundle. Place all the herbs around and on top of the vegetables and add a few drops of argan oil to finish. Blend the hot velouté with a spoonful of goat's curd using a hand blender. Transfer to a sauce jug and serve at the table.

'POTATO AND ROE'
TROUT AND HERRING ROE AND DULSE BEURRE BLANC

Serves: 4

POTATO PREPARATION
4 medium Charlotte potatoes
100 g butter
30 g salted kombu
20 g dulse, finely chopped
5 g salt

VINEGAR REDUCTION
75 g white wine
75 g white wine vinegar
50 g shallots, thinly sliced
1 garlic clove, sliced

2 g white peppercorns
3 sprigs thyme

POTATO CRISPS
2 kg grapeseed oil
1 small Ratte potato
vinegar powder, to taste
salt, to taste

DULSE BEURRE BLANC
Vinegar reduction (left)
50 g double cream

200 g very cold butter, diced
kombu and dulse (reserved from
   the potato preparation, left)
lemon juice, to taste
salt, to taste

ROE MIX
60 g trout eggs
30 g smoked herring eggs
10 g chives, chopped

TO ASSEMBLE
red vein sorrel
sheep's sorrel
butterfly sorrel
sorrel flowers
rocket (arugula) flowers
wild rocket (arugula)
chive tips

POTATO PREPARATION
Preheat a water bath to 98°C/208°F. Add the potatoes to a sous vide bag along with the butter, kombu, dulse and salt, then seal.

Cook in the water bath for 1 hour until the potatoes are cooked through, then cool down in an ice bath. Once chilled, remove and separate the potatoes from the kombu and cooking liquid. Set aside. Top and tail the potatoes then transfer to a new sous vide bag with the cooking liquid. Seal and leave to marinate in the fridge for 24 hours. Finely chop the cooked kombu and dulse and reserve for the beurre blanc.

VINEGAR REDUCTION
Combine all the ingredients in a small saucepan over a medium heat and reduce by half. Pass through a sieve.

POTATO CRISPS
Preheat the oil in a deep-fat fryer to 160°C/320°F. Peel the potato and slice to a thickness of 2 mm (1/16 inch) and deep-fry until golden, then drain on paper towels and season with vinegar powder and salt. Reserve in a dehydrator at 60°C/140°F.

DULSE BEURRE BLANC
Reduce the vinegar reduction in a saucepan until it is a light syrup. Add the double cream, stir and let it come to the boil, then reduce the heat, add one-quarter of the diced butter and whisk gently, creating an emulsion. Repeat these last two steps until all the butter is added, then remove from the heat, add the chopped kombu and dulse, and mix. Leave to infuse for 5 minutes, then season to taste with lemon juice and salt.

ROE MIX
Put the trout and smoked herring eggs into a bowl with the chives and mix gently.

TO ASSEMBLE
Bring a small saucepan of water to the boil over a medium heat. Add the sous vide bag with the potatoes and simmer for 10 minutes. Open the bag and transfer the potatoes to a tray to drain. Place a potato on a plate. Cover the top of the potato with the roe mix. Add the potato crisps so they are standing upright, then place all the herbs and flowers in between the crisps. Finish by pouring the dulse beurre blanc into a sauce jug. Once ready to serve, pour the beurre blanc around the potato.

'LAMB CARROT'
BRAISED LAMB, SHEEP'S MILK YOGURT

Serves: 4

LAMB NECK
grapeseed oil, for searing
1 kg lamb neck, on the bone
100 g celery, diced
200 g carrots, diced
150 g onions, diced
200 g peeled celeriac, diced
50 g garlic cloves
50 g butter
1 g coriander seeds, toasted
5 g black peppercorns
6 sprigs thyme
6 sprigs rosemary
1 bay leaf
1 kg Lamb stock (p. 244)

1 kg Veal stock (p. 244)
salt, to taste

CARROT PREPARATION
4 English carrots with green tops intact
  (13 x 2 cm/5 x ¾ inch)
300 g reduced lamb stock (left)
1 sprig rosemary
2 g salt

CONFIT CARROTS
200 g lamb fat
1 sprig thyme
1 sprig rosemary
1 garlic clove

1 yellow carrot
1 orange carrot
salt, to taste

CARROT-TOP PESTO
20 g chives
20 g chervil
20 g basil
20 g spinach
20 g carrot tops (reserved from
  Carrot preparation, left)
20 g rocket
150 g pomace oil
Barolo vinegar, to taste
salt, to taste

CRISPY LAMB FAT
250 g fatty lamb trim, cut into 2-cm
  (¾-inch) dice
salt, to taste

TO ASSEMBLE
Lamb sauce (p. 245)
1 piece of butter
Barolo vinegar
Carrot tops (left)
sheep's milk yogurt
Lamb buns (p. 238)

LAMB NECK
Heat a dash of grapeseed oil in a medium saucepan over a high heat. Season the lamb neck with salt and sear on all sides. Remove the lamb neck from the pan, set aside, and add the vegetables, garlic and butter to the pan. Sweat until tender, add the spices and herbs, then deglaze the pan with the lamb and veal stock. Transfer the vegetables, stock and lamb neck to a pressure cooker, seal the lid, bring it up to pressure and cook for 1½ hours, then remove from the heat and allow to rest for 30 minutes. Release the pressure and allow the lamb to cool down in its own juices. Carefully remove the meat from the neck bone and reserve. Pass the stock through a fine chinois into a clean saucepan and reduce by half over a low heat.

CARROT PREPARATION
Set a water bath to 98°C/208°F. Wash the carrots and cut off the green tops (reserving the tops for the pesto). Peel and shape the carrots to typical carrot form, then put them into a sous vide bag with the reduced lamb stock, rosemary and salt. Seal to 100% vacuum, place in the water bath and cook for 45 minutes, or until tender, then remove and place in an ice bath. Once the carrots are cold, remove from the ice bath and reserve in the fridge to marinate for 24 hours, keeping them in the bag.

CONFIT CARROTS
Heat the lamb fat in a saucepan to 65°C/150°F and add the herbs and garlic. Peel the carrots and cut them into slices 2 mm (1/16 inch) thick. Using a 2-cm (¾-inch)

cutter, punch cut each slice and lightly season. Add the carrot slices to the pan and cook for 10 minutes or until tender. Drain.

CARROT-TOP PESTO
Wash the herbs and greens and dry them in a salad spinner. Add to a blender with the oil (reserving some of the carrot tops for assembly) and pulse for 30 seconds at a time until smooth. Season with vinegar and salt.

CRISPY LAMB FAT
Render the fat of the lamb trim in a heavy-based saucepan, with salt to taste. Once it's crispy, drain and reserve the liquid fat. Pat the crispy fat dry with paper towels then blend to a crumb in a blender. Reserve in a dehydrator at 60°C/140°F until required.

TO ASSEMBLE
Warm up the lamb neck meat and cooked whole carrots in the lamb sauce in a medium saucepan over a medium heat. Finish with the butter and a dash of Barolo vinegar. Place a carrot on a tray. Lay the lamb neck meat on top, then the crispy lamb fat. Place the orange and yellow confit carrots on top. Place the carrot tops between them. Position the dressed carrot on the left side of the plate. To the right of the carrot, add a quenelle of yogurt with pesto in the middle. Serve with a warm lamb bun and sauce on the side.

'CHEESE AND ONION'

Serves: 4

SPRING ONION OIL
2 bunches of spring onions, washed
  and green tops separated
200 g grapeseed oil

ONION CONSOMMÉ
500 g Beurre noisette (p. 246)
800 g sweet onions, thinly sliced
660 g leeks (white parts only),
  thinly sliced
330 g carrots, thinly sliced
20 g dry sherry
500 g Syrah red wine
2 kg cold water
sherry vinegar, to taste
salt, to taste

CHEESE PURÉE
60 g double cream
140 g whole milk
40 g 4-year-old Parmesan, grated
25 g 5-year-old or other aged
  Cheddar, grated
0.5 g Gellan LT100

0.4 g Gellan F
0.5 g guar gum
6 g Metilgel

RED WINE REDUCTION
350 g red wine
2 sprigs thyme
1 garlic clove

ONION PREPARATION
2 medium English brown onions
20 g Red wine reduction (above)
20 g Cabernet Sauvignon vinegar
12 g salt
Cheese purée (left)

PICKLED ONION RIBS
150 g Onion consommé (left)
50 g dry sherry
50 g sherry vinegar
salt, to taste
onion layers (from the onion
  preparation, above, reserving
  150 g for the Onion Purée)

ONION PURÉE
150 g onion layers (reserved from
  the onion preparation, left)
onion liquid (reserved from the onion
  preparation, left)
2 g Cabernet Sauvignon vinegar
salt, to taste

PUFFED PARMESAN RIND
200 g Parmesan rinds, cut into 1-cm
  (½-inch) cubes
30 g Parmesan powder (p. 242)

PICKLED RED ONION
250 g water
200 g white wine vinegar
10 g caster sugar
½ red onion, thinly sliced
salt, to taste

FRIED SHALLOT RINGS
1 kg grapeseed oil
1 banana shallot
20 g plain flour

20 g Onion powder (p. 242)
10 g vinegar powder
10 g Parmesan powder (p. 242)
salt, to taste

TO ASSEMBLE
alyssum flowers
allium flowers
onion flowers
chive tips
Onion buns (p. 239)

SPRING ONION OIL
Put the green tops into a blender with the oil and blend until the mix resembles a purée. Pass the purée through a fine chinois into a bowl set over an ice bath, then pour the oil into a sous vide bag, seal and hang at an angle in the fridge for 24 hours to allow the water and oil to separate. Once the water has drained to the bottom corner of the bag, cut a small hole in the bag to allow the water to slowly escape, leaving only the oil. Reserve in a squeeze bottle. Cut the white part of the onions at a bias to 1 mm (scant 1/16 inch) thick.

ONION CONSOMMÉ
Gently heat the beurre noisette in an open pressure cooker pot and add the onions, leeks and carrots. Sweat until tender. In a separate large saucepan bring the dry sherry and wine to the boil and reduce by two-thirds. Add the reduction and the cold water to the pressure cooker. Bring to the boil and skim off any impurities that rise to the surface. Secure the lid and cook on full pressure for 2½ hours. Allow the pressure cooker to cool down slowly. Strain the broth through a fine chinois into a large saucepan and reduce by half, season with the sherry vinegar and salt to taste and reserve in a container in the fridge overnight. The next day, remove the fat that has separated from the broth.

CHEESE PURÉE
Put the double cream and milk into a temperature-controlled blender set to a low speed and bring it to 90°C/195°F. Stir in the Parmesan and Cheddar, then bring the temperature back up to 90°C/195°F. Add the LT100, Gellan F and guar gum and bring the mixture back up to 90°C/195°F. Blend on medium speed for 2 minutes, then remove the lid and scrape down around the sides and at the bottom of the jug. Add the Metilgel and blend on full power for 30 seconds. Pour into a tray and place in the fridge to set for at least 1 hour. Remove the mixture from the fridge and blend in a blender until smooth. Transfer to a piping bag fitted with a 5-mm (¼-inch) nozzle.

RED WINE REDUCTION
Bring the red wine to the boil with the thyme and garlic in a medium saucepan over a medium heat and reduce by three-quarters. Pass through a sieve and let it cool.

ONION PREPARATION
Preheat a water bath to 95°C/200°F. Peel the onions (without cutting off the tip or the root) and place into a sous vide bag with the red wine reduction and Cabernet Sauvignon vinegar. Seal and cook in the water bath for 1 hour until the onions are tender. Remove and place in an ice bath. Once cold, drain the onions and reserve the onion liquid for the onion purée. Cut the onions in half lengthways and burn the flat halves with a blowtorch. Carefully remove every other layer of the onion while keeping the remaining layers intact and attached to the root. (Reserve the layers/petals that were removed to be used for the onion ribs and onion purée.) Replace the missing onion layers with the cheese purée. Lightly press each layer and level with a palette knife for a flat onion surface.

PICKLED ONION RIBS
Put the onion consommé, dry sherry, sherry vinegar and salt into a small saucepan and bring to the boil. Meanwhile, julienne the onion trim and add to the boiling liquid, then reduce the heat and simmer for 5 minutes or until the onions are tender. Season to taste. Transfer the pickled onion ribs to a container.

ONION PURÉE
Julienne the onion trim. Add it to a saucepan with a dash of the reserved onion liquid and cook over medium heat for 30 minutes until tender. Transfer to a blender with the vinegar and salt and blend until smooth. Season to taste with more salt and vinegar, if needed.

PUFF PARMESAN RIND
Place the Parmesan rinds onto a plate covered with parchment paper and microwave on medium power for 1 minute, checking after 30 seconds to see if they have puffed. Remove from the microwave and sprinkle with the Parmesan powder.

PICKLED RED ONION
Put all the ingredients, except the onion, into a saucepan and bring to the boil. Pull apart the red onion layers, add them to the saucepan and boil for 1 minute. Transfer to a container and leave to cool. Cut the cooled layers into diamonds with 1-cm (½-inch) edges.

FRIED SHALLOT RINGS

Heat the oil in a saucepan until it reaches 160°C/325°F. Peel the shallot (without cutting off the tip or the root) and cut it into rings 5 mm (¼ inch) thick, then gently separate the rings from each other. Mix the shallot rings in a bowl with a dusting of flour, then add to the saucepan to deep-fry. Once they're crispy, remove the shallots from the oil with a slotted spoon and drain on paper towel. Dust with onion powder, vinegar powder and Parmesan powder, and season with salt. Reserve in a dehydrator at 60°C/140°F until required.

TO ASSEMBLE

Heat the onion halves in a steamer for 5 minutes. In separate saucepans, warm up the onion purée, cheese purée and pickled onion ribs. In the middle of a plate, create a complete 5-cm (2-inch) circle of onion purée, pipe one dot of cheese purée in the middle, then cover with the onion ribs. Place the onion on top of the cheese purée. Add all the flowers, puffed Parmesan, chive tips, fried shallot rings, sliced spring onion white and the pickled red onion in a circle around the steamed onion. Add them on the left side of the onion, too. Warm the consommé in a saucepan and add to a sauce jug. Serve with a warm onion bun and the onion consommé topped with the spring onion oil.

JERUSALEM ARTICHOKE
MUSHROOM, TRUFFLE, MALT AND CHEDDAR

Serves: 4

JERUSALEM ARTICHOKE CRISPS
4 large Jerusalem artichokes, scrubbed
2 kg grapeseed oil
salt, to taste

INFUSED ARTICHOKE LIQUID
300 g whole milk
200 g double cream
Jerusalem artichoke flesh, chopped (reserved from above)

JERUSALEM ARTICHOKE ROYALE
500 g Infused artichoke liquid (above)
6 g salt
100 g Parmesan, grated
80 g Cheddar, grated
1 g LT100
0.2 g Gellan F
1 g guar gum

PICKLED JERUSALEM ARTICHOKE
50 g Jerusalem artichokes
25 g Elderflower cordial (p. 248)
50 g Chardonnay vinegar
1 g salt

JERUSALEM ARTICHOKE PURÉE
20 g butter
200 g Jerusalem artichokes, scrubbed and thinly sliced
1 shallot, thinly sliced
50 g whole milk
50 g double cream
salt, to taste

BLACK TRUFFLE PURÉE
20 g butter
100 g chestnut mushrooms, thinly sliced
100 g closed cup mushrooms, thinly sliced
50 g preserved black truffle, finely chopped
75 g black truffle juice
75 g Chicken stock (p. 244)
25 g black truffle oil
salt, to taste

JERUSALEM ARTICHOKE CONSOMMÉ
1 kg Jerusalem artichokes, scrubbed
1.3 kg water
15 g salt, plus extra to taste

TO FINISH THE SAUCE
200 g Jerusalem artichoke consommé (above)
50 g black truffle juice
50 g butter

JERUSALEM ARTICHOKE PREPARATION
1 kg Jerusalem artichokes, scrubbed
250 g 15% Herb brine (p. 247)

JERUSALEM ARTICHOKE FONDANT
50 g grapeseed oil
4 brined Jerusalem artichokes (above)
500 g butter
8 sprigs thyme
2 garlic cloves
150 g Chicken stock (p. 244)

ARTICHOKE CRUMB
100 g almond flour
75 g dried breadcrumbs
10 g maltodextrin (Zorbit)
5 g malt powder
7 g Cep powder (p. 242)
7 g Shiitake powder (p. 242)
Dried artichoke skin (from Jerusalem artichoke preparation, left)
15 g grapeseed oil
3 g black truffle oil
salt, to taste

TO ASSEMBLE
mizuna
parsley cress
nasturtium cress
marjoram cress
thyme cress
tiny tagete flowers
chervil leaves
chive tips

JERUSALEM ARTICHOKE CRISPS
Preheat the steam oven to 100°C/210°F. Cook the Jerusalem artichokes in the steam oven for 1 hour–1 hour 20 minutes, until cooked through, then allow to cool to room temperature. Score the artichokes lengthways and gently peel off the skin, keeping it intact. Reserve the flesh. Transfer the skins to a dehydrator and dehydrate at 60°C/140°F until they're completely dry.

Heat the oil in a deep-fat fryer to 160°C/325°F, then fry each skin until golden. Immediately after removing each piece from the fryer, drain on paper towels and reshape the Jerusalem artichoke skin into a dome shape. Season with salt and reserve in a dehydrator at 60°C/140°F until required.

INFUSED ARTICHOKE LIQUID
Put all the ingredients into a saucepan and simmer for 5 minutes, then remove from the heat and allow to infuse for 2 hours. Strain and discard the artichoke flesh.

JERUSALEM ARTICHOKE ROYALE
Add the infused artichoke liquid and salt to a temperature-controlled blender set to a low speed and bring it to 90°C/195°F. Add the Parmesan and Cheddar and bring the temperature back up to 90°C/195°F. Add the LT100, Gellan F and guar gum and bring it back to 90°C/195°F, then blend on a medium speed for 2 minutes. Scrape down the sides and around the bottom of the blender jug with a spatula. Replace the lid and blend on full power for 30 seconds. Immediately pour the liquid into a tray and place in the fridge to set for 1 hour. Cut out four discs 4 cm (1½ inches) in diameter from the royale using a ring cutter and place on a tray.

PICKLED JERUSALEM ARTICHOKE
Peel the artichokes and slice them thinly using a mandoline. Heat the elderflower cordial in a saucepan with the vinegar and salt, stir and bring to the boil. Add the sliced Jerusalem artichoke, then immediately remove from the heat. Transfer to a container and leave to cool.

JERUSALEM ARTICHOKE PURÉE
Melt the butter in a saucepan over a medium heat. As it starts to foam, add the artichokes and shallot. Reduce the heat and sweat without colouring. Cover the mixture with the milk and cream and cook until the artichokes are soft, then remove from the heat. Drain the artichokes and reserve the liquid. Add the cooked artichokes to a blender and blend until smooth, adding some of the reserved liquid if needed, to make the purée smooth. Pass through a fine chinois and season to taste with salt. Transfer to a container set over an ice bath and cover with cling film.

BLACK TRUFFLE PURÉE
Melt the butter in a saucepan over a medium heat, add the sliced mushrooms and cook until lightly browned, then add the preserved truffle. Add the truffle juice and chicken stock and bring back to a simmer, then reduce the liquid by half. Season to taste. Place the mixture in a blender and blend until smooth, add the truffle oil, then check the seasoning. Pass the purée through a fine chinois into a container. Place a layer of cling film over the surface of the mushroom purée to prevent it from forming a skin.

JERUSALEM ARTICHOKE CONSOMMÉ
Cut the Jerusalem artichokes into small dice, leaving the skin on. Transfer to a blender and blend with the water and salt until it forms a pulp. Transfer the mixture to a medium saucepan, set over a low heat and cook until it naturally clarifies. Pass through a chinois lined with muslin cloth into another clean saucepan, bring to the boil and cook until it reduces to 200 g, then season to taste.

TO FINISH THE SAUCE
Combine the artichoke consommé and truffle juice in a medium saucepan and bring to the boil, then whisk in the butter to make a smooth sauce.

JERUSALEM ARTICHOKE PREPARATION
Peel the Jerusalem artichokes, place the skin in a dehydrator at 60°C/140°F and dehydrate until dried. Cut the top and bottom of the artichokes to create a flat surface, then transfer to a sous vide bag with the brine. Seal and compress for

20 minutes. Remove the artichokes from the bag and rinse under cold running water for 5 minutes. Dry thoroughly with paper towels.

JERUSALEM ARTICHOKE FONDANT
Heat a heavy black-bottomed pan over a medium heat. Once hot, add the grapeseed oil. Add the brined Jerusalem artichokes and cook until golden. Add half of the butter and allow it to foam, then add the thyme, garlic and the remaining butter. Deglaze with the chicken stock and reduce by half. Cover with a cartouche and cook over a low heat for 15–20 minutes, until the artichokes are tender. Check constantly to ensure the artichokes don't stick to the pan while cooking. Once cooked, remove from the heat and leave to cool.

ARTICHOKE CRUMB
Blend all the ingredients, except the oils and salt, in a food processor. While blending, slowly add the grapeseed oil and black truffle oil until mixed, then season to taste.

TO ASSEMBLE
Preheat the oven to 180°C/350°F (fan). Reheat the Jerusalem artichoke fondant in its cooking liquid in a small saucepan. Warm up the Jerusalem artichoke purée and place in a squeeze bottle. Do the same with the truffle purée. In another small saucepan gently heat the Jerusalem artichoke sauce. Put the Jerusalem artichoke royale in a small tray lined with parchment paper and reheat in the oven for 3 minutes. In the middle of a plate, add a dot of Jerusalem artichoke purée followed by the Royale disc. Sprinkle the Jerusalem artichoke crumb to cover the royale. Place the Jerusalem artichoke fondant on top followed by three dots each of the artichoke and truffle purée, then the pickled artichokes. Position the herbs and flowers circling the fondant and finish by covering the fondant with the whole artichoke crisp. Place the Jerusalem artichoke sauce into a sauce jug. To serve, pour the sauce around the artichoke.

'BEANS ON TOAST'

Serves: 4

TO COOK THE COCO BEANS 500 g coco de Paimpol beans 1.5 kg Chicken stock (p. 244) 2 garlic cloves, wrapped in muslin cloth 5 sprigs thyme, wrapped in muslin cloth salt, to taste	**SOAKING LIQUID FOR THE BRIOCHE** 300 g whole milk 3 eggs salt, to taste white pepper, to taste truffle oil, to taste	6 white peppercorns 500 g whole milk 500 g double cream 200 g aged Parmesan, grated salt, to taste	chive tips parsley tips chervil plush rondelles of spring onion white black truffle slices salt and pepper, to taste
COCO BEAN PURÉE 200 g coco beans (reserved from above) 100 g double cream extra virgin olive oil, to taste Barolo vinegar, to taste salt, to taste	**PARMESAN SAUCE** ½ head garlic 500 g Chicken stock (p. 244) 4 medium shallots, sliced 25 g thyme	**TO FINISH AND ASSEMBLE** 4 brioche discs (10 x 2.5 cm/4 x 1 inch) grapeseed oil, for frying butter, for frying 1 garlic clove 2 sprigs thyme 4 eggs	

TO COOK THE COCO BEANS
Place a medium saucepan over a medium heat and add all the ingredients. Bring the stock to the boil, then reduce the heat and simmer for about 30 minutes or until the beans are tender. Season to taste, then transfer 300 g of the beans to a container. Cover the beans with some of the stock and allow to cool. Keep the remaining half of the beans in the pan for the purée.

COCO BEAN PURÉE
Return the pan of beans to a medium heat and cook for 20 minutes until they are completely soft, then remove from the heat, drain in a sieve and reserve the stock. Discard the garlic and thyme and transfer the beans to a blender. Cover with some of the reserved stock, add the cream, and season with salt. Blend on full speed until smooth, then add some olive oil and blend again to incorporate the oil and until it reaches a smooth consistency. Pass the purée through a fine chinois into a container and add vinegar and salt to taste.

SOAKING LIQUID FOR THE BRIOCHE
Combine all the ingredients in a bowl and blend, using a hand blender, until everything is incorporated.

PARMESAN SAUCE
Preheat the oven to 180°C/350°F (fan). Wrap the head of garlic in foil and roast in the oven for 30 minutes until soft, then remove the skin. Put the chicken stock into a large saucepan over a high heat, add the shallots, thyme, peppercorns and a pinch of salt and reduce by half. Once it has reduced, add the milk, cream and roasted garlic pulp and reduce by a third, then add the Parmesan. Remove the pan from the heat and set aside for 20 minutes, then blend using a hand blender. Pass through a fine chinois.

TO FINISH AND ASSEMBLE
Put the brioche into a container and cover with the soaking liquid, then place into a sous vide machine and compress once. Transfer the brioche to a rack for 1 minute to allow excess liquid to drain off. Heat a little grapeseed oil in a non-stick frying pan over a medium-high heat and fry the brioche for a minute on each side until lightly golden. Add the butter, garlic and thyme and cook for another 2 minutes on one side until golden brown. Remove the brioche from the pan and drain on paper towels. Heat some grapeseed oil in a small non-stick frying pan over a low heat and fry the eggs. Season with salt and pepper. Cut the egg yolks with a 5-cm (2-inch) ring cutter. In two separate small saucepans gently heat the cooked beans and bean purée. Centre a brioche on the plate, spoon some bean purée on top and evenly spread it over. Place an egg yolk at the centre, then arrange the beans individually to form a circle around the egg yolk. Position the herbs and spring onion rondelles along the inner circle and cover the egg yolk with sliced truffle. In a small saucepan gently warm the Parmesan sauce. Mix with a hand blender until it foams, then transfer to a sauce jug and pour around the beans on toast.

CELERIAC
ROASTED OVER WOOD WITH BLACK TRUFFLE AND HAZELNUT

Serves: 4

MUSHROOM CRUMB
15 g extra virgin olive oil
500 g portobello mushrooms,
  roughly sliced
1 head garlic, cloves peeled and crushed
lemon juice, to taste
12 g flat-leaf parsley, finely chopped

CELERIAC POWDER
250 g celeriac, peeled

CELERIAC CRISP
grapeseed oil, for frying
100 g celeriac
salt, to taste

CELERIAC CONSOMMÉ
2 kg celeriac, washed
2.3 kg water
15 g salt, plus extra to taste
4 long peppercorns

MISO BUTTER
20 g brown miso paste
20 g butter, softened

YOUNG CELERIAC
4 young celeriac
250 g 10% Herb brine (p. 247)
40 g Miso butter (above)

CELERIAC FARCE
4 celeriac, plus reserved trimmings
25 g hazelnuts, toasted and
  coarsely chopped
50 g Parmesan
10 g Black truffle purée (p. 248)
Barolo vinegar, to taste
salt, to taste

CELERIAC VELOUTÉ
30 g unsalted butter, diced
1 celeriac, peeled and diced

200 g whole milk
200 g double cream
Celeriac consommé (left), if needed
salt, to taste

CELERIAC 'RISOTTO'
1 celeriac, peeled
50 g butter
Celeriac consommé (left)
20 g Black truffle purée (p. 248)
50 g Parmesan
20 g crème fraîche
50 g spring onions
salt, to taste
Barolo vinegar, to taste

TRUFFLE CRUMB
100 g Mushroom crumb (left)
100 g dried breadcrumbs
25 g toasted hazelnuts, chopped
10 g black truffle, chopped

HAZELNUT DRESSING
100 g hazelnut oil
30 g sherry vinegar
salt, to taste

TO ASSEMBLE
Celeriac top powder (p. 242)
picked yellow celery leaves
red endive leaves, turned
yellow endive leaves, turned
picked flat-leaf parsley leaves
black truffle, sliced

MUSHROOM CRUMB
Heat the oil in a non-stick frying pan over a medium heat, add the mushrooms and sauté until lightly browned. Just before the mushrooms are cooked, add the garlic and a small splash of lemon juice, then remove from the heat. Add the chopped parsley. Transfer to a tray lined with paper towels and dehydrate in a dehydrator at 60°C/140°F for at least 24 hours. Crush the mushroom mix to a fine powder in a mortar with a pestle.

CELERIAC POWDER
Set a dehydrator to 65°C/150°F. Slice the celeriac as thinly as possible with a mandoline. Place the sliced celeriac on a dehydrator tray and allow to fully dry for 12 hours. Check to ensure the celeriac slices have retained their crisp, white colour, then place in a blender and blend to a powder.

CELERIAC CRISP
Heat some grapeseed oil in a deep-fat fryer to 160°C/325°F. Slice the celeriac to a thickness of 2 mm (1/16 inch) with a mandoline. Deep-fry until lightly golden, drain on paper towels, then season with salt and reserve in a dehydrator at 60°C/140°F until required.

CELERIAC CONSOMMÉ
Cut the celeriac into 2-cm (3/4-inch) dice, leaving the skin on. Transfer to a blender with the water and salt and blend until smooth, then place the mixture in a large pan, set over a low heat and cook until it naturally clarifies. Pass through a chinois lined with muslin into another clean saucepan with the peppercorns and bring to the boil over a high heat, then cook until it reduces by half. Remove from the heat and season to taste.

MISO BUTTER
Combine the miso and softened butter in a small bowl and mix well.

YOUNG CELERIAC
Set a water bath to 98°C/208°F. Peel and turn each celeriac into a perfect ball. Place the balls in a sous vide bag, add the brine to cover and seal. Set aside for 30 minutes. Drain the brine, then transfer the celeriac into a new sous vide bag, add the miso butter and seal. Cook in the water bath for about 45 minutes until soft, then chill over an ice bath. Set up your grill with wood and get it burning hot. Remove the celeriac from the sous vide bag, discard the butter, and dry them well. Place the celeriac on the grill to roast for about 5 minutes so they take on a light,

smoky flavour. Once roasted, remove from the grill. Hollow out each single ball from the bottom using a Parisienne scoop and chop the scooped-out trimmings to make the farce.

CELERIAC FARCE
Combine all the ingredients in a medium bowl and mix well. Check the seasoning and transfer to a piping bag fitted with a 5-mm (1/4-inch) nozzle. Fill each hollowed-out celeriac ball with the farce, place each ball into a sous vide bag and seal with no compression.

CELERIAC VELOUTÉ
Melt the butter in a saucepan over a medium heat, add the diced celeriac, season with salt and sweat without colouring for 5 minutes. Pour in the milk and cream and simmer for 30 minutes until the celeriac is soft, then transfer to a blender and blend to a velouté consistency. If needed, add some of the celeriac consommé to reach a smooth consistency. Pass through a fine chinois.

CELERIAC 'RISOTTO'
Cut the celeriac into 5-mm (1/4-inch) dice. Heat a medium saucepan over a medium heat, add the butter and diced celeriac and cook gently for 1 minute. Gradually add a little of the celeriac consommé, as if making a risotto. Once the consommé is absorbed, add some more until the celeriac is just tender. This should take only 5–6 minutes. Add the truffle puree and cook for 1 minute. Remove from the heat and add the Parmesan, crème fraîche and spring onions, then season to taste with salt and Barolo vinegar.

TRUFFLE CRUMB
Combine all the ingredients in a bowl and mix.

HAZELNUT DRESSING
Mix all the ingredients in a bowl.

TO ASSEMBLE
Bring a saucepan of water to the boil. Reduce the heat to a simmer, place the bag with the celeriac balls into the water and heat for 15 minutes to ensure it's hot all the way through. Add the celeriac velouté to a separate saucepan and start to heat through.

In another small pan warm the celeriac 'risotto'. Remove a celeriac ball from the bag, dust a good amount of celeriac powder over the whole of it and finish with a small amount of celeriac top powder on the top. Spoon the celeriac risotto into the presentation bowl, then add two spoons of the truffle crumb to cover the 'risotto'. Place the celeriac ball on top. Dress the leaves and herbs with the hazelnut dressing then position them on top of the ball, pointing up, and leaving enough space to place the celeriac crisps and truffle slices on top. Place a glass cloche on top of the dish and serve the warm velouté in a sauce jug on the side.

MOREL TART
WITH WILD GARLIC AND VIN JAUNE

Serves: 4

SHORTCRUST PASTRY
225 g T45 flour, plus extra for dusting
110 g butter, chilled and diced
40 g Parmesan, grated
20 g Dijon mustard
6 g whole milk
26 g whole egg
3 g salt

WILD GARLIC SAUCE
20 g butter
50 g onions, thinly sliced
2 g picked thyme leaves
100 g whole milk
75 g double cream
100 g Chicken stock (p. 244)
30 g picked wild garlic leaves

VIN JAUNE SAUCE
300 g butter
400 g sand carrots, thinly sliced
60 g button mushrooms, thinly sliced
1 x 750-ml bottle of vin jaune
2 kg Chicken stock (p. 244), reduced
   to 250 g
500 g double cream
salt, to taste

WILD GARLIC INFUSION
30 g butter
250 g onions, thinly sliced
2 g picked thyme leaves
200 g whole milk
100 g double cream
200 g Vegetable nage (p. 243)
150 g picked wild garlic leaves

WILD GARLIC ROYALE
500 g Wild garlic infusion (above)
10 g Parmesan, grated

10 g Cheddar, grated
1.2 g LT100
0.3 g Gellan F
1.2 g guar gum

VIN JAUNE ROYALE
500 g Vin jaune sauce (left)
1.5 g LT100
0.8 g Gellan F
1.2 g guar gum
Set wild garlic royale (left)

MUSHROOM DUXELLES
50 g grapeseed oil
120 g onions, brunoised
120 g leeks, brunoised
300 g large closed-cup mushrooms,
   diced
50 g Parsley butter (p. 246)
150 g Mushroom purée (p. 246)

30 g Parmesan, grated
16 g flat-leaf parsley, finely chopped
sherry vinegar, to taste
salt, to taste

BRAISED MORELS
200 g morels
grapeseed oil, for frying
25 g shallots, finely chopped
50 g dry white wine, plus a dash
   to finish
200 g Chicken stock (p. 244)
25 g Parsley butter (p. 246)
salt, to taste

TO ASSEMBLE
Parmesan shavings
wild garlic shoots
picked thyme leaves
wild garlic flowers

SHORTCRUST PASTRY
Put all the ingredients into a food processor and process for 3 minutes, then wrap in cling film and leave to rest in the fridge for 1 hour 30 minutes.

Preheat the oven to 160°C/325°F (fan). Remove the dough from the fridge and roll it out on a flour-dusted work surface to a thickness of 4 mm (⅛ inch). Using an 8-cm (3-inch) ring cutter, cut out four discs then add them to four fluted moulds that measure 6 cm (2½ inches) across the top, 3 cm (1¼ inches) deep and 2.5 cm (1 inch) across the base. Press another four moulds on top. Trim away any excess dough with a small knife and bake the pastry between the moulds for 8 minutes. Remove the tart shells from the moulds and reserve in an airtight container.

WILD GARLIC SAUCE
Melt the butter in a medium saucepan over a medium heat, add the onions and thyme and sweat for 5 minutes. Add the milk, cream and chicken stock and bring to the boil, then simmer for 5 minutes. Remove the thyme, add the wild garlic and cook for 1 minute. Transfer to a blender and blend on full speed until smooth. Pass the sauce through a chinois and chill quickly over ice.

VIN JAUNE SAUCE
Melt the butter in a medium saucepan over a medium heat, add the carrots and cook gently without letting them colour. Season with salt and continue to cook the carrots until the water has evaporated from them, then add the mushrooms and repeat the process. As soon as the water from the mushrooms has evaporated, increase the heat to high, add the vin jaune and reduce it by half, then add the reduced chicken stock and cream. Stir, bring to the boil and season to taste. Pass through a chinois into a container and chill over ice.

WILD GARLIC INFUSION
Melt the butter in a medium saucepan over a medium heat, add the onions and thyme and sweat for 5 minutes. Add the milk, cream and vegetable nage, bring to the boil and simmer for 5 minutes. Remove the thyme and blend briefly using a hand blender. Pass the liquid through a chinois, pressing well, into another saucepan. Bring the liquid back to the boil, add the wild garlic and cook for 1 minute. Transfer to a blender and blend on full speed until smooth and green. Pass it through a chinois and chill quickly over ice.

WILD GARLIC ROYALE
Pour the wild garlic infusion into a temperature-controlled blender with the cheese, blend on a medium speed and bring to 90°C/195°F. Add the LT100,

Gellan F and guar gum, bring the mixture back to 90°C/195°F and blend for another 2 minutes. Remove the lid, scrape the mixture down from the sides and around the bottom of the jug with a rubber spatula, replace the lid and blend on full power for 30 seconds. Immediately transfer into two 20 x 15-cm (8 x 6-inch) trays, 4 cm (1½ inches) deep, and leave to set at room temperature.

VIN JAUNE ROYALE
Pour the vin jaune sauce into a temperature-controlled blender on a medium speed and bring to 90°C/195°F. Add the LT100, Gellan F and guar gum, bring the mixture back up to 90°C/195°F and blend for another 2 minutes. Remove the lid, scrape the mixture down from the sides and around the bottom of the jug with a spatula, replace the lid and blend on full power for 30 seconds. Immediately pour on top of the set wild garlic royale. Leave in the fridge to set for 1 hour, then use a 4-cm (1½-inch) ring cutter to cut the royale into four discs and transfer to a tray.

MUSHROOM DUXELLES
Heat the oil in a medium saucepan over a medium heat, add the onion, season lightly with salt and sweat without letting it take on any colour. Add the leeks and sweat them down (also with no colour), then add the mushrooms and cook until all the liquid has evaporated. Add the parsley butter and cook for another 2 minutes, then transfer the mixture to a large bowl and combine with the remaining ingredients. Mix and check the seasoning.

BRAISED MORELS
Remove the morel stalks using a turning knife in a circular motion. Wash the morels in room-temperature water to remove any dirt and grit, repeat this process twice more, then check to ensure all the grit and dirt has been removed. Drain on paper towels.

Heat the oil in a medium saucepan over a medium heat, add the shallots and sweat down. Add the morels, season lightly and sweat until they're just tender. Deglaze with the white wine, cover with a lid, and let it braise and reduce the wine. Once reduced by two-thirds, add the chicken stock so it is halfway up the morels and let them braise for 10 minutes or until the morels are cooked. Add the parsley butter to create an emulsion, check the seasoning and add a dash of white wine to finish.

TO ASSEMBLE
Preheat the oven to 180°C/350°F (fan). Place the royale disc on a tray lined with parchment paper and warm in an oven for 3 minutes or until hot. Heat the remaining vin jaune sauce and the wild garlic sauce in two separate saucepans.

Gently heat the mushroom duxelles in a saucepan. Once it's hot, spoon it into the tart cases and place a hot royale disc on top. Spoon the morels generously on top. Add Parmesan shavings, wild garlic shoots, thyme and wild garlic flowers and place each tart on a plate. Finish by aerating the two sauces separately with a hand blender and pouring them into two sauce jugs. Once ready to serve at the table, pour one sauce on the left and the other on the right.

GIROLLE AND TOASTED BUCKWHEAT TART
WITH FRESH ALMONDS

Serves: 4

PICKLED GIROLLES
10 g hazelnut oil
50 g girolles, cleaned
25 g sherry vinegar
salt, to taste

SHORTCRUST PASTRY
225 g plain flour, plus extra for dusting
110 g butter, chilled and diced
40 g Parmesan, grated
20 g Dijon mustard
6 g whole milk
26 g egg
3 g salt

MUSHROOM DUXELLES
50 g grapeseed oil
120 g onions, brunoised
120 g leeks, brunoised
300 g large closed-cup mushrooms, diced
50 g Parsley butter (p. 246)
150 g Mushroom purée (p. 246)
30 g Parmesan, grated
16 g flat-leaf parsley, finely chopped
sherry vinegar, to taste
salt, to taste

BUCKWHEAT INFUSION
200 g whole milk
40 g toasted buckwheat

BUCKWHEAT ROYALE
100 g Buckwheat infusion (left)
400 g Chicken consommé (p. 244)
1.2 g LT100
0.3 g Gellan F
1.2 g guar gum

MUSHROOM VELOUTÉ
300 g Mushroom purée (p. 246)
300 g Mushroom juice (p. 242)
salt, to taste

EGG PURÉE
200 g egg yolks
2 g salt

SAUTÉED GIROLLES
grapeseed oil, for frying
200 g girolles, cleaned
35 g Parsley butter (p. 246)
25 g Chicken stock (p. 244)
salt, to taste

TO ASSEMBLE
Mushroom purée (p. 246)
fresh almond, sliced
raw girolles, thinly sliced
puffed buckwheat, toasted
chive tips
picked thyme leaves
allium flowers
parsley tips

PICKLED GIROLLES
Heat a medium saucepan over a high heat, add the oil and girolles and cook until tender, without colouring, then season with salt. Once the mushrooms are tender, deglaze the pan with the sherry vinegar. Transfer the girolles to a container and allow to cool. Leave for at least 24 hours in the fridge.

SHORTCRUST PASTRY
Put all the ingredients into a food processor and blend for 3 minutes, then wrap in cling film and leave to rest in the fridge for 1 hour 30 minutes.

Preheat the oven to 160°C/325°F (fan). Remove the dough from the fridge and roll it out on a flour-dusted work surface to a thickness of 4 mm (⅛ inch). Using an 8-cm (3-inch) ring cutter, cut out four discs then add them to four fluted moulds that measure 6 cm (2½ inches) across the top, 3 cm (1¼ inch) deep and 2.5 cm (1 inch) across the base. Press another four moulds on top. Trim away any excess dough with a small knife and bake the pastry between the moulds for 8 minutes. Remove the tart shells from the moulds and reserve in an airtight container.

MUSHROOM DUXELLES
Heat the oil in a medium pan over a medium heat, add the onion, season lightly with salt and sweat without letting it take on any colour. Add the leeks and sweat them down (with no colour), then add the mushrooms and cook until all the liquid has evaporated. Add the parsley butter and cook for another 2 minutes, then transfer the mixture to a large bowl and combine with the remaining ingredients. Mix and check the seasoning.

BUCKWHEAT INFUSION
Bring the milk to a simmer in a medium saucepan, add the toasted buckwheat, then remove from the heat and blend with a hand blender. Leave to infuse for 30 minutes, then pass the liquid through a chinois into a container.

BUCKWHEAT ROYALE
Pour the liquids into a temperature-controlled blender, blend on a medium speed and bring to 90°C/195°F. Add the LT100, Gellan F and guar gum, bring the mixture back to 90°C/195°F and blend for another 2 minutes. Remove the lid, scrape the mixture down from the sides and around the bottom of the jug with a spatula, replace the lid and blend on full power for 30 seconds. Immediately transfer into a 20 x 15-cm (8 x 6-inch) tray that is 1 cm (½ inch) deep and leave in the fridge to set for 1 hour, then use a 4-cm (1½-inch) ring cutter to cut the royale into four discs and transfer to a tray.

MUSHROOM VELOUTÉ
Combine the ingredients in a medium saucepan over a medium heat to warm through and season to taste. Mix well with a hand blender, then set aside to cool.

EGG PURÉE
Preheat a water bath to 68°C/155°F. Place the egg yolks in a small sous vide bag, seal and cook for 30 minutes. Place the bag over an ice bath to cool down as quickly as possible. Season with the salt.

SAUTÉED GIROLLES
Heat a splash of oil in a medium saucepan over a high heat, add the girolles and season to taste. Sauté until the girolles start to release some liquid, then add the parsley butter and roast until it foams and the girolles are cooked. Deglaze with the chicken stock to create an emulsion, then remove from the heat.

TO ASSEMBLE
Preheat the oven to 180°C/350°F (fan). Gently heat the mushroom purée in a small saucepan. Place the royale discs on a tray lined with parchment paper and warm in the oven for 2 minutes. Heat up the mushroom velouté and the mushroom duxelles in separate saucepans. Spoon a layer of mushroom purée into the bottom of each tart, followed by the mushroom duxelles, then place a royale disc on top and finally the egg yolk purée. Add the sautéed girolles in a generous pile, then place the pickled girolles, almond slices and raw sliced girolles on top. Sprinkle with puffed buckwheat. Finish with chive tips, thyme leaves, allium flowers and parsley tips. Place a little mushroom purée on a plate and position the tart on top. Finish by blending the velouté with a hand blender and pouring it into a sauce jug ready to serve.

JERUSALEM ARTICHOKE TART
PÉRIGORD BLACK TRUFFLE, MUSHROOM AND THYME

Serves: 4

ARTICHOKE STOCK
200 g olive oil
300 g onions, cut into slices
    2 cm (1 inch) thick
300 g carrots, cut into slices
    2 cm (1 inch) thick
400 g peeled globe artichoke with
    choke removed
60 g leeks, cut into slices
    2 cm (1 inch) thick
100 g fennel, cut into slices
    2 cm (1 inch) thick
20 g garlic cloves, thinly sliced
7 g coriander seeds
3 g black peppercorns
10 g rosemary
10 sprigs thyme
600 g white wine
100 g white wine vinegar
1 kg water
1 kg Chicken stock (p. 244)
30 g salt
30 g lemon juice
30 g flat-leaf parsley

SHORTCRUST PASTRY
225 g plain flour, plus extra for dusting
112 g butter
20 g Parmesan, grated
20 g ground almonds
20 g Dijon mustard
5 g Shiitake powder (p. 242)
2 g Cep powder (p. 242)
6 g whole milk

25 g whole egg
3 g salt

JERUSALEM ARTICHOKE FONDANT
250 g Jerusalem artichokes
200 g 15% Herb brine (p. 247)
25 g grapeseed oil
200 g butter
2 sprigs thyme
2 garlic cloves
50 g Chicken stock (p. 244)
salt, to taste

BRAISED JERUSALEM ARTICHOKES
150 g Artichoke stock (left)
150 g peeled Jerusalem artichokes,
    cut into 5-mm (¼-inch) dice

JERUSALEM ARTICHOKE PURÉE
30 g butter
250 g peeled Jerusalem artichokes,
    thinly sliced
1 medium shallot, sliced
175 g whole milk
175 g double cream
salt, to taste

JERUSALEM ARTICHOKE ROYALE
300 g Jerusalem artichoke milk
    (reserved from above)
200 g Artichoke stock (left)

30 g Parmesan, grated
15 g Cheddar, grated
1.2 g LT100
0.5 g Gellan F
1.2 g guar gum
5 g salt

JERUSALEM ARTICHOKE VELOUTÉ
15 g butter
250 g Jerusalem artichokes, unpeeled
    and thinly sliced
1 shallot, peeled and sliced
1 garlic clove, wrapped in muslin cloth
2 sprigs thyme, wrapped in muslin cloth
150 g whole milk
150 g double cream
15 g black truffle oil
salt, to taste

JERUSALEM ARTICHOKE CRUMB
200 g ground almonds
150 g toasted Malted sourdough
    (p. 237)
20 g maltodextrin (Zorbit)
10 g malt powder
15 g Cep powder (p. 242)
15 g Shiitake powder (p. 242)
dried Jerusalem artichoke skin
    (reserved from the Jerusalem
    artichoke fondant, left)
30 g grapeseed oil
5 g black truffle oil
salt, to taste

ARTICHOKE FILLING
100 g Jerusalem artichoke purée (left)
100 g Jerusalem artichoke fondant
    (left), diced
100 g Braised Jerusalem artichoke
    (left), diced
7 g picked thyme leaves
25 g Confit shallots (p. 246)
10 g Black truffle purée (p. 248)
5 g black truffle oil
10 g black truffle, finely chopped
salt, to taste

JERUSALEM ARTICHOKE CRISPS
2 kg grapeseed oil
1 Jerusalem artichoke (skin on)
salt, to taste

PICKLED JERUSALEM ARTICHOKE
50 g Jerusalem artichokes
25 g Elderflower cordial (p. 248)
50 g Chardonnay vinegar
1 g salt

TO ASSEMBLE
freshly grated nutmeg
black truffle discs
parsley cress
picked thyme leaves
tagete flowers
chive tips

ARTICHOKE STOCK
Heat 60 g of the olive oil in a large saucepan over a high heat, add the onions, carrots and globe artichokes and sweat until soft. Add the leeks, fennel, garlic and spices and stir, then add the rosemary and thyme. Sweat for 5 minutes before adding the wine and reducing the liquid by half. Add the white wine vinegar, remaining 140 g olive oil, the water, chicken stock and salt. Simmer for 5 minutes, then finish with the lemon juice and parsley. Check the seasoning and transfer to a container set over an ice bath to chill as quickly as possible. Place in the fridge for 24 hours, then strain through a fine chinois.

SHORTCRUST PASTRY
Put all the ingredients into a food processor and process for 3 minutes, then wrap in cling film and leave to rest in the fridge for 1 hour 30 minutes.

Preheat the oven to 160°C/325°F (fan). Remove the dough from the fridge and roll it out on a flour-dusted work surface to a thickness of 4 mm (⅛ inch). Using an 8-cm (3-inch) ring cutter, cut out four discs, then add them to four fluted moulds that measure 6 cm (2½ inches) across the top, 3 cm (1¼ inch) deep and 2.5 cm (1 inch) across the base. Press another four moulds on top. Trim away any excess dough with a small knife and bake between the moulds for 8 minutes. Remove the tart shells from the moulds and reserve in an airtight container.

JERUSALEM ARTICHOKE FONDANT
Peel the Jerusalem artichokes and reserve the skin in a dehydrator at 60°C/140°F until required for the Jerusalem artichoke crumb. Place the artichokes in a sous

vide bag with the brine, seal and brine for 20 minutes. Remove the artichokes and rinse under cold running water for 5 minutes. Dry thoroughly with paper towels. Heat the grapeseed oil in a large saucepan over a medium heat, then add the brined Jerusalem artichokes and cook until golden. Add half of the butter and allow to foam, then add the thyme, garlic and remaining butter, then the chicken stock. Cover with a cartouche and cook over a low heat for 15–20 minutes until the artichokes are tender. Transfer the artichokes and cooking liquid to a container to cool, then cut half the artichokes lengthways into slices 5 mm (¼ inch) thick and cut the rest into 5-mm (¼-inch) cubes. Reserve the cooking liquid to reheat in the assembly.

BRAISED JERUSALEM ARTICHOKES
Bring the stock to the boil in a saucepan, add the diced artichokes and cook until tender. Remove the artichokes, then reduce the stock to a glaze. Return the artichokes to the pan, then remove from the heat and cool.

JERUSALEM ARTICHOKE PURÉE
Melt the butter in a saucepan over a medium heat. As soon as it starts to foam, add the artichokes and shallot and season with salt. Reduce the heat and sweat without colouring for about 15 minutes. Cover the mixture with the milk and cream and cook until the artichokes are soft, then remove from the heat. Pass the mixture through a fine chinois. Reserve 300 g of the milk for the Jerusalem artichoke royale. Add the cooked artichokes to a blender and blend until smooth. Season to taste. Transfer to a container set over an ice bath.

JERUSALEM ARTICHOKE ROYALE

Put the infused milk and artichoke stock into a temperature-controlled blender on a medium speed and bring to 90°C/195°F. Add the Parmesan and Cheddar and bring the temperature back up to 90°C/195°F. Add the LT100, Gellan F, guar gum, and salt, bring the mixture back up to 90°C/195°F and blend on a medium speed for 2 minutes. Remove the lid, scrape the mixture down from the sides and around the bottom of the jug with a spatula, replace the lid and blend on full power for 30 seconds. Immediately transfer the mix to a 20 x 15-cm (8 x 6-inch) tray, 1 cm (½ inch) deep, and leave in the fridge to set for 1 hour, then use a 4-cm (1½-inch) ring cutter to cut the royale into four discs and transfer to a tray.

JERUSALEM ARTICHOKE VELOUTÉ

Melt the butter in a saucepan over a medium heat. As soon as it starts to foam, add the artichokes and shallot and season lightly with salt. Reduce the heat, add the garlic and thyme, and sweat without colouring for about 15 minutes. Cover the mixture with the milk and cream and cook until the artichokes are soft, then remove from the heat and take out the garlic and thyme. Put everything into a blender and blend until smooth. Add the truffle oil, pass through a chinois and check the seasoning.

JERUSALEM ARTICHOKE CRUMB

Blend all the ingredients, except the oils, in a food processor. While blending, slowly add the grapeseed oil and black truffle oil until fully incorporated.

ARTICHOKE FILLING

Mix all the ingredients together in a bowl and check the seasoning.

JERUSALEM ARTICHOKE CRISPS

Heat the oil in a deep-fat fryer to 160°C/320°F. Slice the artichoke to a thickness of 2 mm (1/16 inch) with a mandoline, rinse in cold water and drain on paper towels. Deep-fry until golden brown, drain on paper towels, then season with salt and reserve in the dehydrator at 60°C/140°F until required.

PICKLED JERUSALEM ARTICHOKE

Peel the artichokes and slice them thinly on a mandoline. Combine the elderflower cordial with the vinegar and salt in a saucepan and place over medium heat. Stir and bring to the boil. Add the sliced Jerusalem artichoke, then immediately remove from the heat.

TO ASSEMBLE

Preheat the oven to 180°C/350°F (fan). Gently heat the artichoke purée in a small saucepan, transfer to a squeeze bottle and set aside in a warm place. Put the sliced fondant and royale discs on a tray lined with parchment paper, lightly dust with grated nutmeg, then warm in the oven for 2 minutes. Warm the artichoke filling in a saucepan and place into the tarts. Layer the royale disc on top followed by the sliced fondant. In between, position five pickled artichoke slices and cover with the Jerusalem artichoke crumb. Position the artichoke crisps and black truffle discs upright on top, then place the herbs and flowers all over. Add a dot of purée to the centre of the plate and place the tart on top. Warm the velouté in a saucepan and blend with a hand blender until it foams. Transfer to a sauce jug and pour when serving.

CEP TART
FLUFFETTS FARM EGG YOLK AND WHITE TRUFFLE

Serves: 4

YEAST CRUMBLE
100 g fresh yeast

SHORTCRUST PASTRY
225 g strong bread flour, plus extra
    for dusting
110 g butter, chilled and diced
40 g Parmesan, grated
20 g Dijon mustard
6 g whole milk
26 g egg
3 g salt

MUSHROOM INFUSION
125 g Mushroom juice (p. 242)
100 g whole milk
25 g double cream
10 g fresh yeast
10 g dried ceps
5 drops Douglas fir extract
3 g salt

MUSHROOM ROYALE
250 g Mushroom infusion (left)
0.2 g Gellan F
0.6 g Gellan LT100
0.6 g guar gum

CEP PURÉE
75 g butter
1 shallot, finely chopped
1 garlic clove, chopped
250 g ceps, finely diced
60 g double cream
50 g whole milk
salt, to taste

CEP VELOUTÉ
15 g butter
250 g ceps, thinly sliced
1 medium shallot, sliced
1 garlic clove, sliced
150 g whole milk

150 g double cream
salt, to taste

CONFIT EGG YOLKS
500 g grapeseed oil
4 whole egg yolks

CEP DUXELLES
grapeseed oil, for frying
200 g ceps, finely diced
1 shallot, finely chopped
50 g Parsley butter (p. 246)
100 g Cep purée (left)
2 g flat-leaf parsley
5 g Parmesan, finely grated
2 g sherry vinegar
1 g ground black pepper
salt, to taste

ROASTED CEPS
12 ceps, cut into slices
    1 cm (½ inch) thick
grapeseed oil, for frying
50 g Parsley butter (p. 246)
100 g Chicken stock (p. 244)
Barolo vinegar, to taste
salt, to taste

TO ASSEMBLE
Cep powder (p. 242)
raw cep shavings
shaved white truffle
chive tips
chive flowers
parsley tips
picked thyme leaves
flaky sea salt, to taste
salt, to taste

YEAST CRUMBLE
Set a dehydrator to 65°C/150°F. Crumble the yeast onto a tray and put in the dehydrator for 24 hours until dry and crunchy.

SHORTCRUST PASTRY
Put all the ingredients into a food processor and process for 3 minutes, then wrap in cling film and leave to rest in the fridge for 1 hour 30 minutes.

Preheat the oven to 160°C/325°F (fan). Remove the dough from the fridge and roll it out on a flour-dusted work surface to a thickness of 4 mm (⅛ inch). Using an 8-cm (3-inch) ring cutter, cut out four discs then add them to four fluted moulds that measure 6 cm (2½ inches) across the top, 3 cm (1¼ inches) deep and 2.5 cm (1 inch) across the base. Press another four moulds on top. Trim away any excess dough with a small knife and bake between the moulds for 8 minutes. Remove the tart shells from the moulds and reserve in an airtight container.

MUSHROOM INFUSION
Put all the ingredients into a saucepan, crumbling in the yeast, and bring to the boil. Remove from the heat and leave to infuse for 20 minutes, then transfer to a blender and blend well. Strain through a chinois.

MUSHROOM ROYALE
Pour the mushroom infusion into a temperature-controlled blender, blend at medium speed and bring to 90°C/195°F. Add the Gellan F, LT100 and guar gum, bring the mixture back to 90°C/195°F and blend for another 2 minutes. Remove the lid, scrape the mixture down from the sides and around the bottom of the jug with a spatula, replace the lid and blend on full power for 30 seconds. Immediately transfer into a 20 x 15-cm (8 x 6-inch) tray that's 1 cm (½ inch) deep and leave in the fridge to set for 1 hour, then use a 4-cm (1½-inch) ring cutter to cut the royale into four discs and transfer to a tray.

CEP PURÉE
Melt the butter in a saucepan over a medium-high heat, add the shallot and garlic and sweat until tender. Add the mushrooms, season with salt, and cook until lightly browned. Add the cream and milk and cook for 5 minutes. Transfer to a blender and blend until smooth. Pass through a chinois and season to taste.

CEP VELOUTÉ
Melt the butter in a large saucepan over a medium-high heat, add the ceps and

roast until golden brown and tender. Add the shallot and garlic and cook until lightly browned and tender. Season with salt. Add the milk and cream and cook until the ceps are soft. Remove from the heat, transfer to a blender and blend until smooth. Pass through a chinois and season to taste.

CONFIT EGG YOLKS
Preheat a water bath to 65°C/150°F. In a sous vide bag add the grapeseed oil and carefully add the 4 egg yolks, taking care to keep the yolks whole. Seal and add to the water bath. Cook for 55 minutes until the yolks have a soft texture.

CEP DUXELLES
Heat a dash of grapeseed oil in a saucepan over a medium heat, then add the ceps and shallot, season with salt and roast until golden brown. Add the parsley butter and roast again until the butter foams, then remove from the pan and transfer to a large bowl. Add the remaining ingredients and mix thoroughly. Season to taste.

ROASTED CEPS
Using the tip of a knife, lightly score the flat sides of the ceps, creating a crosshatch effect. Heat a dash of the oil in a roasting pan over a high heat and add the cep slices, scored side down. Frequently check them and once they are golden brown, turn the ceps over and season with salt. Add the parsley butter, and allow it to foam and brown the ceps. Deglaze the pan with the chicken stock to create an emulsion. Check the seasoning and finish with a dash of Barolo vinegar.

TO ASSEMBLE
Preheat the oven to 180°C/350°F (fan) and the water bath to 65°C/150°F. Gently heat the cep purée in a small saucepan. Place the royale discs in a tray lined with parchment paper and warm in the oven for 3 minutes. Gently warm the confit egg yolks in the sous vide bag in the water bath. Warm the duxelles in a small saucepan, then place a small spoonful into a tart and place a royale disc on top. Place a confit egg yolk on the left side of the tart. Sprinkle with some flaky sea salt, cep powder and the yeast crumble. Position the roasted cep slices on the right side of the tart. Season the raw cep shavings with salt, cep powder and yeast crumble, then pile them upright on top of the tart. Add some shaved white truffle and finish by placing the herbs on top. Add a spoonful of warm cep purée to the centre of the plate and add the tart on top. Warm the velouté in a saucepan and mix with a hand blender until it foams, then transfer to a sauce jug. Pour the cep velouté around the tart when serving.

POACHED SEA BASS
COCKLES, CLAMS, COASTAL HERBS AND LOVAGE

Serves: 4

SEA BASS NAGE BRINE
200 g Vegetable nage (p. 243)
20 g salt

SEA BASS PREPARATION
4 x 150-g skinless sea bass portions
Sea bass nage brine (above)
extra virgin olive oil

COCKLES AND RAZOR CLAMS
500 g cockles
500 g razor clams

SEA BASS BROTH
10 g grapeseed oil
80 g carrots, thinly sliced
80 g celery, thinly sliced
40 g banana shallots, thinly sliced

100 g button mushrooms, thinly sliced
4 spring onions, thinly sliced
1 garlic clove, sliced
4 sprigs thyme
50 g white wine
500 g Chicken stock (p. 244)
500 g Fish stock (p. 244)
shellfish cooking liquid (reserved from
   cockles and razor clams, left)
salt, to taste

SEA BASS MOUSSE
160 g skinless sea bass
3 g salt
80 g double cream

PESTO
5 g flat-leaf parsley

5 g basil
5 g spinach
5 g rocket
5 g lovage

SEA BASS DUMPLINGS
Sea bass mousse (left)
Pesto (left)
2 g chervil, finely chopped
2 g chives, finely chopped
salt, to taste

VEGETABLES
4 celery sticks
100 g runner beans
1 fennel head

SEA VEGETABLES
25 g rock samphire
25 g marsh samphire
25 g sea beets
25 g sea purslane

TO FINISH AND ASSEMBLE
Lovage oil (p. 247)
olive oil
baby nasturtium leaves
sea purslane
dill tips
lovage tips
fennel flowers
bronze fennel fronds
sea fennel fronds
salt, to taste
fennel pollen, to taste

SEA BASS NAGE BRINE
Bring the nage and salt to the boil in a pan, then leave to cool.

SEA BASS PREPARATION
Transfer the portions of sea bass into a deep tray, add the brine and let stand for 6 minutes, then drain and pat dry with paper towels. Wrap each portion of fish in cling film with a drizzle of olive oil to hold the shape. Place them into individual sous vide bags and fully seal.

COCKLES AND RAZOR CLAMS
Put the shellfish on a perforated tray with another tray underneath, then steam in the oven at 100°C/212°F. for 3 minutes. Once all the shells have opened, shake the tray to release the liquid. Transfer the shellfish onto another tray and chill as quickly as possible. Pour the liquid from the shellfish into a bowl set over ice to chill immediately. Once chilled, strain through a chinois and a muslin cloth. Remove the meat from the shells. Remove and discard the skirt from the razor clams and cut the clams on a bias. Transfer to a container with some of the chilled cooking liquid. Remove the foot from the muscle of the cockles and discard the muscle. Transfer to a container with some of the chilled cooking liquid.

SEA BASS BROTH
Heat the oil in a saucepan over a medium heat, add the vegetables and garlic (reserving half the mushrooms and spring onions for later), season lightly, and sweat them down without any colour until tender. Add the thyme and white wine and reduce by half, then add both stocks and bring to the boil. Reduce by half again, then pass the liquid through a fine chinois into a medium saucepan. To finish the broth, add the reserved mushrooms and spring onions and allow to infuse for 5 minutes. Season to taste with the shellfish cooking juices and salt.

SEA BASS MOUSSE
Place an empty blender jug into the freezer. Once chilled, add the sea bass and blend on full speed for 30 seconds, then stop and scrape down the mixture from the sides of the jug and blend again for 30 seconds. Repeat this process once more. Scrape down the sides again, add the salt, and blend for another 30 seconds until smooth. Pass the purée through a fine tamis sieve into a bowl set over ice, then beat the purée using a spatula. Gradually add the cream, ensuring it is fully incorporated before adding more.

PESTO
Blanch the leaves in a medium saucepan of boiling water for 1 minute, then immediately refresh in ice water and squeeze dry. Place the blanched leaves in a mortar and mix with a pestle until smooth.

SEA BASS DUMPLINGS
Bring a small saucepan of water to a simmer. Combine all the ingredients in a mixing bowl and season to taste. Using two teaspoons, shape the mixture into quenelles. Place them in the simmering water for 6 minutes, a few at a time, turning them every couple of minutes. Remove the dumplings from the water and place on a metal tray set over ice.

VEGETABLES
Peel the celery, runner beans and the inner leaves of the fennel to remove the fibrous strands, then cut each vegetable into 1-cm (½-inch) diamonds. Blanch the vegetables in a pan of seasoned boiling water until tender and refresh in ice water.

SEA VEGETABLES
Wash, trim and pick the sea leaves. Blanch them in a small saucepan of salted boiling water for 30 seconds, then immediately transfer to ice water.

TO FINISH AND ASSEMBLE
Preheat a water bath to 60°C/140°F. Poach the sea bass in the water bath for 14 minutes. Combine the blanched vegetables and sea vegetables in a small saucepan over a medium heat with a dash of sea bass broth and a drizzle of lovage oil to heat through. Season with salt and fennel pollen. In a small pan gently warm the sea bass dumplings with a dash of cockle and clam cooking liquid and a drizzle of the lovage oil until they are hot. In a separate pan gently heat the cockles and razor clams with a dash of cockle and clam cooking liquid. In another small saucepan, gently warm the sea bass broth. Remove the sea bass from the water bath and place in a medium saucepan over a low heat with 100 g sea bass broth and a dash of olive oil.

In the centre of the plate, spoon the vegetables and sea vegetables, creating a flat circle (and reserving a few). Lay the sea bass on top and add the reserved vegetables. Position two dumplings around the base of the fish and one on top in the centre. Finish by placing the cockles and razor clams on top and around the fish, followed by the herbs and flowers. Add a dessertspoonful of the lovage oil into a sauce jug, then add the broth. Once you're ready to serve, pour it around the fish.

ROASTED MONKFISH
MORECAMBE BAY SHRIMPS, SWISS CHARD AND BROWN BUTTER

Serves: 4

KELP OIL
100 g grapeseed oil
200 g kelp seaweed, chopped
10 g sea lettuce
salt, to taste
caster sugar, to taste

SHRIMP OIL
200 g shrimp heads
50 g carrots, diced
50 g white onions, diced
50 g celery stick, diced
1 garlic clove, sliced
5 coriander seeds
5 fennel seeds
½ star anise
5 white peppercorns
4 sprigs thyme
50 g butter
15 g tomato purée
150 g grapeseed oil, plus a dash
   for frying
salt, to taste

MONKFISH PREPARATION
4 x 150-g skinless monkfish tail
   portions
1 kg 10% Herb brine (p. 247)

SWISS CHARD PREPARATION
2 Swiss chard stalks
50 g Chicken stock (p. 244)
5 g lemon juice
salt, to taste

SWISS CHARD MIX
grapeseed oil, for frying
50 g shallots, brunoised
50 g leeks, brunoised
50 g button mushrooms, brunoised
100 g peeled brown shrimp, brunoised
50 g squid, brunoised
cooked Swiss chard leaves and trim
   (above)
grated lemon zest, to taste
finely chopped marjoram, to taste
freshly ground mace, to taste

freshly ground nutmeg, to taste
salt, to taste

SHRIMP PURÉE
10 g butter
20 g Shrimp oil (left)
100 g peeled brown shrimp
freshly ground mace, to taste
freshly ground nutmeg, to taste

MONKFISH SAUCE
500 g whole milk
100 g slice Malted sourdough (p. 237)
250 g Beurre noisette (p. 246)
100 g lemon juice
salt, to taste

SLICED SQUID
125 g squid, cleaned

NUTMEG EMULSION
50 g Chicken stock (p. 244)
50 g butter

finely grated lemon zest, to taste
freshly grated nutmeg, to taste
salt, to taste

SOURDOUGH CRISPS
½ loaf Malted sourdough (p. 237),
   frozen
100 g Beurre noisette (p. 246)
10 g thyme
5 g garlic cloves, sliced
salt, to taste

TO FINNISH AND ASSEMBLE
butter, for frying
freshly grated nutmeg, to taste
grapeseed oil
brown shrimp
purslane
nasturtium leaves
sea olive leaf
sea fennel
samphire
salt, to taste

KELP OIL
Heat the oil in a saucepan to 60°C/140°F, add the kelp, then remove the pan from the heat and infuse for 1 hour. Add the kelp, oil and remaining ingredients to a blender and blend on full power for 5 minutes. Place the mixture in a muslin cloth and hang in the fridge with a bowl underneath to catch the oil overnight. The next day, pour the liquid into a sous vide bag, seal and hang it at an angle in the fridge overnight, allowing the water and the oil to separate. Once the water has drained to the bottom corner of the bag, cut a small hole in the bag to allow the water to slowly escape, leaving only the clear green oil.

SHRIMP OIL
Preheat the oven to 180°C/350°F (fan). Place the shrimp heads on a tray and roast in the oven for 10 minutes. Heat a dash of oil in a saucepan over a medium heat, add the vegetables, cook and season with salt. Add the spices and thyme and cook until nicely browned. Add the roasted shrimp heads to the pan and crush them with a rolling pin, then add the butter and allow it to foam and roast. Reduce the heat, add the tomato purée and grapeseed oil and cook for 30 minutes. Pass through a fine chinois lined with muslin cloth into a container.

MONKFISH PREPARATION
Put the fish into a container with the brine and leave for 20 minutes, then drain well and pat dry with paper towels.

SWISS CHARD PREPARATION
Preheat a water bath to 98°C/208°F. Separate the white stems from the green leaves of the Swiss chard and reserve the leaves. Place the white stems in a sous vide bag with the chicken stock, lemon juice and salt. Fully seal and cook in the water bath for 20 minutes until the stems are tender. Remove the bags from the water and cool down in an ice bath. Remove the stems from the bag, peel away the fibres, then cut into 8-cm (3-inch) discs (reserve the trim). Blanch the reserved green leaves in a saucepan of seasoned boiling water for 1 minute. Cool them down in an ice bath, then remove and pat dry.

SWISS CHARD MIX
Heat a drizzle of the grapeseed oil in a saucepan over a medium heat, add the vegetables, season and sweat, without letting them colour. Remove from the pan and drain on paper towels. Heat a dash of oil in another small saucepan over

a medium heat, add the shrimp and squid, season and cook for about 2 minutes until opaque. Remove from the pan and drain on paper towels. Finely chop the cooked Swiss chard leaves and white stem trim, then add to the rest of the cooked ingredients and combine in a bowl. Mix and season with lemon zest, marjoram, mace, nutmeg and salt to taste.

SHRIMP PURÉE
Melt the butter in a medium saucepan over a high heat with the shrimp oil and cook until the butter browns. Add the shrimp, reduce the heat and cook for 3 minutes. Transfer to a blender and blend on full speed for 1 minute. Check the consistency and add water if needed, then blend again to make a smooth purée. Season with ground mace and nutmeg to taste. Transfer to a squeeze bottle.

MONKFISH SAUCE
Heat the milk in a saucepan over a medium heat. Toast the slice of sourdough to a dark brown colour. Add the toasted bread to the warm milk, remove the pan from the heat and leave to infuse for 15 minutes. Pass the liquid through a fine chinois into a bowl, then add the beurre noisette to the infused milk, along with the lemon juice and salt to taste. Mix with a hand blender and check the seasoning.

SLICED SQUID
Rinse the squid under cold running water and pat dry with paper towels. Cut the squid down one side to create a flat sheet. Place one sheet of squid on top of the other then place in the freezer until it's solid. Slice the frozen squid on a mandoline to a thickness of 2 mm (1/16 inch).

NUTMEG EMULSION
Boil the chicken stock in a small saucepan over a high heat until reduced by half. Add the butter and, using a hand blender, blend until smooth and emulsified, then add the lemon zest, nutmeg and salt to taste.

SOURDOUGH CRISPS
Preheat the oven to 180°C/350°F (fan). Slice the frozen sourdough lengthways on a slicer to a thickness of 2 mm (1/16 inch) then cut into 2.5-cm (1-inch) discs with a ring cutter. Melt the beurre noisette in a small saucepan, then remove from the heat and add the thyme and garlic. Allow to infuse for 5 minutes. On a tray lined with parchment paper, brush a layer of the infused beurre noisette then lay

the sourdough discs on top and season with salt. Cover with another sheet of parchment paper followed by another tray. Toast in the oven between the trays for 5 minutes until the bread is crisp. Transfer the crisps to an airtight container.

TO FINISH AND ASSEMBLE

Heat a non-stick frying pan over a medium-high heat with a good spoonful of butter. When it begins to foam, add the portion of monkfish and baste the fish all over until cooked and golden brown. Remove the fish from the pan and set aside to rest in a warm place. Gently warm the white Swiss chard disc in a steamer, then place on a tray and glaze with the nutmeg emulsion. Warm the brown shrimp in the shrimp oil in a small pan over a low heat, and warm the Swiss chard mix in another small pan over a low heat for 2 minutes until hot, then set both pans aside. Once the shrimp are removed from the heat, finish with grated nutmeg.

In a third small pan over a low heat, gently cook the sliced squid in a dash of grapeseed oil with a pinch of salt, then reserve until required.

Place an 8-cm (3-inch) ring at the centre of the plate, spoon the Swiss chard mix into the ring and spread it evenly to a thickness of 5 mm (¼ inch). Place the white Swiss chard disc on top of the mix then remove the ring. Place the monkfish on a tray, add dots of shrimp purée on top, then position the sourdough crisps upright. Add the shrimp and squid between the crisps, drizzle with shrimp oil and finish with the herbs. Position the dressed monkfish on top of the white Swiss chard disc. Gently warm the monkfish sauce in a saucepan then use a hand blender to create a foam. Add the shrimp and kelp oils to a serving jug, pour in the sauce and finish with a spoon of foam. Once ready to serve, pour the sauce around the monkfish.

CORNISH TURBOT
SMOKED MUSSELS, RED APPLE, CABBAGE AND CIDER

Serves: 4

TURBOT PREPARATION
4 x 150-g turbot portions
250 g 10% Herb brine (p. 247)

INFUSED CHICKEN
CONSOMMÉ
3 medium shiitake mushrooms, cleaned
20 g grapeseed oil
100 g Chicken consommé (p. 244)
5 g bonito flakes
salt, to taste

TO FINISH THE BROTH
100 g Infused chicken consommé
  (above)
100 g Mussel broth (p. 243)
50 g Dashi stock (p. 243)

CIDER EMULSION
10 g grapeseed oil
2 Braeburn apples, cored and diced
500 g Somerset cider
100 g apple juice
50 g butter, diced

KELP VINEGAR
50 g apple cider vinegar
15 g kelp seaweed

APPLE PURÉE
4 English red apples, peeled
  and chopped
5 black peppercorns
200 g cold-pressed apple juice
salt, to taste

MUSSELS PREPARATION
250 g mussels
20 g maple wood chips

MUSSEL CREAM
500 g mussels
50 g butter
1 garlic clove
100 g leeks, thinly sliced
2 medium shallots, thinly sliced
25 g white wine
5 g chervil
5 g flat-leaf parsley

4 sprigs thyme
150 g double cream
500 g whole milk

TO SET THE MUSSEL CREAM
500 g Mussel cream (left)
1.8 g LT100
1.5 g Gellan F
1.8 g guar gum
15 g Metilgel
1 g xanthan gum
lemon juice, to taste
salt, to taste

MUSSEL FARCE
500 g Set mussel cream (above)
10 g flat-leaf parsley, finely chopped
10 g chives, finely chopped
10 g chervil, finely chopped
prepared mussels
salt, to taste

CABBAGE AND FENNEL
BALLOTINE
½ hispi cabbage
½ fennel head
20 g Confit shallots (p. 246)
5 g fennel pollen
salt, to taste

TO FINISH AND ASSEMBLE
50 g butter
red apple batons
samphire
sea fennel
nasturtium leaves
oyster leaves
borage leaves
fennel flower
brassica flower
green fennel top
bronze fennel

TURBOT PREPARATION
Put the fish into a container with the brine and leave for 10 minutes, then drain well and pat dry with paper towel. Chill in the fridge.

INFUSED CHICKEN CONSOMMÉ
Season the shiitakes with salt and brush with the grapeseed oil. Heat a small saucepan over a high heat, add the shiitakes and cook until golden brown. Warm the chicken consommé in a medium saucepan over a medium heat until it reaches 80°C/176°F. Add the roasted shiitakes and allow to infuse for 5 minutes. Remove the pan from the heat, add the bonito flakes and allow to infuse for 5 minutes, then strain the consommé through muslin cloth into a container.

TO FINISH THE BROTH
Put all the ingredients into a medium saucepan over a high heat and reduce by half to a broth consistency.

CIDER EMULSION
Heat the grapeseed oil in a saucepan over a medium heat, add the apples and sweat until tender. Add the cider and reduce by half. Pour in the apple juice and bring to the boil, then remove the pan from the heat, add the butter and stir until melted. Pass the liquid through a chinois into a clean pan, then use a hand blender to thoroughly mix to an emulsion.

KELP VINEGAR
Bring the apple cider vinegar and seaweed to the boil in a saucepan, then remove from the heat and let it infuse for 5 minutes. Strain and discard the seaweed.

APPLE PURÉE
Put the chopped apples into a sous vide bag. Wrap the black peppercorns in a tied piece of muslin cloth and crush with a rolling pin to release their aroma. Add the crushed pepper and apple juice to the apples, seal the bag and place in a pan of boiling water. Cook until the apples are completely soft. Remove the apples and discard the peppercorns. Transfer the apples to a blender and blend on full speed for about 3 minutes until smooth. Pass the purée through a chinois and add salt to taste. Transfer to a squeeze bottle.

MUSSELS PREPARATION
Place the mussels in a perforated tray with a tray underneath and steam at 100°C/210°F until the mussels open. Drain the juices from the tray into a container and chill the mussels as quickly as possible. Using scissors, remove the foot and digestive gland, keeping the muscle intact. Place the mussels in an airtight container. Fill the smoking gun (food smoker) with the wood chips. Start the machine and light the chips. Insert the pipe into the airtight container and fill with smoke. Seal the lid of the container and leave for 20 minutes.

MUSSEL CREAM
Wash the mussels thoroughly under cold running water. Pull out the tough fibrous beards protruding between the tightly closed shells and remove any barnacles with a knife. Rinse the mussels once more to remove any small pieces of shell. Put the butter, garlic, leeks and shallots in a large saucepan over a medium heat and sweat until the vegetables are soft and tender. Add the wine and reduce the liquid to a glaze, then add the herbs. Add the mussels to the pan, increase the heat to high, cover and steam them in their own juices for 4 minutes, shaking the pan every 30 seconds. Add the cream and milk and cook for a further 5 minutes. Strain and reserve the juice.

TO SET THE MUSSEL CREAM
Put the mussel cream into a temperature-controlled blender, set to a low speed and bring to 90°C/195°F. Add the LT100, Gellan F and guar gum. Bring the mixture back up to 90°C/195°F and blend on a medium speed for 2 minutes. Remove the lid, scrape the mixture down from the sides and around the bottom of the jug with a spatula, replace the lid and blend on full power for 30 seconds. Pour the liquid into a tray and place in the fridge to set for at least 1 hour. Transfer to a blender with the Metilgel and xanthan gum and blend until smooth.

MUSSEL FARCE
Combine all the ingredients except the smoked mussels in a bowl, stir and check the seasoning. Transfer the mixture to a piping bag fitted with a 5-mm (¼-inch) nozzle, then pipe the mix into the centre of the smoked mussels until they're full. Chill in the fridge.

CABBAGE AND FENNEL BALLOTINE

Remove the first few dark green leaves of the cabbage, then take the light green leaves and remove the spine. Place the cabbage in a pan of boiling water and blanch until tender. Chill in an ice bath then lightly roll the leaves with a rolling pin to flatten them out. Using a mandoline, slice the fennel to a thickness of 2 mm (1/16 inch). Blanch the sliced fennel in a pan of boiling water until tender, then chill in an ice bath, drain and squeeze out the excess water. In a bowl, combine the fennel with the confit shallots and fennel pollen. Mix and season to taste. On a sheet of cling film, place a layer of cabbage, then the fennel mix. Roll into a ballotine and reserve in the fridge to set for 1 hour, then cut into slices 2 cm (3/4 inch) thick.

TO FINISH AND ASSEMBLE

Melt the butter in a medium saucepan over a medium heat. When it begins to foam, add the portion of turbot and baste until cooked and golden brown. Place the stuffed mussels and the cabbage and fennel ballotine slices in a steamer and heat gently. Warm the cider emulsion in a small saucepan over a low heat. Once the mussels and the cabbage and fennel ballotine slices are hot, add them to the pan with the emulsion, add the kelp vinegar and baste for 1 minute. Warm the consommé in a small saucepan over a medium heat, then pour into a sauce jug.

Position the ballotine slice on the top left side of the plate. Add 8 dots of apple purée: 4 on top of the slice, 3 at the front and 1 at the back. Position one mussel on top of the ballotine slice and one at the front. Garnish with apple batons and the samphire, sea fennel, nasturtium and oyster and borage leaves. Position the turbot on the right side of the plate and top with a final mussel. Add the fennel flower, brassica flower, bronze fennel and green fennel on top. Once ready to serve, pour the broth in the middle.

CORNISH BRILL
OYSTERS, CUCUMBER AND CAVIAR

Serves: 4

BRILL PREPARATION	5 g thyme	**COMPRESSED CUCUMBER**	Pickled Buddha's hand (p. 248),
4 x 150-g brill portions	1 head garlic	½ cucumber	thinly sliced
1 kg 10% Herb brine (p. 247)	50 g chicken fat	150 g mineral water	olive oil cress
2 sprigs thyme	salt, to taste		baby oyster leaves
grated zest of 1 lemon		**TO FINISH AND ASSEMBLE**	salad burnet
extra virgin olive oil	**OYSTER SAUCE BASE**	Braisage (p. 246)	cucumber flowers
	500 g Fish stock (p. 244)	grapeseed oil, for frying	Buddha's hand lemon
OYSTER PREPARATION	10 g shallots, sliced	Confit shallots (p. 246)	caviar
4 large raw oysters	40 g dry white vermouth	chives, finely chopped	Oyster leaf oil (p. 247)
	100 g double cream	4 large raw oysters, removed from	salt, to taste
SPIRAL POTATO	salt, to taste	the shell	lemon juice, to taste
1 large potato, peeled			

BRILL PREPARATION

Put the fish into a container with the brine and leave for 10 minutes, then drain well and pat dry with paper towels. Place the fillets in a sous vide bag with the thyme, lemon zest and a drop of olive oil and seal. Chill in the fridge.

OYSTER PREPARATION

Preheat a water bath to 62°C/144°F. Wrap the oysters individually in parchment paper and place in a sous vide bag, then seal. Cook in the water bath for 50 minutes. Remove from the bag and cool in an ice bath. Open each oyster and reserve the meat and juice.

SPIRAL POTATO

Preheat a water bath to 98°C/208°F. Using a Japanese vegetable slicer, sheet the peeled potato and lay it flat on a work surface. Season all over with salt, then roll up tightly lengthways into a cylinder. Line the work surface with a 30-cm (12-inch) sheet of cling film, then place the cylinder at the closest side of the cling film. Tightly roll the cylinder in the cling film and tie up the ends with a knot. Pierce the cling film with a small knife. Place the potato cylinder in a sous vide bag along with the thyme, garlic and chicken fat, then fully seal. Cook in the water bath for 25–30 minutes, or until the potato is completely cooked. Remove the bag and chill in an ice bath. Unwrap the cylinder from the cling film and cut it into four slices 2 cm (3/4 inch) thick.

OYSTER SAUCE BASE

Bring the fish stock to the boil in a saucepan over a high heat, season to taste and reduce by three-quarters. Put the shallots into another saucepan with the dry white vermouth and bring to the boil, then remove from the heat. Once the stock has reduced, add the shallot and dry white vermouth to the same pan, then add the cream and let it reduce by half. Remove from the heat and strain the liquid through a chinois into a container.

COMPRESSED CUCUMBER

Peel the cucumber and reserve the trim. Cut the cucumber in half lengthways, remove the seeds and reserve. Combine the cucumber trim, seeds and the mineral water in a bowl and blend using a hand blender. Pass the liquid through a fine chinois and set aside. Brunoise the cucumber flesh and place in a container with the skin juice. Place the container in a sous vide machine and close on full pressure. Compress twice more.

TO FINISH AND ASSEMBLE

Preheat a water bath to 60°C/140°F. Place the brill in the water bath to heat through for 8 minutes. Put the braisage into a small saucepan over a medium heat and bring to 80°C/175°F. Gently warm the cooked oysters in their juice in a small saucepan. Heat a dash of grapeseed oil in a small non-stick frying pan over a high heat, add the spiral potato slices and cook until golden brown, then flip over and colour the opposite side. Gently warm the diced compressed cucumber, confit shallots and chives in a small saucepan. Heat the oyster sauce base in a separate small saucepan over a medium heat, then add the raw oysters and blend for 1 minute using a hand blender. Pass the mixture through a fine chinois into a pan, then season with salt and lemon juice. Remove the fish from the water bath, drain, then place in the warm braisage and baste to finish the cooking.

Place a roasted spiral potato on a tray and position a warmed oyster on top and to one side and a spoon of the diced cucumber on the other. Add the pickled Buddha's hand and finish with the olive oil cress, baby oyster leaves, salad burnet and cucumber flowers on top. Place the potato on the left hand side of the bowl. Coat the fish with a final layer of braisage, then remove from the pan. Grate the zest the Buddha's hand lemon on top and add a spoon of caviar. Place the fish to the right of the potato. Pour the oyster sauce into a jug and finish with a drizzle of the oyster leaf oil.

DOVER SOLE
BLACK TRUFFLE, LEEKS AND CHAMPAGNE SAUCE

Serves: 4

MUSHROOM DUXELLES
grapeseed oil, for frying
10 g shallots, brunoised
25 g green spring onions, thinly sliced
200 g button mushrooms, diced
10 g Parsley butter (p. 246)
30 g Mushroom purée (p. 246)
salt, to taste
sherry vinegar, to taste

SOLE PREPARATION
2 gutted sole (800 g)
200 g 10% Herb brine (p. 247)
Mushroom duxelles (above)

CHAMPAGNE SAUCE
500 g Fish stock (p. 244)
grapeseed oil, for frying
50 g shallots, thinly sliced
50 g button mushrooms, thinly sliced
4 sprigs thyme
1 garlic clove, sliced
40 g dry, white vermouth
200 g Champagne
100 g double cream
salt, to taste

SOLE MOUSSE
200 g gutted, skinned sole
3 g salt
100 g double cream

LEEK BALLOTINE
2 large leeks
100 g Chicken stock (p. 244)
2 sprigs thyme
1 garlic clove, sliced
Sole mousse (left)
black truffle
salt, to taste

LEEK PURÉE
60 g butter
100 g onions, diced
100 g potato, diced
200 g Chicken stock (p. 244)
Leek tops (reserved from above)

100 g spinach
salt, to taste

TO FINISH AND ASSEMBLE
Braisage (p. 246)
Black truffle discs
   (2.5 x 4 cm/1 x 1½ inches)
Button mushroom discs
   (2.5 x 4 cm/1 x 1½ inches)
chive flowers
chive tips
spring onion tops
Champagne

MUSHROOM DUXELLES
Heat a dash of the grapeseed oil in a medium saucepan over a medium heat, add the shallots, season, and sweat them down (without any colour). Add the spring onions and let them soften, then add the mushrooms and cook until all the liquid has evaporated. Add the parsley butter and cook for another 2 minutes. Transfer the mixture to a large bowl with the mushroom purèe, mix and check the seasoning. Reserve in a piping bag fitted with a 5-mm (¼-inch) nozzle.

SOLE PREPARATION
Skin and fillet the sole. Put the fish into a container with the brine and leave for 4 minutes, then drain well and pat dry with paper towels. Match each sole fillet with its opposite side, but with the skin sides (the sides where the skin was removed) touching, then open them up like a book. Pipe a quarter of the mushroom duxelles in a line down the middle of one fillet on the skin side, then place the other fillet on top (with the flesh side up). Wrap each fillet in cling film, tie the ends, and place into a sous vide bag. Seal to 30 bars and allow to rest in the fridge for at least 2 hours before cooking.

CHAMPAGNE SAUCE
Bring the fish stock to the boil in a saucepan over a high heat, season to taste and reduce by three-quarters. Heat a dash of the grapeseed oil in a separate saucepan, add the shallots, season lightly, and sweat them down until tender (without any colour). Add the mushrooms, thyme and garlic to the pan of shallots, cook until tender, then add the dry white vermouth and Champagne. Bring to the boil and reduce by three-quarters, then add the reduced fish stock and cream and reduce by half. Remove the pan from the heat, strain the liquid through a chinois into a container and season to taste.

SOLE MOUSSE
Place an empty blender jug into the freezer. Once chilled, add the sole and blend on full speed for 30 seconds, then stop and scrape down the mixture from the sides of the jug and blend again for 30 seconds. Repeat this process once more. Scrape down the sides again, add the salt, and blend for another 30 seconds until smooth. Pass the purée through a fine tamis sieve into a bowl set over ice, then beat the purée using a spatula. Gradually add the cream, ensuring it is fully incorporated before adding more.

LEEK BALLOTINE
Preheat a water bath to 98°C/208°F. Remove the tops of the leeks and reserve for the purée. Wash the leeks under cold running water, then place them in a sous vide bag with the chicken stock, thyme and garlic, seal and cook in the water bath for 12 minutes until tender. Remove the bag and chill in an ice bath. Drain the leeks and cut them lengthways but only halfway through. Separate the layers, dry them with paper towels and gently roll a rolling pin over them. Layer each sheet of leek halfway on top of the other until you have a continuous 25-cm (10-inch) line of leek. Spread a thin layer of sole mousse over the leek, shave the truffle over the top, lightly season, then roll into a tight spiral. Wrap in cling film and tie at both ends. Place the ballotine into the water bath for 6 minutes, then transfer to an ice bath. Remove the leek from the cling film and cut into four slices 1 cm (½ inch) thick on a bias.

LEEK PURÉE
Put the butter, onions and potato into a medium saucepan over a high heat, season lightly and sweat (without any colour). Add the stock and cook until the vegetables are tender, then add the leek tops and cook for 2 more minutes. Set a metal tray over an ice bath. Add the spinach to the leek mixture and quickly stir. Transfer to a blender and blend on full power for 2 minutes until it reaches a smooth, thick consistency. Pass the purée through a fine chinois straight into the metal tray to chill it as quickly as possible.

TO FINISH AND ASSEMBLE
Preheat a water bath to 60°C/140°F. Place the chilled sole in the water bath for 6 minutes. Warm the leek purée in a small saucepan over a medium heat, then transfer to a squeeze bottle. Warm the Champagne sauce in a saucepan, and the leek ballotine in the braisage stock in a separate saucepan. Remove the sole from the bag and add to the braisage with the leek ballotine to heat through. Alternate the truffle and mushroom discs so they lay halfway on top of each other until you have a continuous line of 15 cm (6 inches), reserving some of the discs for garnish. Remove the sole from the pan and place onto a small tray. Lay the line of truffle and mushroom on top of the sole and cut each end on a bias.

Place two leek ballotine slices on the left-hand side of the plate and pipe dots of leek purée in a random fashion between and around the slices. Dress the leek with the truffle and mushroom discs and add the flowers and herbs. Place the dressed sole on the right-hand side of the plate. Finally, add a dash of Champagne to the sauce and blend using a hand blender. Pour into a sauce jug and serve in the middle of the plate.

DUCK AND NECTARINE
THYME, HONEY AND TIMUT PEPPER

Serves: 4

DUCK PREPARATION
1 whole duck
1 kg 10% Herb brine (p. 247)

DUCK LEGS
1 kg duck fat
2 garlic cloves
10 g thyme, leaves picked
2 white peppercorns
2 duck legs
20 g salt

DUCK HEARTS
1 g juniper berries
1 g allspice berries
1 small sprig rosemary
2 sprigs thyme, leaves picked
36 g rock salt
25 g duck hearts
20 g duck fat

DUCK TART FILLING
grapeseed oil, for frying
50 g carrots, brunoised
50 g celery, brunoised
100 g red wine
150 g Madeira duck sauce (p. 245)
1 Confit duck leg (left),
   meat shredded
1 Crispy duck leg (left), chopped
50 g tinned duck gizzards, diced
50 g duck hearts, diced
20 g cornichons, diced
20 g smoked duck ham, diced
20 g Confit shallots (p. 246)
salt, to taste

DUCK TART
350 g T45 flour, plus extra for dusting
6 g salt
3 g baking powder
180 g butter, chilled and diced
150 g whole eggs
30 g egg yolks
15 g Parmesan, finely grated

TO ASSEMBLE
duck fat
Madeira duck sauce (p. 245)
ripe nectarine
thyme leaves
Nectarine and honey gel (p. 248)
alyssum flowers (small)
Timut pepper

DUCK PREPARATION
Preheat the oven to 98°C/208°F (fan). Remove both the wings and legs of the duck, leaving as much skin as possible attached to the crown. Turn the duck over and remove the back by cutting in between the second and third ribs. Render the duck skin with a blowtorch. Using butcher's string, truss the duck crown and tie with a double knot. Put the duck in a large sous vide bag with the herb brine, seal and marinate for 2 hours. Remove the duck from the brine and pat dry with paper towels. Transfer the duck to a baking tray. Add a probe to the centre of the duck breast and set the probe to a core temperature of 49°C/120°F. Cook in the oven for 45 minutes–1 hour. Remove the duck from the oven and chill, then remove the breasts and transfer them to a tray.

DUCK LEGS
Preheat the oven to 88°C/190°F (fan). Melt the duck fat in a deep oven tray, then add the garlic, thyme and peppercorns. Season the duck legs with the salt and add to the tray of duck fat. Cover with parchment paper and cook for 8 hours, until tender. Remove the duck from the oven and allow to cool in the fat. Drain the legs and reserve the duck fat. Pick the meat from one leg and reserve until required. De-bone the other leg, leaving it whole, then press the de-boned leg between two layers of parchment paper, with a tray on top and underneath. Chill in the fridge for 2 hours. Heat a dessertspoonful of duck fat in a non-stick frying pan over a medium heat and place the pressed duck leg into the pan, skin side down. Cook until crispy and golden, then turn the leg over and repeat. Remove the leg from the pan and drain on paper towels.

DUCK HEARTS
Blend all the spices and herbs to a fine powder and add the salt. Trim any veins attached to the duck hearts and wash the hearts thoroughly in cold water. Pat dry with paper towels and coat the hearts evenly with the salt mixture. Place on a tray and leave in the fridge for 30 minutes. Preheat a water bath to 65°C/150°F. Rinse the salt off the hearts and pat dry with paper towels. Place the hearts into a sous vide bag with the duck fat, seal on full pressure and place in the water bath for 2 hours. Chill in an ice bath.

DUCK TART FILLING
Heat a dash of oil in a medium saucepan over a medium heat, add the vegetables and sweat until tender (without any colour). Add the red wine and reduce the liquid to a glaze, then add the duck sauce and let it reduce by half. Remove the pan from the heat and add all the remaining ingredients. Mix well, check the seasoning and keep in the fridge.

DUCK TART
Put the flour, salt, baking powder and butter into the bowl of a stand mixer fitted with the paddle attachment. Mix on speed 1 until it forms a crumble, then slowly add the whole eggs, egg yolk and Parmesan and continue to mix until a dough is formed. Remove the dough and lightly work it by hand, then wrap it in cling film and leave to rest in the fridge for 1½ hours. Preheat the oven to 160°C/325°F (fan level 3). Remove the dough from the fridge and roll it out on a work surface lightly dusted with flour to a thickness of 4 mm (⅛ inch). Cut out four 9 x 5-cm (3½ x 2-inch) ovals from the dough. Using eight 8 x 3-cm (3 x 1¼-inch) boat-shaped moulds, position one oval of dough in between two moulds and press down. Trim away any excess dough with a small knife and bake for 8 minutes. Remove the tarts from the moulds and reserve in an airtight container.

TO ASSEMBLE
Heat a dessertspoonful of duck fat in a non-stick frying pan over a medium heat and place the duck breast skin side down with a heavy weight on top. Gently heat the tart filling and the Madeira sauce in two separate small saucepans. Slice the nectarine in half and remove the stone. Cut the nectarine halves lengthways, so you're left with four equal pieces. Using a mandoline, slice the nectarine pieces to a thickness of 1 mm (scant 1/16 inch), creating half-moon-shaped slices. Layer the slices halfway on top of each other until you have a continuous line about 25 cm (10 inches) long. Using a pair of tweezers, roll up the line of nectarine slices so that it resembles a rose. Remove the duck breast from the pan and leave to rest. Add the duck tart filling up to the rim of the tart and cover with the nectarine rose, skin side up, then top with thyme leaves. Cut the duck breast in half and brush with duck fat. Pipe dots of the nectarine and honey gel on top, then place thyme leaves and alyssum flowers in a random pattern. Place the tart on the left side of the plate and the duck breast on the right. Finish by grinding Timut pepper over the duck. Pour the Madeira duck sauce into a sauce jug and serve at the table.

'BEEF AND OYSTER'

Serves: 4

WAGYU TONGUE
1 Wagyu tongue
500 g 8% Herb brine (p. 247)

WAGYU BEEF
1 x 600-g piece F1 sirloin
salt, to taste

BEEF CONSOMMÉ
100 g Wagyu beef fat (reserved
  from above)
500 g Wagyu beef trim (reserved
  from above), diced
150 g onions, thinly sliced
150 g carrots, thinly sliced
200 g button mushrooms, thinly sliced
7 g garlic cloves, thinly sliced
25 g shallots, thinly sliced
80 g fresh shiitake mushrooms, grilled
7 g dried shiitake mushrooms
6 sprigs thyme
10 black peppercorns
150 g Guinness
1 kg Beef stock (p. 244)
salt, to taste

TO FINISH THE CONSOMMÉ
500 g Beef consommé (left)
10 g white soy sauce
30 g oyster juice
salt, to taste

BEEF SHIN
grapeseed oil, for searing
250 g beef shin, de-boned
1 medium carrot, diced
1 large onion, diced
2 celery sticks, diced
2 garlic cloves
60 g butter
6 sprigs thyme
1 bay leaf
8 black peppercorns
1 bottle of full-bodied red wine
3 cans Guinness
4 kg Beef stock (p. 244)
salt and pepper, to taste

BEEF AND OYSTER PIE
grapeseed oil, for frying
50 g carrot, cut into 5-mm (¼-inch) dice

50 g celery, cut into 5-mm (¼-inch) dice
100 g red wine
Beef and Guinness glaze (reserved
  from the beef shin, left)
Braised beef shin (left)
Wagyu tongue (left)
50 g Confit shallots (p. 246)
salt and pepper, to taste

POTATO
400 g Ratte potatoes
160 g butter
80 g whole milk
salt, to taste

OYSTERS
6 oysters

OYSTER EMULSION
4 oysters
dash of lemon juice
250 g grapeseed oil
salt, to taste

OYSTER CRISPS
100 g oyster meat
260 g oyster juice
100 g tapioca flour
3 g silver powder
5 kg grapeseed oil, for deep-frying
dash of gin
2 g algae powder
10 g fried sea lettuce, ground
salt, to taste

OYSTER SAUCE
2 oysters
250 g Fish stock (p. 244)
2 medium shallots, thinly sliced
50 g dry white vermouth
200 g double cream
lemon juice, to taste
salt, to taste

TO FINISH AND ASSEMBLE
coastal herbs
small and large oyster leaves
Cabernet Sauvignon vinegar, to taste
salt, to taste

WAGYU TONGUE
Preheat a water bath to 65°C/150°F. Place the Wagyu tongue in a bowl and rinse under cold running water until the water runs clear and the excess blood has been removed. Place the tongue in a sous vide bag with the brine, fully seal, then cook in the water bath for 48 hours. Chill the bag in an ice bath and remove the tongue. Using a paring knife, remove the fat and hard outer layer.

WAGYU BEEF
Remove all the fat from the beef and reserve for the consommé, and trim the beef of any sinew. Cut it into five 100-g portions and reserve any trim for the consommé. Freeze one portion of beef, then thinly slice and reserve in the fridge for the grilled oysters.

BEEF CONSOMMÉ
Melt the beef fat in a saucepan over a medium heat. Add the diced beef trim, season, and cook until browned all over. Remove the beef trim from the pan and set aside. Add the onions, carrots, mushrooms, garlic and shallots, season lightly and roast until lightly browned all over, then add the grilled and dried shiitakes, thyme and peppercorns. Return the beef trim to the pan, deglaze with the Guinness, add the beef stock and bring to the boil. Skim off the impurities, then simmer for 2 hours, continuing to skim off impurities frequently throughout. Strain the stock through a chinois into a deep tray set over an ice bath. Once the stock has cooled and the fat has solidified, remove any fat from the surface and transfer the stock to a large pan over a high heat. Bring to the boil and reduce by half. Pass through a muslin cloth and pour 500 g into a saucepan.

TO FINISH THE CONSOMMÉ
Add the remaining ingredients to the consommé in the saucepan.

BEEF SHIN
Heat a dash of grapeseed oil in a large saucepan over a high heat. Season the shin with salt and pepper then sear on all sides. Once the shin is browned all over, remove from the pan and set aside. Add the vegetables, garlic and butter to the same pan, season with salt, and sweat them down until browned all over. Add the thyme, bay leaf and peppercorns, then return the beef to the pan. Deglaze with

the red wine and reduce to a glaze, then add two cans of the Guinness and reduce again to a glaze. Pour in the beef stock and braise the shin until tender, then allow it to cool in its stock. Remove the shin, press between two trays and reserve in the fridge. Pass the stock through a fine chinois into a large pan, add the final can of Guinness and reduce again to a glaze.

BEEF AND OYSTER PIE
Heat a dash of oil in a medium saucepan over a medium heat, then add the carrot and celery, season with salt, and sweat until tender (with no colour). Deglaze with the wine and reduce to a syrup, then transfer to a bowl. Warm the beef and Guinness glaze in a small saucepan. Dice the beef shin and tongue to 5-mm (¼-inch) squares and add to the bowl of vegetables with the confit shallots. Mix and check the seasoning. Add the beef and Guinness glaze, mix and check the seasoning again.

POTATO
Bring a large saucepan of salted water to the boil. Add the potatoes and boil for about 20 minutes, or until tender, then drain and peel. Pass them through a fine drum sieve, transfer to a saucepan and cook over a very low heat for 2 minutes, until no moisture remains. Add the butter, milk, and salt to taste. Mix until completely smooth.

OYSTERS
Preheat a water bath to 62°C/144°F. Wrap each oyster individually in parchment paper and place each one in a sous vide bag. Fully seal the bags and cook in the water bath for 50 minutes. Remove the bags and place in an ice bath. Open each oyster, reserving the oyster shells. Dice two of the oysters into 5-mm (¼-inch) cubes and reserve the remaining oysters in their juice.

OYSTER EMULSION
Open the oysters and reserve the juice in a separate bowl. Place the oysters, half their juice (discard the rest) and a dash of lemon juice into a small blender and blend on full power. Add the oil in a slow, steady stream until a thick, creamy emulsion forms. Season with salt and lemon juice and reserve in a squeeze bottle.

OYSTER CRISPS

Place the oyster meat and juice into a temperature-controlled blender and blend until smooth. Season to taste with salt. Add the tapioca flour and 2 g of the silver powder and blend for another 30 minutes at 90°C/195°F. Preheat the oven to 70°C/160°F (no fan). Spread the mixture out onto a silicone mat and dry in the oven for 20 minutes. Remove from the oven and break into 5-cm (2-inch) shards. Heat the oil in a deep-fat fryer to 180°C/350°F and fry the dried oyster crisps until they puff and double in size. Drain on paper towels, then – while they're still warm – flatten and cut into an oyster-lid shape. In two separate bowls mix a dash of gin with 1 g of the algae powder and the remaining silver powder. Paint rings on the crisps so they look like oyster shells. Sprinkle with fried sea lettuce and the remaining algae powder and reserve in a dehydrator at 60°C/140°F until required.

OYSTER SAUCE

Preheat a water bath to 60°C/140°F. Open the oysters and reserve the juice in a bowl. Bring the fish stock to the boil in a medium saucepan and reduce by three-quarters. Combine the shallots and dry white vermouth in another saucepan and bring to the boil, then remove from the heat and add to the reduced fish stock. Add the cream, bring to the boil and reduce by half, then pass the liquid through a fine chinois into a clean saucepan. Add the oysters and their juice, season with lemon juice and salt and blend with a hand blender. Pass through a chinois into a siphon, seal and charge with 2 cartridges. Reserve in the water bath.

TO FINISH AND ASSEMBLE

Set up a small Japanese barbecue with very hot charcoal. Season the Wagyu with salt on both sides. Cook the beef on the grill until both sides are seared – the core temperature should be 50°C/120°F. Remove from the grill and allow to rest. Trim all sides to make a square and position on the left side of the plate. Reheat the potato and the beef and oyster pie in two separate saucepans. To finish the pie, add the diced oyster, oyster juice and vinegar to taste. To assemble the oyster shell, place the potato in the bottom of it followed by the pie. Finish with the coastal herbs and finally the oyster crisp. Place the whole poached oysters on the grill to heat through, then wrap with a raw Wagyu slice and place on top of the grilled wagyu. Blanch the oyster leaves in a small saucepan of boiling water and place on top of the beef. Add a dot of oyster emulsion in the centre of the plate, with a dot of Guinness glaze in the centre. Heat the beef consommé in a small pan, then pour into a serving jug. Top the consommé with the oyster sauce and serve at the table.

LAMB, HOGGET AND MUTTON
CELTUCE, SAVORY AND BLACK CARDAMOM

Serves: 4

MUTTON LOIN PREPARATION
2 x 250-g mutton loin portions
2 sprigs thyme
2 sprigs rosemary
50 g grapeseed oil

LAMB BELLY
2 kg duck fat
5 garlic cloves
5 sprigs thyme
5 sprigs rosemary
1 small boneless lamb belly
salt, to taste

LAMB TONGUE
4 lamb tongues
100 g 8% Herb brine (p. 247)

HERB-INFUSED SHEEP'S CURD
1 kg whole milk
20 g thyme
10 g rosemary
15 g mint
22 g parsley

250 g sheep's yogurt
20 drops of vegetable rennet
salt, to taste

HOGGET SHOULDER
grapeseed oil, for frying
1 carrot, halved
1 white onion, halved
4 celery sticks, halved
300 g boneless hogget shoulder
5 sprigs rosemary
5 sprigs thyme
5 garlic cloves
2 kg Lamb stock (p. 244)
2 kg Chicken stock (p. 244)
salt, to taste

ACIDULATED ONIONS
grapeseed oil, for frying
100 g white onions, thinly sliced
20 g white wine
18 g Chardonnay vinegar
20 g butter
salt, to taste

HOGGET SHOULDER MIX
Shredded hogget shoulder (left)
Acidulated onions (left)
sherry vinegar, to taste
salt, to taste

LITTLE GEM LETTUCE
4 Little Gem lettuces, including
  the root
Hogget shoulder mix (above)

CELTUCE PREPARATION
1 celtuce
salt, to taste

MINT VINAIGRETTE
60 g Mint oil (p. 247)
20 g Chardonnay vinegar
salt, to taste

INFUSED MUTTON FAT
50 g mutton fat, cut into small,
  equal-sized pieces
10 g thyme
10 g rosemary
1 garlic clove
1 black cardamom pod
salt, to taste

TO ASSEMBLE
grapeseed oil, for searing
piece of butter
1 garlic clove
2 sprigs thyme
Mint oil (p. 247)
Mutton sauce (p. 245)
baby mint cress
savory leaves
thyme leaves
marjoram leaves
garlic flowers
lovage cress
black cardamom pod
flaky sea salt, to taste

MUTTON LOIN PREPARATION
Place the loin portions in a sous vide bag with the thyme, rosemary and oil and fully seal. Chill in the fridge.

LAMB BELLY
Preheat the oven to 98°C/208°F. Melt the duck fat in a deep oven tray, then add the garlic, thyme and rosemary. Season the lamb belly with salt and add it to the tray of duck fat. Cover with parchment paper and cook for 8 hours, until tender. Remove the belly from the oven and allow it to cool in the fat, then remove it from the fat and place it between two sheets of parchment paper. Place between two baking trays and chill in the fridge for 24 hours. Cut the pressed belly into four 10 x 2-cm (4 x ¾-inch) rectangles.

LAMB TONGUE
Preheat a water bath to 67°C/153°F. Place the tongues in a bowl and rinse under cold running water until the water becomes clear and the excess blood has been removed. Place the tongue in a sous vide bag with the brine, fully seal, then cook in the water bath for 24 hours. Chill the bag in an ice bath and remove the tongue. Using a paring knife, remove the fat and hard outer layer. Cut the tongue into 1-cm (½-inch) dice.

HERB-INFUSED SHEEP'S CURD
In a medium saucepan heat the milk to 90°C/195°F. Add the herbs, then remove from the heat, transfer to a container and allow to cool to 35°C/95°F. Add the yogurt and allow to cool to 30°C/86°F, then add the rennet. Leave the mixture at room temperature for 8 hours to separate, then drain and hang in a muslin cloth over a bowl for 12 hours in the fridge. Remove the curd from the cloth and transfer to a mixing bowl. Whisk until smooth and season with salt. Transfer to a squeeze bottle.

HOGGET SHOULDER
Light a charcoal grill, making sure the charcoal is nice and hot. Heat a dash of the oil in a medium pressure cooker over a high heat, add the vegetables, season with salt, and roast until a light brown colour. Season the shoulder all over with salt and seal on the grill until it is browned on all sides, then add it to the pressure cooker followed by the herbs, garlic and both stocks. Cover and cook under full

pressure for 2 hours. Allow the shoulder to cool down in the stock, then remove the shoulder and pick the meat. Pass the stock through a fine chinois into a clean saucepan and bring to the boil, then reduce by half.

ACIDULATED ONIONS
Heat a dash of the oil in a medium saucepan over a low heat, add the onions, season with salt, and sweat until tender (with no colour). Add the wine and vinegar and reduce to a glaze, then add the butter and cook for another 10 minutes. Remove the onions from the pan and chill.

HOGGET SHOULDER MIX
Put the shoulder and acidulated onions into a large bowl, mix together, and season with vinegar and salt.

LITTLE GEM LETTUCE
Remove the stem at the bottom of the lettuce while keeping the gem intact, then remove two layers of the external leaves. Open up the lettuce with your hand to expose the core and, using a knife, carve the core out. Use a paring knife to turn the root of the lettuce. Wash the lettuce hearts three times to completely remove any excess dirt. Stuff each lettuce with 50 g of the hogget shoulder mix.

CELTUCE PREPARATION
Bring a medium saucepan of salted water to the boil. Wash and peel the celtuce and cut into 1-cm (½-inch) cubes. Blanch the celtuce until tender, then immediately cool in an ice bath and drain on paper towels.

MINT VINAIGRETTE
Combine the oil and vinegar in a bowl, season to taste and whisk to emulsify. Transfer to a squeeze bottle.

INFUSED MUTTON FAT
Render the fat with a splash of water and a pinch of salt in a small saucepan over a medium heat. Add the herbs and garlic and grate in the whole cardamom pod. Remove the pan from the heat and allow to infuse for 30 minutes. Pass through a fine chinois.

TO ASSEMBLE

Preheat the oven to 180°C/350°F (fan). Light a wood-fired grill, ensuring it gets nice and hot. Place a small oak log on top until it begins to smoke and burn. Transfer the burning log to a tray and reserve in a warm place. Remove the mutton loins from the oil and allow to rest for 20 minutes. Heat a dash of oil in a cast-iron pan over a high heat, add the mutton, season with salt and sear all sides. Add the butter, garlic and thyme. Once the butter begins to foam, baste the loin all over and cook for about 2 minutes. Transfer the mutton to the grill and roll it on top until it reaches a core temperature of 47°C/116°F. Place the loin on top of the log and allow to rest for a minimum of 10 minutes. Heat the infused mutton fat in a small saucepan. Heat a small amount of oil in a small non-stick frying pan over a high heat and fry the lamb belly on both sides until browned all over, then place in the oven for 4 minutes. Combine the mint vinaigrette, celtuce and lamb tongue in a small saucepan and gently heat through. In a separate saucepan, gently warm the mutton sauce, then pour into a sauce jug. Place the Little Gems in a steamer and steam for 4 minutes, then transfer onto a tray and dress with the mint vinaigrette. Remove the belly from the oven. Create a chequerboard with the celtuce, tongue and sheep's curd on top of the belly and finish by placing the herbs on top. To finish the mutton, trim each end and brush with melted mutton fat. Carve directly down the middle, brush again with fat, season with flaky sea salt and grated black cardamom. Place the dressed lamb belly on the left hand side of the plate and the mutton loin on the right. Finish by placing a Little Gem on top of the loin and serve the mutton sauce at the table.

DEXTER SHORT RIB
OXTAIL, ONION AND BONE MARROW

Serves: 4

SHORT-RIB PREPARATION
1 kg beef short ribs (Jacob's ladder)
50 g beef fat
4 sprigs thyme
1 garlic clove
salt and pepper, to taste

OXTAIL PREPARATION
grapeseed oil, for frying
500 g oxtail
1 carrot, halved
4 celery sticks, halved
1 white onion, peeled and halved
4 garlic cloves
4 sprigs thyme
10 black peppercorns
250 g red wine
1 kg Beef stock (p. 244)
1 kg Chicken stock (p. 244)

ONIONS
250 g red wine
4 x 80-g English red onions (each,
    with a 6-cm/2½-inch diameter)
half of the reduced oxtail stock
    (reserved from the oxtail
    preparation, left)
salt, to taste

LYONNAISE ONIONS
60 g butter
onion flesh (reserved from above),
    thinly sliced
2 g thyme, leaves picked
sherry vinegar, to taste
salt, to taste

OXTAIL MIX
half of the reduced oxtail stock
    (reserved from Oxtail preparation, left)
Braised oxtail (from Oxtail preparation,
    left), coarsely chopped
Lyonnaise onions (left)
5 g thyme, leaves picked
sherry vinegar, to taste
salt and black pepper, to taste

ONION GLAZE
100 g cooking liquid (reserved from
    Onions, left)
100 g Beef sauce (p. 245)
Cabernet Sauvignon vinegar, to taste

BEEF POTATOES
500 g large King Edward potatoes
100 g beef fat
1 garlic clove
2 sprigs thyme
5 black peppercorns
salt, to taste

CRISPY SHALLOTS
25 g crispy shallots
5 g chives, finely chopped
salt, to taste

TO ASSEMBLE
Onion purée (p. 245)
200 g beef fat
bone marrow discs
chive tips
nasturtium leaves
thyme leaves
onion flowers
spring onion shoots
Beef sauce (p. 245)
Cabernet Sauvignon vinegar, to taste
black pepper, to taste

SHORT-RIB PREPARATION
Preheat a water bath to 68°C/154°F. Light a charcoal grill, making sure the charcoal gets nice and hot. Remove the bones from the short rib. Season the short rib well with salt and pepper and seal on the grill, making sure the meat is sealed all over, then chill. Place in a sous vide bag with the beef fat, thyme and garlic, and fully seal. Place in the water bath for 48 hours. Cool the bag in an ice bath for 20 minutes, then press between two trays for 12 hours in the fridge. Portion the short rib into four 8 x 5 x 2-cm (3 x 2 x ¾-inch) rectangles weighing 120 g. Chill in the fridge.

OXTAIL PREPARATION
Heat a dash of the oil in a large pressure cooker over a high heat. Season the oxtail, put in the cooker and roast all over, then remove. Add the vegetables to the cooker and roast until lightly browned. Return the oxtail to the cooker with the garlic, thyme and peppercorns, add the wine, bring to the boil and reduce by half. Pour in both the stocks, seal and bring the cooker to pressure and cook for 2 hours. Allow the oxtail to cool in its stock, then remove the oxtail and pick the meat from the bones. Pass the stock through a fine chinois into a large saucepan and reduce by half.

ONIONS
Preheat a water bath to 98°C/208°F. Bring the wine to the boil in a small saucepan and reduce by half, then allow to cool. Peel the red onions, keeping the tips intact, then place in a sous vide bag with the wine reduction, oxtail stock and a small amount of salt. Seal the bag on full pressure and cook in the water bath for 1 hour until tender, then cool in an ice bath. Drain the onions and reserve the liquid for the onion glaze. Peel the outer two layers and remove the centre of the onions. Set the 'shells' aside for filling with the oxtail mix and save the rest of the onion flesh to use in Lyonnaise onions below.

LYONNAISE ONIONS
Melt the butter in a small saucepan over a medium heat, add the onions and cook until caramelized, then add the thyme and vinegar and salt to taste. Set aside to cool.

OXTAIL MIX
Heat the oxtail stock in a small saucepan over a medium heat and reduce to a glaze. Add all the remaining ingredients, season to taste and place in a piping bag. Cut a 2-cm (¾-inch) hole in the piping bag and very carefully fill the empty onion shells.

ONION GLAZE
Combine all the ingredients in a small saucepan and bring to the boil, then reduce to a glaze and season with vinegar.

BEEF POTATOES
Preheat a water bath to 98°C/208°F. Peel the potatoes and cut them lengthways into slices 3.5 cm (1½ inch) thick. Transfer them to a sous vide bag with the remaining ingredients, season to taste, seal on full pressure and cook in the water bath for 30 minutes until tender. Chill in an ice bath, then punch-cut four rounds with a 5-cm (2-inch) ring mould. Using a Parisienne scoop, remove a ball of potato from the top.

CRISPY SHALLOTS
Preheat the oven to 180°C/350°F (no fan). Place the crispy shallots on a tray and toast for 1 minute. Allow to cool. Chop the toasted shallots and place in a mixing bowl with the chives and season to taste.

TO ASSEMBLE
Light a charcoal grill, making sure the coals get very hot. Warm up the onion glaze in a small saucepan and set aside. Gently warm the stuffed onion in a steamer for 10 minutes, then place in the onion glaze. Warm up the onion purée in a small saucepan, then transfer to a squeeze bottle. Heat the beef fat in a medium saucepan to 60°C/140°F and hold it at this temperature. Lightly season the short rib, place on the grill and sear on all sides, then place in the warm beef fat with the potato rounds to heat through. Place a small non-stick frying pan over a high heat, lightly season the bone marrow and fry on both sides, then remove from the pan. Remove the potato from the beef fat. Place the bone marrow into the recess in the potato and pipe a dot of onion purée on top. Finish with 3 chive tips. Remove the beef from the fat, carve off both ends and brush the top with onion glaze, then finish with a layer of crispy shallots and a grind of black pepper. Cover the top with the nasturtium leaves so they overlap. Baste the onion with the glaze, then place on a tray. Place the thyme leaves and onion flowers on the skin of the onion and place 2 spring onion shoots coming out of the top. Heat up the beef sauce in a small saucepan and finish with the vinegar to taste, then pour into a sauce jug. Place the stuffed onion on the bottom left of the plate, then the potato at the top, and the beef on the right, keeping an equal distance between the three. Finish the dish by pouring the sauce at the table.

ROAST GROUSE
RED CABBAGE AND BELL HEATHER

Serves: 4

GROUSE PREPARATION
2 whole grouse
100 g bell heather
200 g 10% Herb brine (p. 247)

GROUSE LEGS
500 g duck fat
2 garlic cloves
4 sprigs thyme
2 white peppercorns
4 grouse legs (reserved from above)
20 g salt

RED-WINE PICKLED CABBAGE
250 g red wine
250 g ruby port

25 g Cabernet Sauvignon vinegar
4 baby red cabbages
salt and sugar, to taste

GROUSE FARCE
25 g Chicken mousse (p. 248)
Grouse legs (left)
150 g minced pork
20 g Confit shallots (p. 246)
5 g brandy
5 g chervil
5 g chives
4 chicken livers, trimmed and cleaned
Red-wine pickled cabbage (left)
grapeseed oil, for frying
salt and pepper, to taste

BREAD SAUCE
12 g butter
100 g onions, thinly sliced
1 g clove, grated
ground white pepper, to taste
freshly grated nutmeg, to taste
freshly ground Voatsperifery
  pepper, to taste
1 bay leaf
75 g Chicken stock (p. 244)
75 g whole milk
4 slices of white bread (pain de mie)
salt, to taste

BREAD CRISPS
½ loaf white sourdough (pain de mie),
  frozen
100 g Beurre noisette (p. 246)
5 g thyme, picked
salt, to taste

TO ASSEMBLE
grapeseed oil, for frying
Grouse sauce (p. 246)
Confit shallots (p. 246)
Swiss chard leaves, cut into ovals
thyme tips
chive flowers
sherry vinegar, to taste

GROUSE PREPARATION

Remove both the wings and legs of the grouse, leaving as much skin as possible attached to the crown. Set the legs aside. Remove the wishbone. Turn the grouse over and remove the back by cutting in between the second and third ribs. Remove the innards, leaving a clean crown. Torch the skin lightly with a blowtorch. Place the heather in the cavity and set it on fire with the blowtorch, allowing it to smoke for 10 minutes. Put both grouse into a large sous vide bag with the herb brine, seal fully and marinate for 1 hour. Preheat a water bath to 65°C/150°F. Remove the grouse from the brine and place into a new sous vide bag and cook in the water bath for 45 minutes, then chill in an ice bath.

GROUSE LEGS

Preheat the oven to 98°C/208°F (fan). Melt the duck fat in a deep oven tray, then add the garlic, thyme and peppercorns. Season the grouse legs with the salt and add to the oven tray, cover with parchment paper and cook for 4 hours until tender. Leave the grouse to cool in the duck fat, then pick the meat and reserve the fat.

RED-WINE PICKLED CABBAGE

Bring the red wine and port to a boil in a saucepan over a medium heat and reduce by half. Add the vinegar and set aside to cool. Open the first three layers of leaves of each cabbage, keeping the root intact. With a small knife, remove the centre and separate the leaves to be pickled. Reserve the external leaves and root for the presentation later. Transfer the cabbage centre leaves to a container and pour over the wine and port reduction. Place the container inside a vacuum-pack machine and close on full pressure. Compress 4–5 times.

GROUSE FARCE

Put all the ingredients, except the livers, red cabbage, oil and seasoning, into a large bowl and mix thoroughly. Portion the mixture into four 40-g balls and place in the fridge. Preheat a non-stick frying pan over a high heat with a dash of oil. Butterfly the livers and season them with salt and pepper, then sear in the pan until browned all over. Remove the livers from the pan and chill as quickly as possible. Lay out a square of cling film on a work surface, place 1 cabbage leaf in the centre, followed by the liver, then the grouse farce. Taking all four corners of the cling film, pull up to the centre. Close the cling film around the ball and tie a knot. Repeat to make four balls. Poach the balls in a saucepan of boiling water for 10 minutes, then chill in an ice bath.

BREAD SAUCE

Melt the butter in a large saucepan over a medium heat, add the onions and sweat (with no colour) until tender. Add the spices and bay leaf and cook for 30 seconds, then add the chicken stock and milk and bring the mixture to the boil. Reduce the heat and simmer for 10 minutes, then season to taste and remove the pan from the heat. Pass the liquid through a fine chinois into a blender jug. Add the bread and blend on full power until completely smooth. Transfer to a squeeze bottle.

BREAD CRISPS

Preheat the oven to 180°C/350°F (fan). Cut the frozen sourdough lengthways on a slicer to slices 2 mm (1/16 inch) thick, then cut 4-cm (1½-inch) discs with a ring cutter. Spread a layer of beurre noisette on a tray lined with parchment paper, lay the discs of sourdough on the tray and season with salt and the thyme leaves. Cover with a sheet of parchment paper followed by another tray and toast in the oven for 5 minutes until golden. Remove from the oven, remove from the tray, and leave to cool.

TO ASSEMBLE

Light a wood-fired grill, making sure it is nice and hot. Heat a dash of oil in a medium cast-iron pan over a high heat, add the grouse crown, skin side down, and roast all over. Transfer the grouse to the grill and slowly finish off the cooking until the core temperature reaches 55°C/130°F, then remove from the heat and rest in a warm place. Warm the bread sauce in a small saucepan over a medium heat, then transfer to a squeeze bottle. Bring a medium saucepan of water to the boil, then reduce the heat and simmer. Place the grouse farce in the pan of simmering water, then remove the pan from the heat for 2 minutes. Heat the grouse sauce in a small saucepan and finish with a dessertspoonful of the confit shallots. Add a small amount of grouse sauce to a small pan and place over a medium heat. Remove the grouse farce from the water, unwrap, and add to the sauce to heat through. Place the grouse farce onto the presentation plate, cover with a glass cloche and smoke with bell heather. Reserve the sauce. Remove the breasts from the crown, trim and check for shot, then place on a tray with a rack underneath. Add a dash of vinegar to the reserved grouse sauce and glaze the breast. In a small pan of seasoned boiling water, blanch the Swiss chard ovals, then drain on paper towels. Place the Swiss chard on the right hand side of the plate, followed by the grouse and top with thyme tips and chive flowers. Pipe a dot of bread sauce on the left hand side and top with the bread crisp. To finish, place the sauce into a sauce jug and serve at the table with the grouse farce.

RHUG ESTATE VENISON
'HAGGIS', PEARL BARLEY AND LAGAVULIN WHISKY

Serves: 4

PICKLED CELERIAC
1 small celeriac, peeled
200 g Pickle liquor (p. 248)
salt, to taste

VENISON PREPARATION
4 x 130-g venison loins
2 sprigs thyme
4 black peppercorns
2 juniper berries
100 g grapeseed oil

SPICE MIX FOR 'HAGGIS'
5 g coriander seeds
5 g fennel seeds
5 g white peppercorns

BACON STOCK
grapeseed oil, for frying
150 g smoked bacon, diced
50 g carrots, finely chopped
50 g celery, finely chopped
5 sprigs thyme
2 garlic cloves
100 g butter
100 g white wine
500 g Chicken stock (p. 244)
salt, to taste

BRAISED VENISON NECK
grapeseed oil, for frying
500 g bone-in venison neck
1 carrot, peeled and halved
4 celery sticks, halved
1 white onion, halved
5 sprigs thyme
2 garlic cloves
250 g red wine
1 kg Chicken stock (p. 244)
500 g Veal stock (p. 244)
salt, to taste

MISO BUTTER
20 g pearl barley miso
20 g butter, at room temperature

CELERIAC
1 celeriac
250 g 10% Herb brine (p. 247)
40 g Miso butter (above)

PEARL BARLEY
250 g Bacon stock (left)
100 g pearl barley, washed

VENISON HEART
1 small venison heart
500 g 8% Herb brine (p. 247)

VENISON 'HAGGIS'
grapeseed oil, for frying
20 g smoked bacon, diced
10 g carrots, diced
10 g white leeks, diced
10 g shallots, diced
20 g cooked chestnuts, diced
Braised venison neck (left)
Venison heart (left), diced
20 g Venison sauce (p. 245)
2 g thyme, chopped
5 g chives, chopped
Pearl barley (left)
50 g Chicken mousse (p. 248)
1 g ground mace
1 g grated nutmeg
20 g Spice mix (left)
80 g minced pork
15 g minced pork back fat
white wine, to taste
brandy, to taste
whisky, to taste
salt, to taste

CHESTNUT PURÉE
250 g Bacon stock (left)
100 g butter, diced
150 g Smoked chestnuts (p. 247)
100 g double cream
salt, to taste

CELERIAC PURÉE
½ medium celeriac, peeled
  and diced
30 g butter, diced
100 g whole milk
100 g double cream
salt, to taste

TO FINISH AND ASSEMBLE
grapeseed oil, for frying
2 pieces of butter
garlic clove
sprig thyme
Venison sauce (p. 245)
Cabernet Sauvignon vinegar, to taste
16-year-old Lagavulin whisky, to taste
5 Smoked chestnuts (p. 247), diced
smoked bacon, diced
onion flowers
thyme leaves
chive tips
Beurre noisette (p. 246)
flaky sea salt, to taste

PICKLED CELERIAC
Using a mandoline slicer, turn the celeriac into a sheet and cut into 10 x 2.5-cm (4 x 1-inch) strips. Place into a container. Bring the pickle liquor to the boil in a small saucepan, pour it over the celeriac and season to taste. Leave in the fridge for 24 hours.

VENISON PREPARATION
Place the venison loin into a sous vide bag with the thyme, peppercorns, juniper berries and oil. Seal on full pressure and reserve in the fridge.

SPICE MIX FOR 'HAGGIS'
Place all the spices in a mortar and grind with a pestle to a fine powder.

BACON STOCK
Heat a dash of oil in a medium saucepan over a high heat, add the bacon, season and sear until browned all over. Remove from the pan. Add the vegetables to the same pan and cook until lightly browned all over and tender. Return the bacon to the pan and add the thyme and garlic, then add the butter and let it foam for 2–3 minutes. Deglaze with the wine, then add the chicken stock and cook for 30 minutes over a medium heat. Pass the liquid through a fine chinois.

BRAISED VENISON NECK
Heat a dash of oil in a large pressure cooker over a high heat, season the venison neck with salt, then sear all over. Remove from the pressure cooker, add the vegetables to the cooker and cook until lightly browned. Return the neck to the cooker and add the thyme and garlic. Pour in the wine, bring to the boil and reduce by half, then add both stocks, seal, bring the cooker to high pressure and cook for 2 hours. Allow the meat to cool in the stock. Remove the neck and pick the meat. Pass the stock through a fine chinois into a large saucepan and bring to the boil, then reduce by half.

MISO BUTTER
Combine the miso and softened butter in a small bowl.

CELERIAC
Preheat a water bath to 98°C/208°F. Set up a wood-fired grill and get it burning hot. Peel and cut the celeriac in half and shape into an oblong. Place into a sous vide bag, add the brine to cover, and fully seal. Brine for 20 minutes. Drain the celeriac then transfer to a new bag, add the miso butter, and fully seal. Cook in the water bath for 45 minutes until tender, then place in an ice bath. Remove the celeriac from the bag and cut it into slices 5 mm (¼ inch) thick, then into eight 7 x 3-cm (2¾ x 1¼-inch) rectangles. Place each rectangle over the grill and grill on one side until golden brown. Remove from the grill.

PEARL BARLEY
Bring the bacon stock to the boil in a medium saucepan. Add the pearl barley, reduce the heat and simmer until cooked. Allow the barley to cool in the stock, then drain.

VENISON HEART
Place the heart in a bowl and rinse in cold water for 30 minutes. Place the heart in a sous vide bag with the brine, fully sealed, for 3 hours. Rinse the brined heart in cold water for 1 hour. Preheat a water bath to 60°C/140°F. Place the brined heart in a sous vide bag, seal and cook in the water bath for 3½ hours.

VENISON 'HAGGIS'
Preheat a water bath to 65°C/150°F. Heat a dash of oil in a medium non-stick frying pan over a high heat, add the bacon and fry until golden, then remove and allow to cool. Put the bacon into a large bowl with all the remaining ingredients and mix thoroughly. Season to taste with wine, brandy, whisky and salt. Place the mixture into a 20 x 16-cm (8 x 6½-inch) sous vide bag and seal 3 cm (1¼ inches) from the

opening, then roll flat. Place the bag in the water bath for 15 minutes. Chill in an ice bath for 10 minutes, then place between two trays and chill in the fridge for 6 hours. Remove the mixture from the bag. Cut the 'haggis' into four 7 x 3-cm (2¾ x 1¼-inch) rectangles, then place each one in between 2 grilled celeriac rectangles. Carefully place them into a sous vide bag and seal with no pressure.

CHESTNUT PURÉE
Bring the bacon stock to the boil in a medium saucepan over a high heat. Add the butter and smoked chestnuts and simmer for 30 minutes. Drain the chestnuts from the liquid, reserving both. Place the chestnuts into a blender and add the reserved cooking liquid to cover. Blend on full power, adding the cream until it becomes a smooth purée. Season to taste. Pass the purée through a fine chinois.

CELERIAC PURÉE
Put the diced celeriac and butter into a saucepan over a high heat, season with salt and sweat for 5 minutes (with no colour). Pour in the milk and cream and simmer for 30 minutes until the celeriac is tender. Drain the celeriac and reserve the liquid. Blend the celeriac in a blender on full power, adding the cooking liquid, if needed, to form a smooth purée. Pass the purée through a fine chinois.

TO FINISH AND ASSEMBLE
Preheat a water bath to 80°C/175°F. Light a wood-fired grill, making sure it gets nice and hot. Place a small, wide juniper log on top until it begins to smoke and burn. Transfer the burning log onto a tray and reserve in a warm place. Remove the venison loins from the oil and allow to rest for 20 minutes. Heat a dash of oil in a cast iron-pan over a high heat, season the venison, and sear on all sides. Add the butter, garlic and thyme. When the butter begins to foam, baste the loin all over and cook for 2 minutes until it reaches a core temperature of 47°C/116°F. Transfer the loin to the toasted juniper log and allow to rest. Warm the chestnut purée and celeriac purée in two separate saucepans, then place into squeeze bottles. Place the bag containing the 'haggis' into the water bath and cook for 5 minutes or until hot. Gently warm the venison sauce in a small saucepan and season with the vinegar and whisky, then pour into a sauce jug. In another small pan, gently warm the diced smoked chestnuts and bacon. Once the 'haggis' is hot, remove it from the bag and on top, create a chequerboard with the celeriac and chestnut purée. Add the chestnuts and diced bacon and finish by placing the onion flowers and herbs over the top. Trim the sides of the seared venison, brush with beurre noisette and season with flaky sea salt.

Place the venison on the right side of the plate and the 'haggis' on the left, leaving a space in between. Top the venison with the pickled celeriac ribbon and alyssum flowers and thyme leaves. Finish with the venison sauce at the table.

'CHERRY BAKEWELL'

Serves: **8**

CHERRY COMPOTE	ALMOND MOUSSE	9 g whole eggs	CHOCOLATE CHERRY 'STEMS'
50 g cherry purée	80 g white chocolate	30 g T45 flour	300 g coco powder
50 g Amarena cherry syrup	3.4 g bronze gelatine sheets	1.5 g baking powder	50 g tempered milk chocolate
2 g agar agar	120 g double cream	salt, to taste	1 cherry stem
4 g kirsch	68 g orzata almond syrup		
2 g malic acid	16 g amaretto	CHERRY DIPPING GEL	TO ASSEMBLE
	16 g egg yolk	20 g bronze gelatine sheets	fresh cherries, cut into small dice
CHERRY CENTRES	2 g caster sugar	250 g cherry purée	cherry vinegar
70 g Amarena cherries,	24 g whole milk	5 g malic acid	blanched almond, shaved
cut into small dice		15 g liquid glucose	
Cherry compote (above)	CRUMBLE	25 g kirsch	
	22 g butter	8 frozen mousse-covered cherries (left)	
	20 g caster sugar		

CHERRY COMPOTE

Combine the cherry purée, Amarena syrup and agar agar in a small saucepan over a high heat. Stir, bring to the boil and boil for 2 minutes. Transfer the mixture to a shallow tray and allow to set in the fridge. Place in a small blender, add the kirsch and malic acid and blend on full power until smooth. Pass the compote through a fine chinois and chill until needed.

CHERRY CENTRES

Combine the diced cherries and compote in a bowl and mix well. Portion into eight 14-g balls, lay on a tray lined with parchment paper and reserve in the freezer.

ALMOND MOUSSE

Preheat a water bath to 44°C/111°F. Place the white chocolate in a double sous vide bag, seal and place in the water bath until just melted, then transfer to a bowl. Soften the gelatine in ice water for 10 minutes. Semi-whip the cream with 28 g of the orzata and the amaretto to soft peaks. Whisk the egg yolks and sugar together in a bowl until the sugar dissolves, then add the remaining 40 g of orzata. Heat the milk in a saucepan and pour over the egg yolk mixture, mixing constantly. Return the liquid to the pan and heat gently, mixing all the time until it reaches 80°C/175°F, then remove from the heat. Drain the gelatine, squeeze out the excess water and add it to the pan, stirring until dissolved. Gradually pour this mixture onto the white chocolate, stirring until it's all combined. Let it cool down to 45°C/113°F. Fold in the semi-whipped cream and transfer to a piping bag. Pipe the mousse into eight silicone semi-sphere cherry moulds, 3 cm (1¼ inches) in diameter, until they are three-quarters full. Add one ball of the cherry compote to the centre of the mousse, then pipe more mousse to fill the moulds. Place in the freezer until frozen solid, then remove from the freezer, unmould and stick a cocktail stick in the middle of each cherry. Return to the freezer.

CRUMBLE

Preheat the oven to 150°C/300°F (fan). Cream the butter and sugar together in a bowl, then add the salt and eggs and mix well. Add the flour and baking powder and mix until it's all incorporated and forms a dough. Roll the dough out to a thickness of 2 mm (¹⁄₁₆ inch) and place it between two parchment-paper lined trays to keep it flat. Bake for 6–8 minutes until the crumb is golden brown. Allow to cool, then place in a mortar and crush to a crumble with a pestle.

CHERRY DIPPING GEL

Soften the gelatine sheets in ice water for 10 minutes. Put the cherry purée, malic acid and glucose into a saucepan and bring to the boil, then remove from the heat, add the kirsch and pass through a fine chinois into a bowl. Squeeze out the excess water from the gelatine sheets, add them to the cherry purée and stir gently until all the gelatine has dissolved (it is important not to whisk the mixture). Place over an ice bath until it has cooled to 17°C/63°F.

Hold the cocktail stick and individually dip each frozen mousse-covered cherry into the gel, then place on a wire rack. Dip each cherry for a second and third time. Transfer them onto a flat tray and leave to defrost in the fridge, then remove the cocktail sticks.

CHOCOLATE CHERRY 'STEMS'

Tip the coco powder into a small tray about 2.5 cm (1 inch) deep and smooth out with a spatula. Transfer the tempered chocolate to a piping bag. Make eight indents in the coco powder using the cherry stem, then carefully pipe the chocolate into the indents. Place in the freezer until set, then remove the chocolate 'stems' and reserve in a container.

TO ASSEMBLE

Mix the fresh cherries with a couple of drops of vinegar in a bowl, then place in the middle of a plate and cover with the crumble. Lightly push down the top of the glazed cherry to create a realistic dent where a cherry stem would go. Add the chocolate stem to the top. Position the cherry on top of the crumble, place shaved almonds around the base of the cherry and serve.

'CORE APPLE'

Serves: 6

CARAMELIZED, DICED APPLE
100 g Pink Lady apple
100 g butter, diced
150 g golden caster sugar

APPLE PURÉE
Pink Lady apple trim (reserved from above)
100 g caster sugar
75 g butter

APPLE MOUSSE
9 g bronze gelatine sheets
154 g Granny Smith apple juice
21 g English mead
2.8 g malic acid
130 g Apple purée (left)
35 g 10-year-old Somerset brandy
35 g freeze-dried apple
70 g egg whites
160 g double cream
seeds of 1 vanilla pod

APPLE BRANDY JELLY
13 g bronze gelatine sheets
100 g 10-year-old Somerset brandy
100 g pressed apple juice
100 g English mead
1.5 g malic acid
20 g honey
12 drops green food colouring

GREEN APPLE SKIN
50 g whole milk
5 drops green food colouring

RED APPLE SKIN
50 g 10-year-old Somerset brandy
5 drops red food colouring

TO ASSEMBLE
piece of vanilla pod
  (2 cm x 2 mm / ¾ inch x ¹/₁₆ inch)
small lemon balm leaf

CARAMELIZED, DICED APPLE
Peel the apple and cut it into 1-cm (½-inch) dice. Reserve the trim (peel) and leave both the diced apple and trim in the fridge for 24 hours. Melt the butter in a medium non-stick frying pan over a high heat until it foams, then add the diced apple. Cook off the juice from the apple, then add the golden caster sugar and let it caramelize until it reaches a candy texture. Remove the pan from the heat and allow to cool. Portion the caramelized apple into six 13-g balls and reserve in the freezer.

APPLE PURÉE
Preheat a steamer to 100°C/210°F. Put the apple trim into a sous vide bag and leave it open. Put the sugar into a medium saucepan over a high heat and bring it to 185°C/365°F, to create a dry caramel. Remove from the heat, add the butter and whisk to emulsify, then allow to cool. Add the caramel to the sous vide bag with the apple trim, seal fully, and place in the steamer for 1 hour until cooked. Strain the liquid through a fine chinois, then transfer to a blender and blend on full power to a smooth purée.

APPLE MOUSSE
Soften the gelatine sheets in ice water for 10 minutes. Gently heat the apple juice, mead and malic acid in a saucepan over a medium heat, then remove the pan from the heat and add the gelatine (squeezing out any excess water), and stir. Add the apple purée and allow to cool to 20°C/68°F. Put the brandy and freeze-dried apple into a medium saucepan over a high heat and bring to 118°C/244°F. Whisk the egg whites to soft peaks in a mixing bowl. In another bowl do the same with the double cream and vanilla seeds. Gradually pour the brandy and freeze-dried apple into the beaten egg white, whisking continuously. Add the cooled gelatine mixture and fold in a quarter of the whipped cream, then add the remaining whipped cream and transfer to a piping bag fitted with a 1-cm (½-inch) nozzle. Pipe the mousse into six semi-sphere apple moulds, 3.5 cm (1½ inches) in diameter, until they are three-quarters full. Add one ball of caramelized apple to the centre of the mousse, then pipe more mousse to fill the mould. Place the mousse-filled moulds in the freezer until frozen. Remove from the freezer, unmould and stick a cocktail stick in the centre of each apple. Return to the freezer.

APPLE BRANDY JELLY
Soften the gelatine sheets in ice water for 10 minutes. Put all the remaining ingredients, except the green food colouring, into a large saucepan and bring to the boil over a high heat, then remove the pan from the heat. Drain the gelatine, squeeze out the excess water, then add it to the mixture and stir gently until all the gelatine has dissolved (it is important not to whisk the mixture). Transfer the mixture into a bowl set over an ice bath until it has cooled to 20°C/68°F. Stir in the green food colouring and allow to cool to 17°C/63°F.

GREEN APPLE SKIN
Mix the milk with the green colouring in a small bowl. Place in a spray bottle.

RED APPLE SKIN
Mix the brandy with the red colouring in a small bowl. Place in a spray bottle.

TO ASSEMBLE
Hold the cocktail stick and dip each frozen apple into the brandy jelly, then place on a wire rack. Dip each apple for a second time. Spray one side green and the other side red. Dip each apple for a third time. Place on a flat tray, remove the cocktail sticks and leave to defrost in the fridge.

Position the apple in the middle of the plate. Push down the top of the apple to create an indent where an apple stem would naturally be. Add the vanilla stick to the indent, for a stem. Add the lemon balm leaf to the left side of the stem and serve.

'CORE-TESER'

Serves: 6

CHOCOLATE FEUILLANTINE BASE
13 g 70% dark chocolate, broken into pieces
7 g cocoa butter
17 g Hazelnut praline (p. 249)
23 g feuillantine

AERATED CHOCOLATE
150 g 70% dark chocolate
6 g cocoa butter

MILK CHOCOLATE CRÉMEUX
2 sheets bronze gelatine
12 g egg yolks
36 g whole milk
36 g double cream

66 g 40% milk chocolate, broken into pieces

MALT MOUSSE
2 sheets bronze gelatine
24 g egg yolks
24 g caster sugar
36 g malt powder
110 g double cream

TO ASSEMBLE THE CORE-TESER
Malt mousse (above)
Aerated chocolate (left)
Milk chocolate crémeux (left)

HAZELNUT ICE CREAM
250 g whole milk
81 g double cream

100 g blanched hazelnuts
68 g egg yolks
39 g caster sugar
31 g Frangelico liqueur
salt, to taste

MILK CHOCOLATE FEATHERS
100 g 40% milk chocolate

MALT WATER
15 g water
15 g malt powder

ROYAL ICING
10 g icing sugar
1.5 g egg whites
1 drop of lemon juice

MALT SUGAR PUFF
75 g trehalose
6 g liquid glucose
30 g Malt water (left)
2 g Royal icing (left)

HAZELNUT CARAMEL
5 g caster sugar
16 g double cream
4 g butter
4 g hazelnut oil
salt, to taste

CHOCOLATE SPRAY
330 g 70% dark chocolate
65 g cocoa butter

CHOCOLATE FEUILLANTINE BASE
Melt the chocolate, cocoa butter and hazelnut praline in a bowl over a saucepan of simmering water. Add the feuillantine, then spread the mixture onto a silicone mat to a thickness of 2 mm (1/16 inch). Allow to set in the fridge, then cut out six 4-cm (1½-inch) discs using a round cutter and place in the fridge.

AERATED CHOCOLATE
Melt the chocolate and cocoa butter in a bowl over a saucepan of simmering water until it reaches 50°C/120°F. Temper the chocolate and cocoa butter mixture. Pour into a 1-litre siphon and charge the siphon with 3 cartridges. Spray all the mixture into a half gastronorm tray 10 cm (4 inches) deep. Place the tray into a sous vide vacuum chamber and compress until the chocolate reaches the top of the container. Turn off the machine and leave the mixture for 4 hours to set. Cut the aerated chocolate into slices 1.5 cm (¾ inch) thick, then punch-cut six 4.5-cm (1¾-inch) discs with a ring cutter.

MILK CHOCOLATE CRÉMEUX
Soften the gelatine in ice water for 10 minutes. Whisk the egg yolks in a bowl. Heat the milk and cream in a saucepan and, once it's hot, pour it over the egg yolks while whisking continuously. Return the liquid to the pan and heat gently, stirring constantly, until it reaches 83°C/181°F. Remove the pan from the heat, then drain the gelatine, squeeze out the excess water and stir it into the liquid in the pan. Fold in the chocolate, making sure not to incorporate too much air into the mixture. Allow to cool to 28°C/83°F, then transfer to a piping bag.

MALT MOUSSE
Soften the gelatine in ice water for 10 minutes. Whisk the egg yolks in a small bowl until they double in size. Heat the sugar to 118°C/244°F in a saucepan over a high heat, then pour into the egg yolks, whisking continuously to create a *pâte à bombe*.

Combine the malt powder with 100 g of the double cream in a bowl and whisk to soft peaks. Drain the gelatine, squeezing out the excess water, and gently dissolve it in the remaining 10 g of cream in a saucepan over a low heat, then fold it into the *pâte à bombe*. Fold the malt powder cream mixture into the *pâte à bombe* and transfer to a piping bag fitted with a 5-mm (¼-inch) nozzle.

TO ASSEMBLE THE CORE-TESER
Pipe 24 g of malt mousse into each of six round cavities, 6.5 cm (2½ inches) in diameter and 3 cm (1¼ inches) high, of a silicone mould. Place the aerated chocolate directly in the centre, then pipe the chocolate crémeux around and on top of the aerated chocolate, leaving a 2-mm (1/16-inch) gap for the feuillantine disc. Place in the freezer for 12 hours. Remove from the mould and return to the freezer.

HAZELNUT ICE CREAM
Preheat the oven to 180°C/350°F (fan). Put the milk and cream into a container. Toast the hazelnuts in the oven for 8 minutes until golden brown, then add them to the milk and cream base and blend using a hand blender to break up the nuts. Allow to infuse in the fridge for 12 hours.

Strain the infused hazelnut milk into a medium saucepan and bring to the boil over a high heat. Whisk the egg yolks, sugar and Frangelico together in a bowl, then pour the hazelnut milk over the egg mixture while whisking continuously. Pour the liquid into a clean saucepan, place over a low heat, add salt to taste, and heat, stirring frequently, until it reaches 84°C/183°F. Strain the custard through a fine chinois into a bowl set over an ice bath and allow to cool. Pour into a Pacojet beaker and reserve in the freezer.

MILK CHOCOLATE FEATHERS
Temper the chocolate and transfer it to a tall plastic container. Dip a feather stencil into the container, then allow most of the excess chocolate to drain. Place it onto a sheet of acetate and draw it back to leave a feather shape. Place the acetate inside two rings, giving it a natural curve. Remove the feather from the acetate and, using a warm knife, make three indents down each side of the feather and reserve in the fridge. Repeat to create 24 feathers.

MALT WATER
Mix the water and malt powder in a small bowl.

ROYAL ICING
Whisk all the ingredients together in a bowl. Transfer to a piping bag fitted with a 2-mm (1/16-inch) nozzle.

MALT SUGAR PUFF
Bring the trehalose, glucose and malt water to the boil in a saucepan over a high heat and heat until it reaches 130°C/266°F, then stir in the royal icing. Pour onto a silicone mat and allow to cool, then massage the mixture until it reaches 40°C/100°F. Place into a vacuum chamber and compress until it doubles in size. Turn off the machine and allow to set. Remove the malt puff from the vacuum chamber and portion into eighteen 5-cm (2-inch) shards to use for the top and the base.

HAZELNUT CARAMEL
Heat the sugar in a small saucepan over a high heat and make a dry caramel, light brown in colour. Remove from the heat and pour in the cream while stirring continuously, then add the butter, oil and salt to taste, and mix to emulsify. Transfer to a squeeze bottle.

CHOCOLATE SPRAY

Melt the chocolate and cocoa butter together in a saucepan over a medium heat. Remove the pan from the heat and allow to cool slightly, then pour into a spray gun and spray the frozen portions of the Core-teser. Reserve in the fridge for 20 minutes before serving.

TO ASSEMBLE

Pipe a dot of caramel onto the centre of the plate and add a malt puff shard as the base. Place the sprayed Core-teser on top. Place the container with the ice cream in the Pacojet machine and spin on full power. Add a quenelle of hazelnut ice cream and three more dots of caramel. Add two shards of malt puff, then finish by placing the feathers from the top to the bottom.

LEMONADE PARFAIT
HONEY AND SHEEP'S MILK YOGURT

Serves: 6

LEMON REDUCTION
1 kg lemon purée

LEMONADE PARFAIT
1 sheet bronze gelatine
270 g double cream
75 g egg yolks
90 g caster sugar
20 g water
15 g Lemon reduction (above)
lemon juice, to taste

LEMON SUGAR
1 lemon, zest peeled
200 g caster sugar
5 g tartaric acid

SHEEP'S MILK YOGURT SORBET
30 g liquid glucose
60 g condensed milk
25 g caster sugar
400 g whole milk
5 g Stab 2000
400 g sheep's milk yogurt
30 g lemon juice

CONFIT LEMON
1 frozen lemon
100 g caster sugar
300 g water
2 long peppercorns

BERGAMOT GEL
80 g water
40 g Stock syrup (p. 249)
1.2 g agar agar
2 drops of bergamot extract
bergamot juice, to taste
grated zest of 1 lime

BEE POLLEN SHERBET
28 g icing sugar
4 g citric acid
3 g bicarbonate of soda
10 g bee pollen

TO ASSEMBLE
yellow lemon food colouring spray
honey cress
Honey crisps (p. 249)

LEMON REDUCTION
Reduce the lemon purée in a large saucepan over a high heat to 70°Brix (measured using a refractometer).

LEMONADE PARFAIT
Soften the gelatine in ice water for 10 minutes. Whisk 230 g of the cream in a bowl to soft peaks and reserve in the fridge. Whisk the egg yolks in a separate mixing bowl until light and airy. Combine the sugar with the water in a small saucepan over a high heat and bring to 118°C/244°F. Pour the hot syrup onto the egg yolks and whisk continuously until the mixture is cold and has doubled in volume. Fold in the lemon reduction. Warm the remaining 40 g of cream in a saucepan over a low heat and add the drained gelatine (squeezed of excess water) and stir to dissolve. Add the warm cream to the egg mixture, then fold in the whipped cream and lemon juice to taste. Pour the mixture into six lemon-shaped moulds and freeze for 24 hours. Remove the lemons from the freezer, unmould and return to the freezer.

LEMON SUGAR
Place the lemon zest and half the sugar into a blender and blend to a fine powder. Combine the remaining sugar with the tartaric acid in a bowl and mix with the lemon zest sugar. Spread the mixture onto a tray lined with greaseproof paper and let it dry for 1 day.

SHEEP'S MILK YOGURT SORBET
Dissolve the glucose in the condensed milk with the sugar and half the milk in a small saucepan over a low heat, stirring continuously to avoid the liquid catching at the bottom of the pan. Add the Stab 2000 and bring to the boil for 2 minutes while whisking continuously, then remove from the heat, pass the liquid through a fine chinois into a bowl set over ice and leave to cool. Whisk the yogurt and lemon juice together, then add the mixture to the remaining milk and combine with the condensed milk mixture. Pour into a Pacojet beaker and reserve in the freezer.

CONFIT LEMON
Cut the frozen lemon into slices 4 mm (1/8 inch) thick and remove any seeds. Place all the remaining ingredients in a medium saucepan over a high heat and bring to 90°C/195°F, then add the sliced lemon and cook for 4 hours (maintaining the heat at 90°C/195°F). Remove the pan from the heat and allow the lemons to cool in the liquid, then remove and reserve in a container.

BERGAMOT GEL
Bring the water and stock syrup to the boil in a small saucepan and whisk in the agar agar. Make sure it boils for at least 30 seconds, then pour into a container, add the drops of bergamot extract and place in the fridge to cool. Once cool, transfer to a small blender and blend until smooth. Pass through a fine chinois and add the fresh bergamot juice and lime zest to taste. Transfer to a piping bag fitted with a 2-mm (1/16-inch) nozzle.

BEE POLLEN SHERBET
Blend all the ingredients together in a blender and store in an airtight container.

TO ASSEMBLE
Remove the lemonade parfait from the freezer 15 minutes before serving. Cover the top with a lemon segment stencil, then spray on the yellow food colouring. Cover the bottom half of the lemon with lemon sugar and sprinkle the sherbet on top. Place in the centre of the plate. Pipe five dots of bergamot gel along one edge of the lemon and place honey cress on top of each dot. Place a confit lemon slice on the opposite edge. Add a teaspoon scoop of the sheep's milk yogurt sorbet in the centre and finally top with the honey crisp.

PEAR AND VERBENA
WITH POIRE WILLIAMS SORBET

Serves: 6

LEMON VERBENA MILK AND CREAM INFUSIONS
500 g whole milk
40 g fresh lemon verbena leaves
500 g double cream

LEMON VERBENA MERINGUE
250 g egg whites
450 g caster sugar
10 g egg white powder
7.5 g citric acid
8 drops of lemon verbena essence
1.5 g lemon verbena powder

PASTRY CREAM
4 sheets bronze gelatine
500 g Lemon verbena milk infusion (above)
grated zest of 1 lemon
65 g egg yolks

50 g caster sugar
26 g T45 flour
26 g cornflour
5 g lemon verbena powder
5 drops of lemon verbena essence

LEMON VERBENA CREAM
500 g Lemon verbena cream infusion (left)
8 drops of lemon verbena essence
Pastry cream (left)

PEAR PURÉE
2 pears, peeled, halved, cored and diced
40 g Stock syrup (p. 249)
1.5 g ascorbic acid

PEAR SORBET
250 g water

20 g Trimoline
75 g lemon purée
4 g Stab 2000
500 g Pear purée (left)
50 g Poire William liqueur

LEMON VERBENA JELLY
18 g bronze gelatine sheets
90 g water
40 g caster sugar
120 g Elderflower cordial (p. 248)
18 g lemon purée
8 drops of lemon verbena essence
1 g lemon verbena powder

COMPRESSED PEAR PEARLS
150 g Stock syrup (p. 249)
75 g Poire William liqueur
10 g lemon juice
17.5g Chardonnay vinegar

6 lemon verbena leaves
3 Comice pears

PEAR DISC SOAKING SYRUP
150 g water
50 g Stock syrup (p. 249)
10 g lemon juice
2 Comice pears, peeled

LEMON VERBENA SUGAR
50 g caster sugar
5 g dried lemon verbena leaves

TO ASSEMBLE
nappage
fresh lemon verbena leaves
fresh lemon verbena tips

LEMON VERBENA MILK AND CREAM INFUSIONS
Bring the milk to the boil in a medium pan over a high heat and add 20 g of the fresh lemon verbena leaves. Pour the mixture into a container to cool and leave to infuse for 24 hours. Repeat the same process with the double cream and remaining lemon verbena. Once the milk and double cream infusions are ready, individually pass them through a fine chinois, pressing the leaves and making sure that all the liquid has drained.

LEMON VERBENA MERINGUE
Preheat the oven to 75°C/170°F (0% humidity, full fan). Put the egg whites, caster sugar and egg white powder into a large bowl over a pan of simmering water and whisk the mixture continuously to avoid it sticking to the bottom of the bowl until the sugar has completely dissolved and reaches 73°C/163°F. Pour into the bowl of a stand mixer fitted with the whisk attachment and whisk on high speed for 3 minutes. Add the citric acid and lemon verbena essence and continue to whisk until stiff peaks form. Transfer the meringue into a piping bag fitted with a 5-mm (¼-inch) nozzle and pipe 25 g of meringue into six 8-cm (3-inch) semi-sphere moulds. Use the back of a spoon to press the meringue against the moulds for an even, smooth surface. Place the moulds in the oven for 8 hours until dry. Evenly pipe the remaining meringue onto individual 2-cm (1-inch) circle stencils, with a silicone mat underneath. Scrape off the excess meringue, ensuring the discs are completely covered. Remove the stencil. Using a tea strainer, sprinkle the lemon verbena powder on top of the discs. Place onto a tray and put into the oven for 3 hours until dry, then remove the discs (leaving the sphere moulds in the oven) and store the discs in an airtight container. Remove the sphere meringues, unmould and, using a Microplane, lightly grate the bottom of the meringue domes to create a flat base. Store in an airtight container.

PASTRY CREAM
Soften the gelatine in ice water for 10 minutes, then drain. Bring the lemon verbena milk infusion to a simmer with the lemon zest in a medium saucepan over a high heat. Whisk together the egg yolks, caster sugar, flour, cornflour, verbena powder and essence in a bowl. Temper the egg mixture by gradually adding 200 g of the heated milk into the bowl while whisking constantly, then add this back to the pan with the heated milk and whisk until thoroughly mixed. Simmer the mixture for 3 minutes to ensure the cornflour is cooked. Remove the pan from the heat and add the drained gelatine (squeezed of excess water) and stir to dissolve. Pour into a tray set over ice and chill as quickly as possible.

LEMON VERBENA CREAM
Put the lemon verbena cream and essence into the bowl of a stand mixer fitted with the whisk attachment and whisk on medium speed until it forms soft peaks. Place the pastry cream into a separate stand mixer bowl and whisk until smooth, then fold in the whipped lemon verbena cream. Transfer to a piping bag fitted with a 1-cm (½-inch) nozzle.

PEAR PURÉE
Preheat a water bath to 85°C/185°F. Place all the ingredients into a sous vide bag and seal on full pressure, then place in the water bath and cook until tender. Transfer the pears and cooking liquid to a blender and blend until smooth, then pass through a fine chinois into a squeeze bottle.

PEAR SORBET
Combine the water, Trimoline and lemon purée in a medium saucepan over a high heat and bring to the boil. Add the Stab 2000 and whisk continuously until it returns to the boil, then simmer for 2 minutes. Remove the pan from the heat and blend using a hand blender. Pass the liquid through a fine chinois into a container and allow to cool. Add the pear purée and Poire William liqueur and blend once more with the hand blender, then pour into a Pacojet container and reserve in the freezer.

LEMON VERBENA JELLY
Soften the gelatine in ice water for 10 minutes, then drain. Warm the water and sugar in a small saucepan over a low heat until it's completely dissolved, then add the drained gelatine (squeezed of excess water), remove the pan from the heat, stir to dissolve the gelatine and allow to cool. Add the cordial, lemon purée, lemon verbena essence and lemon verbena powder and pour the jelly into a tray 2 cm (¾ inch) deep and place in the fridge to set. Once it has set, cut it into 5-mm (¼-inch) cubes. Store in the fridge.

COMPRESSED PEAR PEARLS
Put all the ingredients, except the fresh pears, into a container, place the container inside the vacuum-pack machine, set to programme 1, and compress the syrup three times. Peel the skin off the pears and, using a 1.2-cm (½-inch) Parisienne scooper, scoop out the pear flesh, making small pearls. Place the pear pearls into the verbena syrup and compress once more on programme 1. Store the compressed pear pearls in the syrup in the fridge.

PEAR DISC SOAKING SYRUP
Put all the ingredients, except the fresh pears, into a container. Using a mandoline, cut the pears into slices 5 mm (¼ inch) thick. Cut out discs using a 1.5-cm (¾-inch) ring cutter and place them into the syrup.

LEMON VERBENA SUGAR
Blend both the ingredients together in a blender to a fine powder. Add the sugar to a shaker fitted with a fine mesh.

TO ASSEMBLE
Brush the inside of a 10-cm (4-inch) ring with nappage and place in the centre of the plate. Place a 4-cm (1½-inch) ring wrapped in cling film in the centre and dust over the lemon verbena sugar between the rings, leaving you with a ring of verbena sugar. Remove the rings. Pipe the lemon verbena cream inside the walls of the meringue dome. Place the container with the pear sorbet in the Pacojet machine and spin on full power. In the middle of the meringue dome, add the pear purée, verbena jelly, pear pearls and a size-30 scoop of the sorbet. Pipe the lemon verbena cream in a spiral fashion to cover the sorbet. Starting from the base, cover the cream by alternating one pear disc and one meringue disc until you reach the top. Garnish with lemon verbena leaves and tips on top. Once assembled, add a dot of cream in the centre of the sugar ring and place the dessert on top.

WILD STRAWBERRY
MERINGUE AND LEMON VERBENA

Serves: 6

LEMON VERBENA MERINGUE	STRAWBERRY SORBET	STRAWBERRY PURÉE	TO ASSEMBLE
250 g egg whites	250 g water	200 g strawberry purée	nappage
450 g caster sugar	20 g Trimoline	20 g Stock syrup (p. 249)	Lemon verbena sugar (p. 226)
10 g egg white powder	75 g lemon juice	6 g lemon juice	Lemon verbena cream (p. 226)
7.5 g citric acid	125 g Stock syrup (p. 249)	3 g agar agar	Lemon verbena jelly (p. 226)
8 drops of lemon verbena essence	500 g wild strawberry purée		fresh wild strawberries
	4 g Stab 2000	STRAWBERRY SALAD	fresh lemon verbena leaves
	50 g strawberry liqueur	50 g strawberry, brunoised	fresh lemon verbena tips
		5 g icing sugar	
		50 g strawberry liqueur	

LEMON VERBENA MERINGUE
Preheat the oven to 75°C/170°F (0% humidity, full fan). Put the egg whites, caster sugar and egg white powder into a large bowl over a pan of simmering water and whisk the mixture continuously to avoid it sticking to the bottom of the bowl until the sugar has completely dissolved and has reached 73°C/163°F. Pour into the bowl of a stand mixer fitted with the whisk attachment and whisk on high speed for 3 minutes. Add the citric acid and lemon verbena essence and continue to whisk until stiff peaks form. Transfer the meringue into a piping bag fitted with a 1-cm (½-inch) nozzle and pipe 25 g of meringue into each of six 8-cm (3-inch) semi-sphere moulds. Use the back of a spoon to press the meringue against the moulds for an even, smooth surface. Place the moulds in the oven for 8 hours until dry. Unmould the meringues and, using a Microplane, lightly grate the bottom of the meringue domes to create a flat base. Store in an airtight container. Evenly pipe the remaining meringue onto individual 2-cm (1-inch) circle stencils, with a silicone mat underneath. Scrape off the excess meringue, ensuring the discs are completely covered. Remove the stencil. Place onto a tray and put into the oven for 3 hours until dry. Store the discs in an airtight container.

STRAWBERRY SORBET
Combine the water, Trimoline, lemon juice, stock syrup and wild strawberry purée in a medium saucepan over a high heat and bring to the boil. Add the Stab 2000 and whisk continuously until it returns to the boil, then simmer for 2 minutes. Remove the pan from the heat and blend using a hand blender. Pass the liquid through a fine chinois into a container and allow to cool. Add the strawberry liqueur and mix once more with the hand blender, then pour into a Pacojet beaker and reserve in the freezer.

STRAWBERRY PURÉE
Combine all the ingredients in a medium saucepan over a medium heat and bring to the boil, then pour into a shallow tray and place in the fridge to set. Transfer the mixture to a blender and blend until smooth, then pass through a fine chinois into a squeeze bottle.

STRAWBERRY SALAD
Combine all the ingredients in a medium bowl.

TO ASSEMBLE
Brush the inside of a 10-cm (4-inch) ring with nappage and place in the centre of the plate. Place a 4-cm (1½-inch) ring wrapped in cling film in the centre and dust over the lemon verbena sugar between the rings, leaving you with a ring of verbena sugar. Pipe the lemon verbena cream inside the walls of the meringue dome. Place the container with the strawberry sorbet in the Pacojet machine and spin on full power. In the middle of the meringue dome, add the verbena jelly, strawberry purée, strawberry salad and a size-30 scoop of the sorbet. Pipe the lemon verbena cream in a spiral fashion to cover the sorbet. Starting from the base, cover the cream by alternating one wild strawberry and one meringue disc until you reach the top. Garnish with lemon verbena leaves and tips on top. Once assembled, add a dot of cream in the centre of the sugar ring and place the dessert on top.

'THE OTHER CARROT'

Serves: 4

CHEESE MOUSSE
1.5 sheets bronze gelatine
125 g butter, softened
63 g icing sugar
12 g orange blossom water
125 g cream cheese

CARROT CAKE
90 g T45 flour
1.5 g ground cinnamon
0.5 g baking powder
1.5 g bicarbonate of soda
1 g salt
71 g grapeseed oil

104 g caster sugar
seeds from ½ vanilla pod
1 egg
113 g carrots, grated
35 g walnuts, finely chopped

CARROT JELLY
12 g bronze gelatine sheets
150 g blood orange purée
250 g carrot juice, from an
   orange carrot

CARROT SORBET
60 g fructose

25 g caster sugar
3 g pectin jaune
2 g citric acid
2 g Stab 2000
156 g water
7 g vodka
312 g carrot juice, from an
   orange carrot

CARROT SALAD
100 g carrots, grated
10 g Pickled ginger (p. 248)
5 g bee pollen

TO DIP THE CARROT
Carrot jelly (left)
Frozen cheese carrots (left)

TO ASSEMBLE
Pickled ginger (p. 248)
carrot tops
chervil tips
bee pollen
walnut quarters, toasted
small chervil stems

CHEESE MOUSSE
Soften the gelatine in ice water for 10 minutes, then drain. Combine the softened butter and icing sugar in a mixing bowl, then mix in the orange blossom water and cream cheese. Gently melt 50 g of the mixture in a small saucepan over a low heat and add the drained gelatine (squeezed of excess water). Return the contents of the saucepan to the mixing bowl. Transfer the mousse into 2 piping bags fitted with 5-mm (¼-inch) nozzles, one with just 20 g set aside for assembling the carrots later. Using acetate, create cones with a 12-cm (4¾-inch) base and 3-cm (1¼-inch) top. Pipe the cheese mousse into the cones and reserve in the freezer for 12 hours. Remove the cones from the freezer, take off the acetate and, using a knife, cut out a carrot shape, rounding the edges. Return to the freezer.

CARROT CAKE
Preheat the oven to 215°C/420°F (fan level 4). Combine the flour, cinnamon, baking powder, bicarbonate of soda and salt in a bowl. In a separate bowl whisk together the oil, sugar and vanilla. Add the egg to the oil mixture and mix for a minute, then slowly add the dry ingredients, ensuring everything is fully incorporated. Fold in the grated carrot and chopped walnuts. Pour the mixture into a 16-cm (6¼-inch) square cake tin, 8 cm (3½-inches) deep, and bake for 10 minutes. Remove from the oven and leave to cool, then cut into four slices 4 mm (⅛ inch) thick. Cut the slices into rectangles of 10 x 3 cm (4 x 1¼ inches). Using a small knife, cut the rectangles into the shape of a carrot. Crumble the trim and reserve.

CARROT JELLY
Soften the gelatine in ice water for 10 minutes, then drain. Gently warm the blood orange pureé in a medium saucepan over a low heat then, add the drained gelatine (squeezed of excess water). Remove the pan from the heat, stir to dissolve the gelatine, add the carrot juice, then strain through a chinois into a container. Leave to cool to 10°C/50°F.

CARROT SORBET
Put the fructose, sugar, pectin, citric acid and Stab 2000 into a bowl and mix well. Bring the water to the boil in a small saucepan over a high heat and add the fructose mixture, then bring to a simmer and whisk for 2 minutes. Remove the pan from the heat and allow to cool before adding the vodka and carrot juice. Pour into a Pacojet beaker and reserve in the freezer.

CARROT SALAD
Combine all the ingredients in a bowl and mix.

TO DIP THE CARROT
Place the frozen cheese carrot on a wire rack with a tray underneath. Add a cocktail stick into the middle and another stick at the thick end of the carrot. Lift the frozen carrot by the sticks and dip it into the carrot jelly. Repeat 3 times, then leave them to set on the rack. Trim the bottom of the carrots with a palette knife, remove the sticks and transfer them onto a tray. Leave to defrost in the fridge.

TO ASSEMBLE
Place the carrot cake onto a tray and cover with a layer of carrot salad, then position the dipped cheese carrot on top. Pipe a line of cheese mousse down the length of the carrot, then spoon over the crumbled carrot cake trim. Add the ginger, carrot tops, chervil tips, bee pollen and walnuts on top. Position the finished carrot on the left side of the plate. Add a small mound of carrot salad on the right, parallel to the carrot. Add a teaspoon quenelle of carrot sorbet on top. To finish, position the chervil stems at the thick end of the carrot to resemble carrot tops.

'MONT BLANC PAIN PERDU'

Serves: 4

EARL GREY PRUNES
15 g caster sugar
50 g water
1 Earl Grey tea bag
100 g prunes

BRIOCHE
4 brioche slices, 2 cm (¾ inch) thick

CUSTARD
180 g whole milk
24 g golden caster sugar

90 g egg whites
25 g egg yolks
8 g dried yeast
32 g dark rum
seeds of 1 vanilla pod

CHESTNUT PURÉE
60 g chestnut purée
60 g chestnut paste
10 g dark rum

PINE JAM
30 g nappage
2 drops of Douglas fir pine essence

**VANILLA AND RUM
 ICE CREAM**
500 g whole milk
175 g double cream
seeds of 1 vanilla pod
135 g egg yolks
75 g caster sugar
60 g dark rum

TO FINISH AND ASSEMBLE
clarified butter
caster sugar
icing sugar
Smoked chestnuts (p. 247)
olive oil cress
fresh chestnuts, thinly sliced
gold leaf

EARL GREY PRUNES
Bring the sugar and water to the boil in a medium saucepan over a high heat. Remove the pan from the heat, add the Earl Grey tea bag and infuse for 2 minutes. Strain the tea into a container, add the prunes and reserve in the fridge for 24 hours.

BRIOCHE
Cut the brioche into 8-cm (3-inch) rounds using a round cutter. Reserve in an airtight container in the fridge for 12 hours.

CUSTARD
Combine all the ingredients in a large bowl and blend with a hand blender until the sugar is completely dissolved. Place in the fridge for 6 hours.

CHESTNUT PURÉE
Blend all the ingredients in a small blender until smooth. Transfer to a piping bag fitted with a star nozzle.

PINE JAM
Combine both ingredients in a bowl and mix until completely smooth. Transfer to a piping bag.

VANILLA AND RUM ICE CREAM
Bring the milk, cream and vanilla seeds to the boil in a medium saucepan over a high heat. Whisk the egg yolks, sugar and rum in a mixing bowl, then pour the milk over the eggs while whisking continuously. Return to the saucepan over a medium heat and cook, stirring constantly, until the mixture reaches 84°C/183°F. Pass the liquid through a fine chinois into a bowl set over an ice bath to cool it down as quickly as possible. Transfer to a Pacojet beaker and reserve in the freezer.

TO FINISH AND ASSEMBLE
Place the brioche in a container and cover with the custard. Transfer the container to a sous vide machine and compress for 30 seconds. Remove the brioche from the custard and place onto a rack for 5 minutes to allow the excess liquid to drain off. Melt a piece of clarified butter in a non-stick frying pan over a medium heat and fry the brioche until both sides are golden, then remove from the pan. Add enough caster sugar to coat the bottom of another non-stick frying pan and place over a high heat until it becomes a caramel. Add the brioche and coat each side with the caramel. Transfer the brioche to a silicone mat. Using scissors, snip off any stray caramel around the edges. Dust the caramelized brioche with icing sugar and place in the centre of the plate. Top the right side with the Earl Grey prunes and smoked chestnuts in a line. Pipe six dots of pine jam between the prunes and chestnuts as well as five dots of chestnut puree, and add olive oil cress. Arrange the sliced chestnuts on top. Position a quenelle of vanilla and rum ice cream on the left side and finish by adding gold leaf.

'NOTTING HILL FOREST'
CHESTNUT, HAZELNUT, PINE AND WOODRUFF

Serves: 4

EARL GREY PRUNES
250 g water
4 g Earl Grey tea leaves
8 g caster sugar
10 g whisky
8 prunes

HAZELNUT GANACHE
40 g blanched hazelnuts
125 g whole milk
25 G Gelatine mass (p. 249)
50 g gianduja chocolate,
  broken into small pieces
80 g hazelnut paste
225 g double cream

DARK CHOCOLATE
  HAZELNUT GANACHE
40 g blanched hazelnuts
125 g whole milk
25 G Gelatine mass (p. 249)
75 g 70% dark chocolate,
  broken into small pieces
50 g gianduja chocolate,
  broken into small pieces
40 g hazelnut paste
225 g double cream

PASTRY CREAM
2 g gelatine powder
8 g water
75 g whole milk
20 g double cream
seeds of 1 vanilla pod
20 g egg yolk
30 g caster sugar
5 g plain flour
5 g cocoa butter, melted
10 g butter, at room temperature
5 g mascarpone

CHESTNUT CREAM
1 bronze gelatine leaf
25 g egg yolks
12.5 g caster sugar
120 g whole milk
6 g double cream
62.5 g Pastry cream (above)
120 g chestnut paste
4 g cep extract
4 g pine extract
100 g mascarpone

PINE JAM
150 g nappage

4 drops of Douglas fir extract

PUFF PASTRY
1 sheet of all-butter puff pastry

LEAF BASE
200 g egg whites
200 g icing sugar
200 g plain flour
200 g butter, melted

CEP LEAF
50 g Leaf base (above)
2 g cep extract
1 drop of green food colouring
1 drop of red food colouring
Cep powder (p. 242)

YEAST LEAF
50 g Leaf base (above)
1 g pine extract
1 drop of yellow food colouring
1 drop of red food colouring
Yeast crumble (p. 242)

PINE LEAF
50 g Leaf base (above)

1 g pine extract
1 drop of green food colouring
1 drop of yellow food colouring
Yeast crumble (p. 242)

MOSS LEAF
50 g Leaf base (left)
1 g pine extract
1 g cep extract
1 drop of green food colouring
2 drop of red food colouring
Yeast crumble (p. 242)

CHOCOLATE CEP LEAVES
75 g 70% dark chocolate
15 g cocoa butter
2 g Cep powder (p. 242)

CHOCOLATE PINE LEAVES
75 g 70% dark chocolate
15 g cocoa butter
2 g pine extract

TO ASSEMBLE
Woodruff oil (p. 249)
Yeast crumble (p. 242)

EARL GREY PRUNES
Heat the water to 80°C/175°F, add the tea and let it infuse for 3 minutes. Strain, add the sugar to the water, and allow to cool. Add the whisky and prunes and leave them to soak at room temperature for 24 hours. Drain the prunes and reserve.

HAZELNUT GANACHE
Preheat the oven to 180°C/350°F (fan). Toast the hazelnuts in the oven for 8 minutes until golden. Bring the milk to the boil in a medium saucepan over a medium heat, then add the hazelnuts and blend with a hand blender. Remove the pan from the heat and infuse for 30 minutes. Pass the milk through a fine chinois into a clean saucepan over a high heat and bring to the boil, then remove from the heat. Add the gelatine mass, chocolate, hazelnut paste and cream, and mix. Transfer to a container and reserve in the fridge for 6 hours. Place the mixture in a bowl and whisk to stiff peaks, then transfer to a piping bag fitted with a 5-mm (¼-inch) nozzle.

DARK CHOCOLATE HAZELNUT GANACHE
Toast the hazelnuts in the oven for 8 minutes until golden. Bring the milk to the boil in a medium saucepan over a medium heat, then add the hazelnuts and blend with a hand blender. Remove the pan from the heat and infuse for 30 minutes. Pass the milk through a fine chinois into a clean saucepan over a high heat and bring to the boil, then remove from the heat. Add the gelatine mass, dark chocolate, gianduja chocolate, hazelnut paste and cream, and mix. Transfer to a container and reserve in the fridge for 6 hours. Place the mixture in a bowl and whisk to stiff peaks, then transfer to a piping bag fitted with a 5-mm (¼-inch) nozzle.

PASTRY CREAM
Combine the gelatine powder and water in a bowl and set aside for 10 minutes. Bring the milk, cream and vanilla seeds to the boil in a saucepan over a medium heat. Whisk the egg yolks and sugar in a bowl until the sugar dissolves, then add the flour and mix to a smooth paste. Pour the milk over the egg yolk mixture while mixing continuously, then return to the pan and cook for 4 minutes over a medium heat.

Remove the pan from the heat and add the softened gelatine, cocoa butter, butter and mascarpone. Mix well. Transfer to a piping bag fitted with a 5-mm (¼-inch) nozzle and keep in the fridge.

CHESTNUT CREAM
Soften the gelatine in ice water for 10 minutes, then drain. Whisk the egg yolks and sugar together in a bowl until the sugar dissolves. Heat the milk in a saucepan, then pour it over the egg yolk mixture while mixing continuously, then return to the pan and heat gently until the temperature reaches 83°C/181°F. In a small saucepan warm the cream and add the drained gelatine (squeezed of excess water), stir to dissolve, then remove the pan from the heat and allow to cool. Combine the cream with the egg mixture and stir. Transfer the custard to a blender with the pastry cream, chestnut paste, both extracts and the mascarpone, then blend until smooth. Transfer the mix to a container and reserve in the fridge for 2 hours. Whisk the mixture in a mixing bowl until it forms stiff peaks. Transfer to a piping bag fitted with a 5-mm (¼-inch) nozzle and keep in the fridge.

PINE JAM
Put both ingredients into a blender and blend until smooth. Transfer to a piping bag fitted with a 2-mm (⅛-inch) nozzle.

PUFF PASTRY
Preheat the oven to 180°C/350°F (fan). Roll out the puff pastry to a thickness of 7 mm (⅓ inch) and place on a tray lined with parchment paper. When placing in the oven, place a second tray 5 cm (2 inches) above the tray of pastry – this will stop the pastry from rising too far. Bake for 10 minutes until golden. Remove from the oven and, once cooled, break into 3-cm (1¼-inch) shards.

LEAF BASE
Whisk the egg whites and sugar in a bowl until frothy. Stir in the flour, add the melted butter, then mix to a smooth batter. Keep in the fridge until required.

CEP LEAF

Preheat the oven to 160°C/325°F (fan). Put all the ingredients except the cep powder into a bowl and mix. Place a silicone mat on a work surface and, using an oak-leaf template, evenly spread the mixture to create as many leaves as possible, then sprinkle with the cep powder. Transfer the silicone mat to a flat tray and bake for 3–4 minutes until the leaves are just turning golden around the edges. Remove the baking tray from the oven (leave the oven on) and, working very quickly, lift each leaf off the baking tray with a palette knife and place over a raised form to give a natural leaf shape, then leave to cool. Store the leaves in an airtight container.

YEAST LEAF

Put all the ingredients except the yeast crumble into a bowl and mix. Place a silicone mat on a work surface and, using a maple-leaf template, evenly spread the mixture to create as many leaves as possible, then sprinkle with the yeast crumble. Transfer the silicone mat to a flat tray and bake for 3–4 minutes until the leaves are just turning golden around the edges. Remove the baking tray from the oven and, working very quickly, lift each leaf off the baking tray with a palette knife and place over a raised form to give a natural leaf shape, then leave to cool. Store the leaves in an airtight container.

PINE LEAF

Put all the ingredients except the yeast crumble into a bowl and mix. Place a silicone mat on a work surface and, using a bay-leaf template, evenly spread the mixture to create as many leaves as possible, then sprinkle with the yeast crumble. Transfer the silicone mat to a flat tray and bake for 3–4 minutes until the leaves are just turning golden around the edges. Remove the baking tray from the oven and, working very quickly, lift each leaf off the baking tray with a palette knife and place over a raised form to give a natural leaf shape, then leave to cool. Store the leaves in an airtight container.

MOSS LEAF

Put all the ingredients except the yeast crumble into a bowl and mix. Place a silicone mat on a work surface and using a chestnut-leaf template, evenly spread the mixture to create as many leaves as possible, then sprinkle with the yeast crumble. Transfer the silicone mat to a flat tray and bake for 3–4 minutes until the leaves are just turning golden around the edges. Remove the baking tray from the oven, and working very quickly, lift each leaf off the baking tray with a palette knife and place over a raised form to give a natural leaf shape, then leave to cool. Store the leaves in an airtight container.

CHOCOLATE CEP LEAVES AND PINE LEAVES

Temper the chocolate for the cep and pine leaves and transfer to a tall plastic container. Dip a leaf stencil into the container, then allow most of the excess chocolate to drain, before placing it on a sheet of acetate and drawing it back to leave a leaf shape. Sprinkle with cep powder, then place the acetate inside two rings, giving it a natural curve. Once all the cep powder leaves have been made, add the pine extract to the remaining chocolate and repeat the dipping process. After all the leaves have set, remove from the acetate and reserve in the fridge.

TO ASSEMBLE

Pipe a 6-cm (2½-inch) straight line of hazelnut ganache through the centre of the plate. Pipe an identical line, next to the ganache, of the chestnut cream. Place the puff pastry shards evenly spaced on top of the ganache and cream, then place the soaked prunes between the puff pastry. Pipe the dark chocolate hazelnut ganache tightly around the base of each item you previously put on. Drizzle woodruff oil over the prunes and puff pastry. Pipe the chestnut cream over the puff pastry and prunes in a random fashion. Pipe the dark chocolate ganache in between the lines of chestnut cream. Pipe five lines of the pine jam over the mound of creams, then evenly sprinkle the yeast crumble over the top. Place and alternate all the leaves on top to create a natural 'pile of leaves'.

'SNOWBALL'
RUM, PRUNE AND PINE

Serves: 6

RUM COCKTAIL
50 g lemon juice, strained
10 g lemon zest, grated using
  a Microplane
200 g fructose
25 g dextrose
100 g dark rum
25 g vanilla extract
90 g egg yolk
30 g egg white

CHESTNUT CRÉMEUX
22 g egg yolks
10 g caster sugar
138 g whole milk
105 g confit chestnuts
90 g chestnut purée

PASTRY CREAM
2 g gelatine powder
8 g water
75 g whole milk
20 g double cream
seeds of 1 vanilla pod
20 g egg yolks
30 g caster sugar
5 g plain flour
5 g cocoa butter, melted
10 g butter, at room temperature
5 g mascarpone

CHESTNUT PASTRY CREAM
250 g Pastry cream (left)
10 g chestnut purée
10 g chestnut paste

CHESTNUT MOUSSE
2 g bronze gelatine sheet
50 g egg yolks
25 g caster sugar
120 g double cream
270 g Chestnut pastry cream (above)
200 g chestnut paste
250 g mascarpone

PINE SNOW
25 g maltodextrin (Zorbit)
1 drop of Douglas fir pine essence
1 drop of bergamot essence

SPICE MIX
1 tablespoon ground allspice
1 tablespoon ground cinnamon
1 tablespoon ground nutmeg
2 teaspoons ground mace
1 teaspoon ground cloves
1 teaspoon ground ginger

CRUMBLE
250 g plain flour
125 g ground almonds

125 g chestnut flour
250 g butter, chilled and diced
100 g caster sugar
50 g dark muscovado sugar
5 g salt
seeds of 1 vanilla pod
7 g Spice mix (left)

PRUNE PURÉE
50 g caster sugar
1 g pectin jaune
6 g glucose syrup
120 g prune purée
2 g malic acid

CHESTNUT AND PRUNE
COMPOTE
180 g Prune purée (above)
40 g vacuum-packed chestnuts,
  finely chopped
40 g pitted prunes, finely chopped
2 drops of bergamot essence

PINE JELLY
10 g gelatine powder
160 g water
60 g Stock syrup (p. 249)
1 g pine extract
50 g honey
1 g lemon juice, strained

PINE MERINGUE
100 g egg whites
180 g caster sugar
4 g egg white powder
3 g citric acid
3 drops of Douglas fir pine essence

BUILDING THE 'SNOWBALL'
Rum cocktail (left)
cocoa butter
Chestnut and prune compote (left)
Chestnut crémeux (left)
Chestnut mousse (left)

WHITE CHOCOLATE SPRAY
20 g white food colouring
100 g cocoa butter
250 g white chocolate

TO ASSEMBLE
olive oil cress

RUM COCKTAIL
Preheat a water bath to 70°C/160°F. Combine all the ingredients in a sous vide bag and fully seal. Massage the mix and place in the water bath for 30 minutes. Cool in an ice bath and keep in the fridge for 48 hours. Pass the liquid through a fine chinois. Reserve in the fridge.

CHESTNUT CRÉMEUX
Whisk the egg yolk and sugar together in a bowl until the sugar has dissolved. Bring the milk to the boil in a medium saucepan, then pour it over the egg yolk mixture while whisking continuously. Return the liquid to the pan and heat gently, mixing all the time, until it reaches 83°C/181°F. Transfer the mixture to a blender, add the confit chestnuts and chestnut purée and blend on full speed until smooth. Reserve in a piping bag fitted with a 1-cm (½-inch) nozzle.

PASTRY CREAM
Combine the gelatine powder and water in a bowl and set aside for 10 minutes. Bring the milk, cream and vanilla seeds to the boil in a saucepan over a medium heat. Whisk the egg yolk and sugar in a bowl until the sugar has dissolved, then add the flour and mix to a smooth paste. Pour the milk over the egg yolks while mixing continuously, then return to the pan and cook for 4 minutes over a medium heat. Remove the pan from the heat and add the softened gelatine, cocoa butter, butter and mascarpone. Mix well. Transfer to a container and allow to cool in the fridge for 1 hour.

CHESTNUT PASTRY CREAM
Combine all the ingredients in a mixing bowl and mix well. Cover and allow the cream to rest in the fridge for 30 minutes.

CHESTNUT MOUSSE
Soften the gelatine in ice water for 10 minutes, then drain. Whisk the egg yolk and sugar together in a bowl until the sugar is dissolved. Bring the cream to the boil in a saucepan over a medium heat, then pour it over the egg yolk mixture while whisking continuously. Return the pan to the heat, mixing all the time until it reaches 83°C/181°F. Squeeze the excess water from the drained gelatine, add it to the egg yolk mixture, stir to dissolve, then allow to cool. Transfer the custard to a blender, add the chestnut pastry cream and chestnut paste and blend, then add the mascarpone and blend until smooth. Transfer to a container and rest in the fridge for 2 hours. Place in a mixing bowl and whisk the cream to stiff peaks. Transfer to a piping bag fitted with a 5-mm (¼-inch) nozzle and reserve in the fridge.

PINE SNOW
Combine all the ingredients in a small bowl and whisk until the mix resembles snow. Reserve in an airtight container.

SPICE MIX
Combine all the ingredients in a small bowl and mix.

CRUMBLE
Preheat the oven to 185°C/365°F (0% humidity, no fan). Place all the ingredients except the spice mix into the bowl of a stand mixer fitted with the dough hook attachment and mix on a medium speed until it forms a crumble. Transfer to a tray and bake for 7 minutes, then stir the crumble and return to the oven for 7 more minutes. Remove from the oven and break up the crumble with a fork while it is still hot. Add the spice mix, then store in an airtight container.

PRUNE PURÉE
Mix the sugar and pectin in a bowl, then add to a medium saucepan with the glucose and prune purée and bring to the boil over a high heat. Let it reduce to

69° Brix (measured using a refractometer). Remove the pan from the heat, add the malic acid and mix well. Allow to set in the fridge, then blend in a blender until smooth.

CHESTNUT AND PRUNE COMPOTE
Mix all the ingredients in a bowl and chill.

PINE JELLY
Add the gelatine powder to the water in a medium saucepan and gently warm over a low heat until it has completely dissolved, then remove from the heat. Add the remaining ingredients and cool over an ice bath until it reaches 4°C/39°F. Pour the liquid into a tray lined with cling film to a height of 5 mm (¼ inch) and place in the fridge to set. Cut the set jelly into 5-mm (¼-inch) cubes.

PINE MERINGUE
Preheat the oven to 75°C/170°F (0% humidity, full fan). Put the egg whites, caster sugar and egg white powder into a large bowl over a pan of simmering water and whisk the mixture continuously until the sugar has completely dissolved and reaches 73°C/163°F. Pour into the bowl of a stand mixer fitted with the whisk attachment and whisk on high speed for 3 minutes. Add the citric acid and pine essence and continue to whisk until stiff peaks form. Transfer the meringue to a piping bag. Pipe the meringue in a continuous line over a snowflake stencil with a silicone mat underneath. Scrape off the excess meringue, ensuring the snowflakes are completely covered. Remove the stencil. Place onto a tray and put into the oven for 3 hours until the meringue is dry. Store the snowflakes in an airtight container.

BUILDING THE 'SNOWBALL'
Pour the rum cocktail into six 2.5-cm (1-inch) sphere moulds, then place in the freezer. When it's semi-frozen, add a cocktail stick to each ball and continue to freeze until solid. Melt the cocoa butter in a small saucepan and transfer to a tall container. Remove the rum cocktail balls from the moulds and dip into the melted cocoa butter. Transfer to a tray lined with parchment paper and return to the freezer. For each 'snowball' spread a thin layer of chestnut and prune compote in a 3-cm (1¼-inch) semi-sphere mould, then add a dipped ball of rum cocktail into the centre and cover with a thin layer of compote on top. Place in the freezer for 1 hour. Into the bottom of twelve 4-cm (1½-inch) semi-sphere moulds, pipe 20 g of chestnut crémeux. Place a 3-cm (1¼-inch) semi-sphere mould on top and press down gently. Place in the freezer until frozen. Remove from the freezer and place a compote-coated ball of rum cocktail into half the frozen semi-spheres of crémeux and return to the freezer for 1 hour. Once they're frozen, unmould the empty semi-spheres and place on top of the filled ones, then return to the freezer. To the bottom of twelve 5-cm (2-inch) semi-sphere moulds pipe 30 g of chestnut mousse. Place a 4-cm (1½-inch) semi-sphere mould on top and press down gently. Place in the freezer until frozen. Remove from the freezer and add a wrapped ball of rum cocktail into half the semi-spheres of mousse and place in the freezer for 1 hour. Once frozen, unmould the empty semi-sphere and place on top of the filled ones. Return to the freezer. Unmould the finished 'snowballs' and reserve in the freezer until required.

WHITE CHOCOLATE SPRAY
Preheat a water bath to 45°C/113°F. Combine the white food colouring and cocoa butter in a medium bowl and mix well. Put the white chocolate and cocoa butter into a sous vide bag, seal on full pressure and place in the water bath overnight. Transfer to a spray gun and spray the prepared white chocolate onto the assembled 'snowballs'. Store on a tray in the freezer.

TO ASSEMBLE
Remove the 'snowballs' from the freezer and place in the fridge for 20 minutes before serving. Place a dessertspoonful of pine jelly in the centre of the plate and cover, first with the crumble, then the pine snow. Place the 'snowball' on top and arrange the snowflakes as if they are falling. Finish with the cress around the base.

BANYULS WINE GUMS

Serves: 20

WINE GUM PREPARATION

A
30 g liquid glucose
19 g caster sugar
41 g Banyuls wine
1 g tartaric acid

B
6 g gelatine powder
41 g Banyuls wine

C
34 g Banyuls wine

TO ASSEMBLE
Trenwax spray

WINE GUM PREPARATION
Preheat a water bath to 55°C/130°F. Combine all the 'A' ingredients in a small saucepan over a high heat. Using a small whisk, mix well and bring the liquid to 111°C/232°F. Add all the 'B' ingredients to a sous vide bag, fully seal and massage the mix, then place into the water bath for 30 minutes. Remove the pan with the 'A' ingredients from the heat and allow to cool to 80°C/175°F, then add the 'B' ingredients to the pan and stir using a spatula. Allow the mixture to cool to 50°C/120°F before adding the 'C' ingredient and, again, stir using a spatula.

TO ASSEMBLE
Spray a tray of 1.5-cm (¾-inch) sphere moulds with Trenwax spray. Pour the wine gum mixture into the tray, filling each sphere to the rim, then cover with the lid. Place in the fridge to set for 2 hours. Remove the gums from the moulds and place on the presentation, ready to serve.

SAUTERNES WINE GUMS

Serves: 20

WINE GUM PREPARATION

A
30 g liquid glucose
19 g caster sugar
41 g Sauternes wine
1 g tartaric acid

B
6 g gelatine powder
41 g Sauternes wine

C
34 g Sauternes wine

TO ASSEMBLE
Trenwax spray
gold powder

WINE GUM PREPARATION
Preheat a water bath to 55°C/130°F. Combine all the 'A' ingredients in a small saucepan over a high heat. Using a small whisk, mix well and bring the liquid to 111°C/232°F. Add all the contents of 'B' to a sous vide bag, fully seal and massage the mix, then place into the water bath for 30 minutes. Remove the pan with the 'A' ingredients from the heat and allow to cool to 80°C/175°F, then add the 'B' ingredients to the pan and stir using a spatula. Allow the mixture to cool to 50°C/120°F before adding the 'C' ingredient and, again, stir using a spatula.

TO ASSEMBLE
Spray a tray of 1.5-cm (¾-inch) sphere moulds with Trenwax spray. Pour the wine gum mixture into the tray, filling each sphere to the rim, then cover with the lid. Place in the fridge to set for 2 hours. Remove the gums from the moulds, dust with gold powder and place on the presentation, ready to serve.

WARM CHOCOLATE TART

Serves: 20

SHORTCRUST PASTRY CASE
62 g butter, chilled and diced
125 g plain flour
2 g sea salt
30 g egg yolks
50 g icing sugar

CHOCOLATE FILLING
108 g 70% dark chocolate,
  broken into small pieces
125 g double cream
2 whole eggs
52 g egg yolks
50 g caster sugar

SHORTCRUST PASTRY CASE
Preheat the oven to 160°C/325°F (fan level 4). Combine the butter, flour and salt in the bowl of a stand mixer fitted with the paddle attachment and mix until it becomes crumbly in texture. Cream the egg yolks and icing sugar together in a separate bowl with a hand whisk. Add the wet ingredients to the dry ingredients and mix until it comes together as a dough. Roll out the dough between sheets of parchment paper to a thickness of 5 mm (¼ inch). Cut twenty 6-cm (2½-inch) discs from the dough using a round cutter, then, using 5 x 2-cm (2 x ¾-inch) round moulds, position one disc between two moulds and press down. Trim off any excess dough with a small knife. Bake on a tray for 3 minutes, turn the tray and bake for another 3 minutes until the pastry is golden. Let the tart cases cool, then remove them from the moulds.

CHOCOLATE FILLING
Put the chocolate pieces into a heatproof bowl. Bring the cream to 80°C/175°F in a medium saucepan over a high heat. Remove the pan from the heat, pour the cream over the chocolate and mix with a spatula to create a ganache. Whisk the eggs, egg yolks and sugar in a separate bowl until light and fluffy. Slowly fold the ganache into the egg mixture using a spatula until it forms a light brown mousse. Place in a piping bag fitted with a 1-cm (½-inch) nozzle.

TO ASSEMBLE
Preheat the oven to 180°C/350°F (no fan). Pipe the chocolate filling into the tart case until it is level with the rim and bake on a tray for 3 minutes. Remove from the oven and allow to rest, then serve warm.

WARM CHOCOLATE AND LAVENDER TART

Serves: 20

SHORTCRUST PASTRY CASE
62 g butter, chilled and diced
125 g plain flour
2 g sea salt
30 g egg yolks
50 g icing sugar

CHOCOLATE FILLING
108 g 70% dark chocolate,
  broken into small pieces
125 g double cream
2 g lavender essence
2 whole eggs
52 g egg yolks
50 g caster sugar

SHORTCRUST PASTRY CASE
Preheat the oven to 160°C/325°F (fan level 4). Combine the butter, flour and salt in the bowl of a stand mixer fitted with the paddle attachment and mix until it becomes crumbly in texture. Cream the egg yolks and icing sugar together in a separate bowl with a hand whisk. Add the wet ingredients to the dry ingredients and mix until it comes together as a dough. Roll out the dough between sheets of parchment paper to a thickness of 5 mm (¼ inch). Cut twenty 6-cm (2½-inch) discs from the dough using a round cutter then, using 5 x 2-cm (2 x ¾-inch) round moulds, position one disc between two tart moulds and press down. Trim off any excess dough with a small knife and place on a baking tray. Bake for 3 minutes, turn the tray and bake for another 3 minutes until the pastry is golden. Let the tart cases cool before removing them from the moulds.

CHOCOLATE FILLING
Put the chocolate pieces into a heatproof bowl. Bring the cream to 80°C/175°F in a medium saucepan over a high heat, then add the lavender essence. Remove the pan from the heat, pour the cream over the chocolate and mix with a spatula to create a ganache. Whisk the whole eggs, egg yolks and sugar in a separate bowl until light and fluffy. Slowly fold the ganache into the egg mixture using a spatula until it forms a light brown mousse, then place in a piping bag fitted with a 5-mm (¼-inch) nozzle.

TO ASSEMBLE
Preheat the oven to 180°C/350°F (no fan). Pipe the chocolate filling into the tart case until it is level with the rim and bake on a baking tray for 3 minutes. Remove from the oven and allow to rest, then serve warm.

WARM CHOCOLATE AND CLEMENTINE TART

Serves: 20

SHORTCRUST PASTRY CASE
62 g butter, chilled and diced
125 g plain flour
2 g sea salt
30 g egg yolks
50 g icing sugar

CHOCOLATE FILLING
108 g 70% dark chocolate,
    broken into small pieces
125 g double cream
2 whole eggs
52 g egg yolks
50 g caster sugar

TO ASSEMBLE
Clementine purée (p. 248)

SHORTCRUST PASTRY CASE
Preheat the oven to 160°C/325°F (fan level 4). Combine the butter, flour and salt in the bowl of a stand mixer fitted with the paddle attachment and mix until it becomes crumbly in texture. Cream the egg yolks and icing sugar together in a separate bowl with a whisk. Add the wet ingredients to the dry ingredients and mix until it comes together as a dough. Roll out the dough between sheets of parchment paper to a thickness of 5 mm (¼ inch). Cut twenty 6-cm (2½-inch) discs from the dough using a round cutter then, using 5 x 2-cm (2 x ¾-inch) round moulds, position one disc between two tart moulds and press down. Trim off any excess dough with a small knife and place on a baking tray. Bake for 3 minutes, turn the tray and bake for another 3 minutes until the pastry is golden. Let the tart cases cool before removing them from the moulds.

CHOCOLATE FILLING
Put the chocolate pieces into a heatproof bowl. Bring the cream to 80°C/175°F in a medium saucepan over a high heat. Remove the pan from the heat, pour the cream over the chocolate and mix with a spatula to create a ganache. Whisk the whole eggs, egg yolks and sugar in a separate bowl until light and fluffy. Slowly fold the ganache into the egg mixture using a spatula until it forms a light brown mousse. Place in a piping bag fitted with a 5-mm (¼-inch) nozzle.

TO ASSEMBLE
Preheat the oven to 180°C/350°F (no fan). Pipe a small dot of clementine purée into the tart case. Pipe the chocolate filling on top until it is level with the rim and bake on a baking tray for 3 minutes. Remove from the oven and allow to rest, then serve warm.

MALTED SOURDOUGH

Makes: 1 loaf

BREAD STOCK
340 g water
15 g dark treacle
15 g light malt powder
15 g dark malt powder

TO REFRESH THE WHITE STARTER (makes 332 g total)
83 g Mature white starter (p. 249)
83 g water
166 g strong white flour

TO REFRESH THE RYE STARTER (makes 332 g total)
25 g Mature rye starter (p. 249)
12.5 g water
12.5 g dark rye flour

FLOUR MIX
200 g rice flour
100 g strong white flour

BREAD MIX
308 g strong artisan bread flour
13 g malted bran
356 g Bread stock (left), cold
166 g Mature white starter (left)
23 g Mature rye starter (left)
12 g salt

BREAD STOCK
Combine all the ingredients in a large saucepan over a high heat, whisk well and bring to the boil. Remove the pan from the heat, transfer to a container and allow the stock to cool.

TO REFRESH THE WHITE STARTER
Combine all the ingredients in the bowl of a stand mixer fitted with the dough hook and mix for 2–3 minutes until everything is incorporated and smooth. Place in a lidded container and let the dough ferment for 12 hours at 20°C/68°F.

TO REFRESH THE RYE STARTER
Combine all the ingredients in the bowl of a stand mixer fitted with the dough hook and mix for 2–3 minutes until everything is incorporated and smooth. Place in a lidded container and let the dough ferment for 12 hours at 20°C/68°F.

After taking the amount needed for the bread mix, both starters should be refreshed daily, at the same time.

FLOUR MIX
Combine both the flours in a medium bowl and mix.

BREAD MIX
The day after refreshing the starters, mix all the bread mix ingredients apart from the salt in the bowl of a stand mixer fitted with the dough hook attachment for 2 minutes. Leave to rest for 1 hour, then mix on slow for 8 minutes. Add the salt and mix for another 8 minutes. The desired dough temperature is 24°C/75°F. Transfer the dough to a plastic container and allow to rest for 45 minutes.

After 45 minutes, fold the four corners of the dough in to the centre. Let it rest for 45 minutes. After 45 minutes, once more, fold the four corners of the dough in. Let it rest for another 45 minutes, then portion the dough to 750 g and shape it into a ball. Let it rest on the work surface for 30 minutes, then reshape the dough into a ball and place in a floured banneton seam side up (use some of the flour mix). Place the dough in the fridge (3°–5°C/37°–41°F) for 7 hours, then remove and let it prove overnight on the work surface at 12°–18°C (54°–64°F) – the exact time will vary depending on the outside humidity and temperature.

Preheat the oven to 260°C/500°F (30% humidity, fan level 3), with a heavy tray in the oven. Lightly dust the top of the banneton (the bottom of the bread) with some more of the flour mix. Gently turn the dough out of the banneton onto the preheated tray. Score the dough with a blade and place in the oven, saturate with steam and quickly close the door. While the bread cooks adjust the oven temperature as follows: 260°C/500°F for 7 minutes, then 200°C/400°F for 10 minutes (0% humidity, fan level 3) and finally 180°C/350°F for 15 minutes (0% humidity, fan level 3). The total bake time is 32–38 minutes. Remove the bread from the oven and place on a wire rack for a minimum of 2 hours to cool.

LAMB BUNS

Makes: 24 buns

CRISPY LAMB FAT
250 g fatty lamb trim, cut into
  2-cm (¾-inch) cubes
salt, to taste

CONFIT LAMB SHOULDER
2 kg duck fat
2 garlic cloves
4 sprigs thyme
2 white peppercorns
250 g de-boned lamb shoulder
sherry vinegar, to taste
salt, to taste

LAMB BUNS
160 g T45 flour
16 g caster sugar
3 g salt
3.3 g milk powder
1 g Voatsiperifery pepper, crushed
15 g egg, beaten
63 g water

8.8 g fresh yeast
17.5 g olive oil
17.5 g lamb fat, melted
Egg wash (p. 246), for brushing
crushed flaky sea salt, to taste

CRISPY LAMB FAT
Render the fat in a heavy-based saucepan, with salt to taste. Once it's crispy, drain and reserve the liquid fat. Pat the crispy fat dry with paper towels, then blend to a crumb in a blender. Reserve in a dehydrator at 60°C/140°F until needed.

CONFIT LAMB SHOULDER
Heat up a wood-fired grill and preheat the oven to 98°C/208°F (fan). Melt the duck fat in a tray in the oven, then add the garlic, thyme and peppercorns. Season the lamb shoulder with salt and seal on all sides over the hot grill, then add it to the duck fat (it should be fully covered). Cover with parchment paper and cook in the oven for 6 hours until tender. Remove from the oven and leave to cool. Drain the lamb shoulder from the fat and pick the meat. Place the meat in a bowl, mix with vinegar and season with salt. Portion into twenty-four 10-g balls and reserve in the fridge.

LAMB BUNS
Put all the dry ingredients into the bowl of a stand mixer fitted with the dough hook attachment and mix on speed 1, then add the egg. In a separate bowl, combine the water, yeast, olive oil, lamb fat and mix. Pour the wet mixture into the dry mixture and mix to combine, then gradually increase the speed to 4 and mix for 4 minutes. Increase the speed to 6 and mix for another 3 minutes. When the dough is smooth, remove and roll it into a ball. Cover with cling film and leave to prove for 1½ hours.

Knock back the dough and portion it into twenty-four 25-g balls. Fill each ball with a 10-g ball of confit lamb shoulder. Roll the dough to encase the lamb shoulder in the middle of the ball. Place six balls in four 13 x 10 x 6-cm (5 x 4 x 2½-inch) baking pans and leave to prove until they've doubled in size. Preheat the oven to 160°C/325°F (30% humidity, fan level 4). Brush the balls with the egg wash, place the pans onto a baking tray and cook for 10 minutes. Remove the pan from the oven, brush the balls with egg wash again, turn the pans and place back in the oven for another 10 minutes. Remove the buns and leave to cool on a wire rack, then cut into single buns. Brush with the liquid lamb fat reserved from making the crispy lamb fat, sprinkle with crispy lamb fat and finish with crushed flaky sea salt on top.

ONION BUNS

Makes: 12 buns

RED ONION MARMALADE	ONION BUNS	7 g cornflour	284 g butter, cold
100 g grapeseed oil	10 g fresh yeast	2 eggs, separated into whites and yolks	20 g black onion seeds
400 g red onions, thinly sliced	68 g water	54 g caster sugar	Egg wash (p. 246)
salt, to taste	184 g T45 flour, plus extra for dusting	150 g strong white flour	
	70 g whole milk	7 g salt	

RED ONION MARMALADE
Heat the oil in a large saucepan over a high heat, add the onions, season with salt and cook until caramelized. Transfer to a blender and blend until smooth.

ONION BUNS
Crumble the yeast into a mixing bowl, add 34 g of the water and 34 g of the T45 flour and leave to prove for 30 minutes.

Bring the milk to a simmer in a small saucepan over a medium heat, add the cornflour and mix until it has a thick consistency, then pour into a container to cool. Combine the cooled cornflour and milk mixture in a mixing bowl with the remaining 34 g water, 150 g T45 flour and the egg whites, then add the yeast mixture and mix until smooth. Add the egg yolks, sugar, strong white flour and salt and mix in the bowl of a stand mixer fitted with the dough hook until smooth. Add 34 g of the butter and continue to mix until smooth. Remove the dough from the bowl, transfer to a square tray and cover with cling film. Leave in the fridge for 4 hours until doubled in size.

Slice the remaining 250-g block of butter into four equal pieces. Set out the pieces of butter next to each other in one flat square between two sheets of parchment paper, then roll out to 15 x 20 cm (6 x 8 inches) and a thickness of 5 mm (¼ inch). Reserve at room temperature.

To laminate the dough, take the risen dough out of the fridge and roll it out on a flour-dusted work surface to 35 x 20 cm (14 x 8 inches). Add the butter sheet to the centre of the dough. Fold both sides of the dough to cover the top of the butter sheet (book fold) and reserve in the fridge for 30 minutes. Roll the dough back to 35 x 20 cm (14 x 8 inches) to even out the butter between the two layers of dough. Lightly mark the dough sheet into thirds. Fold the outer thirds into the middle, one on top of the other (second book fold). Reserve in the fridge for 30 minutes. Roll the dough out to 40 x 20 cm (15¾ x 8 inches). Lightly mark the dough into quarters. Fold the two outer quarters to meet in the middle. Then fold the dough in half again, creating a double fold. Leave to rest in the fridge for 1 hour. Roll the dough out to 30 x 21 cm (12 x 8¾ inch) and a thickness of 4 mm (⅛ inch). Spread the red onion marmalade onto the dough and sprinkle most of the black onion seeds on top, reserving a small amount for the final stage, then roll up the dough into a spiral. Leave to set in the freezer for 1 hour.

Cut the dough spiral into twelve slices 3 cm (1¼ inch) thick. Leave each slice to prove in a cylinder mould 4 cm (1½ inches) in diameter and 6 cm (2½ inches) high, until it touches the sides of the mould. Preheat the oven to 160°C/325°F (fan level 3). Brush with egg wash and sprinkle the remaining black onion seeds on top of each bun. Bake for 15 minutes until golden.

FIG ROLLS

Makes: 12

FIG JAM
300 g dried figs, quartered
300 g fig purée

FIG LEAF POWDER
20 fig leaves, washed and dried well
  with paper towels

SWEET DOUGH
15 g fresh yeast
250 g whole milk
500 g strong white flour,
  plus extra for dusting
10 g salt
40 g caster sugar
2 eggs

60 g butter, cut into 6 pieces, at room
  temperature, plus extra for brushing
Egg wash (p. 246), for brushing
demerara sugar, to sprinkle

TO ASSEMBLE
3 fig leaves, washed and dried well
  with paper towels

FIG JAM
Put the dried fig quarters into a container with the fig purée, mix and allow to soak in the fridge for 24 hours, then blend in a blender until smooth.

FIG LEAF POWDER
Preheat a dehydrator to 80°C/175°F. Put the fig leaves on a dehydrator tray and dehydrate for 4 hours, then blend the dried leaves in a blender to a powder. Store in an airtight container.

SWEET DOUGH
Crumble the yeast into a bowl, add the milk and stir until the yeast has dissolved. Put the flour, salt and sugar into the bowl of a stand mixer fitted with the dough hook attachment and mix on speed 2 for 2 minutes until fully incorporated. Pour in the eggs and milk and yeast mixture and continue to mix on speed 2 for another 5 minutes. Reduce the speed to level 1 and gradually start to add the butter a few pieces at a time, allowing them to be fully incorporated into the dough before adding the next few pieces. Once all the butter is mixed in, transfer the dough to a large tray and cover with cling film. Rest the dough in the fridge for 12 hours.

Roll out the dough on a work surface lightly dusted with flour to 30 x 21 cm (12 x 8¾ inches) and a thickness of 5 mm (¼ inch). Chill in the fridge for 15 minutes. Spread the fig jam onto the chilled dough and dust some of the fig leaf powder on top (reserving some for sprinkling onto the finished rolls). Roll up the dough into a spiral, cover with cling film and leave to set in the freezer for 1 hour.

Cut the roll into twelve slices 3 cm (1¼ inches) thick. Brush three 7.5 x 10-cm (3 x 4-inch) cast-iron cocottes with butter, then place four fig roll slices inside each, making sure they're all face up. Place cling film over the cocotte and allow the dough to prove for 40 minutes or until doubled in size. Preheat the oven to 160°C/325°F (fan level 3). Brush the rolls with egg wash and sprinkle demerara sugar on top, then bake for 15 minutes until golden. Remove from the cocottes and leave to cool.

TO ASSEMBLE
Preheat the oven to 160°C/325°F (fan). Place the fig leaves inside the cocottes and the fig rolls on top. Sprinkle fig powder on top of the rolls and bake in the oven for 5 minutes. Cover with the lid, ready to serve.

OAT AND PUMPKIN SEED CRACKERS

Makes: 40 crackers

160 g T45 flour, plus extra for dusting
65 g medium oatmeal
7 g salt
5.5 g baking powder
80 g water
35 g olive oil
100 g pumpkin seeds, finely chopped
100 g rolled oats, finely chopped
flaky sea salt, to taste

Put all the ingredients (except the seeds, oats and flaky sea salt) into the bowl of a stand mixer fitted with the dough hook attachment and mix on speed 2 for 4 minutes, until smooth. Roll into a ball and rest in the fridge for 30 minutes.

Preheat the oven to 160°C/325°F (no fan). Cut the dough in half and roll out two sheets using a pasta machine set to 1.5-cm (¾-inch) thickness setting, dusting the dough with flour when necessary, then portion the sheets into two strips 50 cm (20 inch) long. Spray each strip with a light mist of water and sprinkle one strip with pumpkin seeds and rolled oats, then place the second strip on top and press down. Run the sheet through the pasta machine for a final time to a thickness of 2 mm (¹⁄₁₆ inch), then cut into forty 3 x 5-cm (1¼ x 2-inch) rectangles. Season with flaky sea salt, transfer to a baking tray lined with parchment paper and bake in the oven for 4 minutes, then turn up the heat to 180°C/350°F and bake for another 8 minutes. Remove from the oven and allow to cool, then reserve in an airtight container until required.

MULTIGRAIN CRACKERS

Makes: 40 crackers

70 g mixed seeds
  (sunflower, pumpkin and linseed)
130 g T45 flour, plus extra for dusting
20 g light rye flour
3 g salt
34 g honey
24 g olive oil
20 g lard
55 g water
flaky sea salt, to taste

Preheat the oven to 150°C/300°F (no fan). Blend the mixed seeds in a blender for a few seconds to make a coarse powder. Mix the blended seeds with the flours and salt in a bowl, add the honey, olive oil and lard and mix with your fingertips to obtain a crumble. Pour in the water and knead until the dough is homogeneous and forms a ball. Dust the work surface with flour then roll out the dough very thinly to a thickness of 3 mm (1/8 inch). Cut the dough into forty 3 x 4-cm (1¼ x 1½-inch) rectangles, season with flaky sea salt and place them on a baking tray lined with parchment paper. Bake for 10 minutes. Remove from the oven, allow to cool on a wire rack and reserve in an airtight container until required.

TREACLE YOGURT BUNS

Makes: 24 buns

80 g natural yogurt
80 g black treacle
40 g toasted ale
1.5 g caster sugar
55 g T45 flour
5.5 g bicarbonate of soda
1.5 g salt
35 g Beurre noisette (p. 246)

Put all the ingredients into a mixing bowl, reserving 10 g of the beurre noisette, and whisk to a smooth batter. Leave to rest for at least 1 hour in the fridge.

Preheat the oven to 180°C/350°F (fan level 4). Divide the remaining beurre noisette among the cavities of twenty-four 4-cm (1½-inch) semi-sphere silicone moulds, then place on baking trays and heat in the oven for 2 minutes. Fill each cavity two-thirds of the way up with the chilled batter and bake for 8 minutes. Immediately remove them from the moulds and serve warm.

CORE BASICS

These recipes are the foundation of our cuisine, and without attending to the fine details that make these basics what they are, we would be unable to build layers of flavour and complexity in what we cook. These recipes will be of as much use in the home kitchen as the professional one; they are the essentials, and in knowing them and mastering them, you will have the ability to create dishes of your own design, with the confidence that a well-stocked and flavourful larder gives you.

POWDERS

ASPARAGUS POWDER

250 g green asparagus peelings

Preheat a dehydrator to 75°C/165°F. Evenly spread out the peelings onto a dehydrator tray and allow them to fully dry for 8 hours. Once they are dried, place in a blender and blend to a powder. Reserve in an airtight container.

BLACK OLIVE POWDER

250 g black olives, pitted

Preheat a dehydrator to 75°C/165°F. Evenly spread out the olives onto a dehydrator tray and allow them to fully dry for 8 hours. Once they are dried, place in a blender and blend to a powder. Reserve in an airtight container.

BUCKWHEAT POWDER

250 g buckwheat kernels

Toast the buckwheat kernels in a frying pan or on a tray in the oven at 180°C/350°F (no fan) until lightly toasted. Leave to cool, then place in a blender and blend to a powder. Pass through a chinois and reserve in an airtight container.

YEAST CRUMBLE

250 g fresh yeast

Preheat a dehydrator to 75°C/165°F. Crumble the yeast, spread it evenly onto a dehydrator tray and allow it to fully dry for 8 hours. Once it's dried, rub the yeast between your fingers into a fine crumble. Reserve in an airtight container.

CELERIAC TOP POWDER

250 g celeriac leaves

Preheat a dehydrator to 75°C/165°F. Evenly spread out the celeriac leaves onto a dehydrator tray and allow them to fully dry for 8 hours. Once they are dried, place in a blender and blend to a powder. Reserve in an airtight container.

CEP POWDER

50 g ceps

Preheat a dehydrator to 65°C/150°F. Clean the ceps with a brush, then thinly slice. Evenly spread out the ceps onto a dehydrator tray and allow them to fully dry for 24 hours. Once they are dried, place into a blender and blend to a powder. Reserve in an airtight container.

PARMESAN POWDER

250 g Parmesan, grated

Preheat a dehydrator to 75°C/165°F. Evenly spread out the Parmesan onto a dehydrator tray and allow it to fully dry for 8 hours. Once it's dried, place in a blender and blend to a powder. Reserve in an airtight container.

PEA POWDER

250 g fresh peas

Preheat a dehydrator to 75°C/165°F. Evenly spread out the peas onto a dehydrator tray and allow them to fully dry for 8 hours. Once they're dried, place in a blender and blend to a powder. Reserve in an airtight container.

PUMPKIN POWDER

250 g peeled pumpkin flesh, sliced

Preheat a dehydrator to 75°C/165°F. Evenly spread out the pumpkin slices onto a dehydrator tray and allow them to fully dry for 8 hours. Once they're dried, place in a blender and blend to a powder. Reserve in an airtight container.

SHIITAKE POWDER

250 g shiitake mushrooms

Preheat a dehydrator to 65°C/150°F. Clean the shiitakes with a brush, then thinly slice. Evenly spread out the shiitakes onto a dehydrator tray and allow them to fully dry for 24 hours. Once they're dried, place in a blender and blend to a powder. Reserve in an airtight container.

BASIL POWDER

250 g basil leaves
4 kg water
salt, to taste

Preheat a dehydrator to 75°C/165°F. Bring a large saucepan of salted water to the boil and blanch the basil leaves until tender.

Place in an ice bath and pat dry with paper towels. Evenly spread out the leaves onto a dehydrator tray and allow them to fully dry for 6 hours or until crispy. Once they are dried, place in a blender and blend to a powder, then season to taste. Reserve in an airtight container.

GARLIC POWDER

1 kg whole milk
250 g peeled garlic cloves, thinly sliced
salt, to taste

Preheat a dehydrator to 65°C/150°F. Bring the milk to the boil in a medium saucepan and season to taste. Add the cloves of garlic and blanch until tender. Drain and pat dry with paper towels. Evenly spread out the garlic onto a dehydrator tray and allow it to dry for 6 hours or until crispy. Place the dried garlic in a blender and blend to a powder. Season to taste. Reserve in an airtight container.

ONION POWDER

1 kg whole milk
250 g peeled white onions, thinly sliced
salt, to taste

Preheat a dehydrator to 65°C/150°F. Bring the milk to the boil in a medium saucepan and season to taste. Add the sliced onions and blanch until tender. Drain and pat dry with paper towels. Evenly spread out the onions onto a dehydrator tray and allow to dry for 6 hours or until crispy. Place the dried onions in a blender and blend to a powder. Season to taste. Reserve in an airtight container.

TOMATO POWDER

250 g red tomato skins
salt, to taste
caster sugar, to taste

Preheat a dehydrator to 75°C/165°F. Place the tomato skins on a tray and season with salt and sugar. Evenly spread out the skins onto a dehydrator tray and allow them to dry for 6 hours or until crispy. Once the skins are dried, place them into a blender and blend to a powder. Reserve in an airtight container.

STOCKS AND SAUCES

MUSHROOM JUICE

600 g chestnut mushrooms
200 g water
6 g salt

Blend the mushrooms and water in a blender, then transfer the mixture to a large bowl and add the salt. Thoroughly mix until the salt is evenly dispersed.

Prepare a perforated tray lined with a double layer of muslin cloth set over a large gastronorm tray. Spread the mixture onto the muslin cloth, cover with cling film, then place another tray on top to weight it down. Leave in the fridge for 24 hours until all the juice has drained.

DASHI STOCK

1 kg mineral water
12 g dried shiitake mushrooms
15 g large dried kombu
25 g bonito flakes
white soy sauce, to taste
ponzu, to taste
salt, to taste

Combine the water, mushrooms and kombu in a large saucepan over a medium heat. Cover and heat to 60°C/140°F, then remove the pan from the heat and allow to infuse for 1 hour. Line a chinois with a muslin cloth. Discard the kombu and heat the remaining broth to 80°C/175°F. Add the bonito flakes, stir for 15 seconds, then immediately strain through the lined chinois. Season the broth to taste with soy sauce, ponzu and salt.

VEGETABLE NAGE

200 g carrots, cut into 4-cm (1½-inch) dice
200 g onions, cut into 4-cm (1½-inch) dice
200 g celery, cut into 4-cm (1½-inch) dice
300 g leeks, cut into 4-cm (1½-inch) dice
cold water, to cover
1 g black peppercorns
3 g fennel seeds
2 g coriander seeds
1 bay leaf
200 g white wine
1 slice of lemon 2 cm (¾ inch) thick
10 g sprigs parsley
10 g sprigs chervil

Put all the vegetables into a large saucepan and place over a medium heat. Cover with cold water and bring to the boil, then add the aromatics and white wine and simmer for 20 minutes. Remove the pan from the heat, add the lemon slice and fine herbs and leave to infuse in the fridge for 24 hours. Pass the stock through a chinois into a container and reserve until required.

CRAB CONSOMMÉ

2.5 kg cock crab shells (14 medium crabs)
85 g brandy
250 g white wine
100 g grapeseed oil
60 g butter
625 g carrots, thinly sliced
400 g onions, thinly sliced
110 g leeks, thinly sliced
60 g celery, thinly sliced
5 g garlic clove, thinly sliced
40 g lemongrass
½ fennel stalk
5 g fennel seeds

3 g coriander seeds
4 g white peppercorns
1 bay leaf
1 g star anise
5 sprigs thyme
2 kg cold water
2 kg Chicken stock (p. 244)

TO FINISH THE CONSOMMÉ
10 g chervil
5 g parsley
10 g lemongrass
grated zest of 1 lemon

Preheat the oven to 180°C/350°F (no fan). Roast the crab shells in a tray for about 30 minutes until golden. Place into a stand mixer fitted with the paddle attachment and mix to crush the shells. Drain the shells in a colander and reserve the juices.

Flambé the brandy and wine in two separate pans over a medium heat. Once the alcohol has burned off, add the brandy to the wine and let it reduce by half, then set aside.

Put the grapeseed oil, butter, carrots, onions, leeks, celery and garlic into a large pressure cooker and cook over a medium heat until the vegetables have softened and lightly caramelized. Add the roasted crab shells, crab juices, aromatics and flambéed alcohol, then add the water and chicken stock and bring to the boil. While it's coming to the boil, continuously skim off any impurities, then secure the lid and cook on full pressure for 2 hours.

Once the pot has depressurized, pass the stock through a fine chinois, then through a double layer of muslin cloth. Skim the fat from the stock and pour the liquid into a container. Put in the freezer until it becomes an ice block in order to start the ice filtration process.

Place the frozen block into a muslin cloth and onto a perforated tray, with a tray underneath. Allow it to defrost in the fridge for 1–2 days. (Clarification is ready once the liquid has melted and just the impurities are remaining.)

Pour the clarified consommé into a large saucepan over a medium heat and reduce by half, skimming off any impurities as needed, then remove the pan from the heat, add the finishing herbs, lemongrass and lemon zest and let it infuse for 15 minutes, then allow to cool over an ice bath.

LOBSTER CONSOMMÉ

300 g lobster shells
150 g olive oil
50 g butter
25 g carrots, thinly sliced
16 g onions, thinly sliced
20 g leeks, thinly sliced
10 g celery stick, thinly sliced
1 garlic clove, thinly sliced
250 g white wine
100 g brandy
1 kg Fish stock (p. 244)
1 kg Lobster stock (p. 243)

Place the lobster shells in a stand mixer fitted with the paddle attachment and mix to crush the shells. Drain the shells in a colander and reserve the juices.

Preheat a roasting pan over a medium heat with 50 g of the olive oil. Once the oil is hot, add the lobster shells and roast until lightly golden. Drain off the fat.

Heat a medium saucepan over a medium heat, add the remaining olive oil and the butter, carrots, onions, leeks, celery and garlic and cook until soft and lightly browned. Add the roasted lobster shells, reserved lobster juice, white wine and brandy and reduce the liquid to a syrup consistency over a high heat. Add both stocks and bring to the boil. While it's coming to the boil, continuously skim off any impurities, then reduce the heat and simmer gently for 1 hour.

Pass the liquid through a fine chinois, then through a double layer of muslin cloth into a deep gastronorm tray and put in the freezer until frozen, in order to start the ice filtration process.

Place the frozen block into a muslin cloth and onto a perforated tray, with a tray underneath. Allow it to defrost in the fridge for 1–2 days. (Clarification is ready once the liquid has melted and just the impurities are remaining.)

Pour the clarified consommé into a large saucepan over a medium heat and reduce by half, skimming off any impurities as needed. Allow to cool over an ice bath.

LOBSTER STOCK

grapeseed oil, for roasting
400 g crushed lobster shells
100 g carrots, diced
100 g onions, diced
100 g celery, diced
20 g tomato purée (paste)
cold water, to cover
4 sprigs thyme
2 garlic cloves

Heat the oil in a medium saucepan over a high heat, then add the crushed lobster shells and cook until lightly roasted. Add the vegetables and tomato purée, cover with cold water and add the thyme and garlic. Bring the liquid to the boil, then reduce the heat and simmer gently for 2 hours, skimming off any impurities that rise to the surface. Pass the stock through a chinois into a container and place in the fridge.

MUSSEL BROTH

1.2 kg cleaned, debearded mussels
25 g olive oil
2.5 g garlic cloves, chopped
180 g shallots, chopped
120 g celery, chopped
120 g leeks, chopped
300 g carrots, chopped
24 g thyme
2 g bay leaves
1.2 kg white wine
3 kg Fish stock (below)
salt, to taste

222 g egg whites
120 g mussel meat

Place the mussels onto a perforated tray with a tray underneath and steam at 100°C/210°F until the mussels open. Drain the juices into a container and plunge the mussels into an ice bath. Pick the meat and reserve for later.

Heat the olive oil in a large saucepan over a medium heat, add the garlic and shallots, lightly season, and cook for 1 minute, then add the remaining vegetables and herbs. Stir and cook until soft, without any colour, then pour in the wine and let it reduce until only a few spoonfuls of liquid remain. Add the fish stock and mussel juice and simmer until the liquid has reduced by two thirds, skimming off any impurities as needed. Strain the liquid through a chinois into a container placed over an ice bath.

To clarify the broth, put 72 g of the egg whites and the mussel meat into a blender and blend for 3 minutes, then transfer the mixture to a bowl. Whisk the remaining 150 g of the egg whites to soft peaks, then fold them into the mussel mixture.

Put the reduced mussel stock and egg white mixture in a large saucepan over a medium heat, whisk to combine, then bring to a gentle simmer, whisking occasionally to stop the egg whites from sticking to the bottom of the pan. Simmer for 40 minutes, or until the stock is clear. Siphon off the stock and pass through a muslin cloth into a container. Chill over an ice bath.

FISH STOCK

3 kg white fish bones
5 kg water
500 g white wine
150 g white onions, sliced
150 g fennel, sliced
150 g celery, sliced
150 g leeks, sliced

Rinse the fish bones until the water runs clear, then put them into a large saucepan with the water and wine and bring to the boil. Once it is boiling, remove the pan from the heat, skim off the impurities that rise to the surface and add the vegetables. Allow to cool for 30 minutes. Strain through a chinois, then through muslin cloth.

CHICKEN STOCK

2 kg chicken wings
cold water, to cover
150 g onions, diced
125 g carrots, diced
125 g celery, diced
125 g leeks, diced
2 g garlic clove
8 sprigs thyme
1 bay leaf
2 g black peppercorns

Place the chicken wings in a large pot, cover with cold water and bring to the boil, then remove the chicken wings and rinse under cold running water to remove impurities. Transfer the chicken wings to a large saucepan, place over a high heat, cover with cold water and bring to a simmer, skimming to remove any impurities that rise to the surface. Add the vegetables, garlic, herbs and peppercorns and bring the liquid back up to the boil, then reduce the heat and simmer for 8 hours. Pass the stock through a muslin cloth, then a chinois, into a container. Let it cool over an ice bath.

BEEF STOCK

grapeseed oil, for roasting
2 kg beef bones
2 kg beef chuck, diced
100 g white onions, diced
100 g leeks, diced
100 g carrots, diced
30 g garlic head, cut in half
10 sprigs thyme
1 g bay leaf
1 g black peppercorns
5 kg water
salt, to taste

Preheat the oven to 180°C/350°F (fan). Heat an oven tray with a dash of grapeseed oil. Once it's hot, add the beef bones and roast until golden.

Heat a little oil in a large saucepan over a medium heat, add the diced beef and cook until browned all over. Remove the beef from the pan and drain off the excess fat. Add the vegetables and garlic to the same pan, lightly season, and cook until golden brown, then add the herbs and peppercorns. Return the beef to the pan and add the roasted bones. Using a spatula, scrape the bottom to prevent the beef from sticking. Add the water, bring to the boil, then reduce the heat and simmer gently for 8 hours, skimming off any impurities. Strain the liquid through a fine chinois, then through a muslin cloth into a clean saucepan. Reduce the stock by half. Remove from the heat and allow to cool.

VEAL STOCK

grapeseed oil, for roasting
4 kg veal bones
2 onions, diced
2 leeks, diced
4 celery sticks, diced
2 large carrots, diced
1 garlic head, cut in half
100 g tomato purée (paste)
10 sprigs thyme
2 bay leaves
20 black peppercorns
6 kg water
salt, to taste

Preheat the oven to 180°C/350°F (fan). Heat an oven tray with a dash of grapeseed oil. Once the oil is hot, add the veal bones and roast in the oven until golden brown.

Heat a little oil in a large stock pot over a medium heat and cook all the vegetables and garlic, then lightly season. Once the vegetables are browned, add the tomato purée, herbs and peppercorns. Add the roasted bones to the pot, cover with the water and bring to the boil, skimming off any impurities that rise to the surface. Reduce the heat and simmer for 24 hours. Strain the liquid through a fine chinois, then through a muslin cloth into a clean pan and reduce by half. Remove from the heat and allow to cool over ice.

LAMB STOCK

grapeseed oil, for roasting
2 kg lamb bones
2 kg lamb rump, diced
100 g white onions, diced
100 g leeks, diced
100 g carrots, diced
25 g garlic head, cut in half
2 g thyme
2 g rosemary
1 bay leaf
1 g black peppercorns
4 kg water

Preheat the oven to 180°C/350°F. Heat an oven tray with a dash of grapeseed oil. Once it's hot, add the lamb bones to roast until golden.

Heat a little oil in a large saucepan over a medium heat, add the diced lamb and cook until browned all over. Remove the lamb from the pan and drain off the excess fat. Add the vegetables and garlic to the same pan and cook until browned, then add the herbs and peppercorns. Return the lamb to the pan and add the roasted bones. Using a spatula, scrape the bottom to prevent the meat from sticking. Add the water, bring to the boil, then reduce the heat and simmer gently for 8 hours. Strain the liquid through a fine chinois, then through a muslin cloth into a clean saucepan. Reduce the stock by half. Remove from the heat and allow to cool.

CHICKEN CONSOMMÉ

150 g grapeseed oil
300 g chicken wings, diced
25 g carrots, thinly sliced
16 g onions, thinly sliced
20 g leeks, thinly sliced
10 g celery, thinly sliced
1 garlic clove, thinly sliced
50 g butter
4 sprigs thyme
1 bay leaf
5 g black peppercorns
2 kg Chicken stock (p. 244)
1 whole chicken, quartered

TO CLARIFY
100 g chicken breast
25 g shallots
25 g leek
25 g celery
100 g egg whites
salt, to taste

Heat the oil in a large saucepan over a medium heat, add the chicken wings and cook until golden brown. Drain off any excess fat. Add the vegetables and garlic and cook until lightly brown, then add the butter, herbs and black peppercorns. Add the stock and bring to the boil, then add the pieces of whole chicken. Reduce the heat and simmer for 2 hours, continuously skimming off any impurities that rise to the surface. Pass through a chinois into a clean saucepan and cool to room temperature.

To clarify the broth, first blend the chicken breast, shallots, leeks and celery in a food processor until minced. Add a good pinch of salt. Whisk the egg whites to soft peaks, then add to the chicken mixture. Add the mixture to the stock and whisk well. Bring the stock to a simmer, gently whisking as it heats up to make sure that the egg white mixture does not stick to the bottom of the pan. Once the raft begins to form, stop whisking and leave it to cook, making sure it does not boil.

Make a small hole in the raft and, when the stock is clear, remove the pan from the heat. Using a ladle, carefully pass the consommé through a muslin cloth into a container. Chill over ice and reserve until required.

BEEF SAUCE

100 g beef fat
3 kg beef chuck, diced
700 g shallots, sliced
100 g garlic cloves
100 g butter
1 bay leaf
8 sprigs thyme
10 g black peppercorns
50 g Cabernet Sauvignon vinegar
100 g Cognac
750 g red wine
2 kg Beef stock (p. 244)
2 kg Veal stock (p. 244)
roasted bones (reserved from stocks above)
salt, to taste

Melt the beef fat in a large pot over a medium heat, add the diced beef, season with salt, and cook until browned. Remove the beef from the pan, drain through a sieve, and set aside. Add the shallots and garlic to the pot with the butter, season with salt, and brown, then add the herbs, peppercorns and the beef back to the pot, pour in the vinegar and reduce to a glaze, using a spatula to scrape the bottom to prevent the meat from sticking. Repeat with the Cognac. Add the wine and let it reduce to a thick, syrupy consistency. Add both the stocks and the roasted bones and bring to the boil, then reduce the heat and simmer for 2 hours, continuously skimming off any impurities that rise to the surface. Pass the stock through a fine chinois into a clean saucepan and reduce until it reaches a velvet consistency. Season to taste. Transfer to a container and reserve until required.

MADEIRA DUCK SAUCE

grapeseed oil, for roasting
3 kg duck bones, chopped
100 g butter
200 g shallots, thinly sliced
4 garlic cloves
10 g white peppercorns
750 g Madeira
750 g port
2 kg Veal stock (p. 244)
2 kg Chicken stock (p. 244)
1 g sprig thyme
1 bay leaf
cherry vinegar, to taste
spoonful of Confit shallots (p. 246)
salt, to taste

Preheat the oven to 180°C/350°F (fan). Heat an oven tray with a dash of grapeseed oil. Once it's hot, add the duck bones, season with salt and roast until golden.

Melt the butter in a large saucepan over a medium heat, add the shallots and garlic and cook until browned. Add the roasted bones and peppercorns, then pour in the Madeira and reduce it to a glaze. Add the port and reduce it to a glaze too. Add both stocks and the aromatics and bring to the boil, then reduce the heat and simmer for 2 hours, continuously skimming off any impurities that rise to the surface. Pass the liquid through a fine chinois, then through a muslin cloth into a container. Before serving, season with cherry vinegar and the confit shallots.

MUTTON SAUCE

250 g lamb fat
3 kg mutton trim, diced
250 g butter
200 g carrots, thinly sliced
200 g onions, thinly sliced
200 g celery, thinly sliced
50 g garlic cloves
10 sprigs thyme
50 g sprigs rosemary
4 kg Lamb stock (p. 244)
1 kg Veal stock (p. 244), reduced
1 g white peppercorns
salt, to taste
sherry vinegar, to taste

SAUCE INFUSION
200 g Mutton sauce (above)
8 g mint
2 g rosemary
6 sprigs thyme

Melt the lamb fat in a large saucepan over a medium heat, then add the diced mutton trim and cook until browned all over. Remove the mutton from the pan, drain in a colander and set aside. Add the butter, vegetables and garlic to the pan, season with salt, and cook until browned, then add the herbs and return the mutton to the pan. Using a spatula, scrape the bottom to prevent the trim from sticking. Add both stocks and the peppercorns and bring to the boil, then reduce the heat and simmer for 2 hours, continuously skimming off any impurities that rise to

the surface. Pass the stock through a chinois into a container and season with sherry vinegar.

SAUCE INFUSION
Bring the sauce to the boil in a small saucepan over a medium heat. As soon as it reaches the boil, add the herbs and remove the pan from the heat. Allow to infuse for 20 minutes, then strain through a chinois.

LAMB SAUCE

150 g lamb fat
1.5 kg lamb trim, diced
150 g butter
1 carrot, diced
1 onion, diced
1 celery stick, diced
2 garlic cloves
6 sprigs thyme
35 g sprigs rosemary
10 g coriander seeds
1 g white peppercorns
700 g Lamb stock (p. 244)
200 g Veal stock (p. 244)
sherry vinegar, to taste
salt, to taste

Melt the lamb fat in a large saucepan over a medium heat, add the diced lamb trim and cook until browned all over. Remove the trim from the pan and set aside. Add the butter, vegetables and garlic and cook until browned. Add the aromatics, except the rosemary, and return the lamb trim to the pan. Using a spatula, scrape the bottom to prevent the trim from sticking. Add both the stocks and bring to the boil, then reduce the heat and simmer for 2 hours, continuously skimming off any impurities that rise to the surface. Strain the sauce through a fine chinois into a container and season with salt and sherry vinegar. Add the rosemary sprigs and let it infuse for 10 minutes. Pass through a chinois into a container over ice.

VENISON SAUCE

200 g grapeseed oil, plus extra for roasting
3 kg venison bones
3 kg venison trim
250 g butter
1 white onion, chopped
1 carrot, chopped
2 celery sticks, chopped
100 g garlic cloves
4 sprigs thyme
1 bay leaf
1 x 750-ml bottle port
1 x 750-ml bottle red wine
2 kg Chicken stock (p. 244)
2 kg Veal stock (p. 244)
4 sprigs rosemary
10 juniper berries
60 g Cabernet Sauvignon vinegar
salt, to taste

Preheat the oven to 180°C/350°F (fan). Heat an oven tray with a dash of grapeseed oil. Add the venison bones and cook until golden.

Heat the grapeseed oil in a stock pot over a medium heat. Add the venison trim, lightly season and cook until browned all over. Remove the trim, set aside and remove any excess fat. Add the butter, vegetables and garlic, lightly season and cook until browned, then add the thyme and bay and return the venison trim to the pan. Using a spatula, scrape the bottom to prevent the trim from sticking. Pour in the port and let it reduce completely. Add the wine and again let the liquid reduce to a syrupy consistency. Add both stocks and the roasted bones and bring to the boil, then reduce the heat and simmer for 2 hours, regularly skimming off the impurities that rise to the surface. Pass the stock through a fine chinois then through a muslin cloth into a clean pan and place over a medium heat. Reduce to a velvety consistency, then remove from the heat, add the rosemary and juniper berries and leave to infuse for 5 minutes. Pass through a chinois into a clean bowl over ice. Season with the Cabernet Sauvignon vinegar. Leave to cool.

DUCK STOCK

25 g grapeseed oil, plus extra for roasting
2.5 kg duck bones
25 g butter
125 g carrots, coarsely chopped
125 g onions, coarsely chopped
125 g celery, coarsely chopped
2 garlic cloves
10 sprigs thyme
5 g white peppercorns
3 kg Chicken stock (p. 244)
1 kg Veal stock (p. 244)
salt, to taste

Preheat the oven to 180°C/350°F (fan). Heat an oven tray with a dash of grapeseed oil, add the duck bones and cook until browned all over.

Heat the grapeseed oil in a stock pot over a medium heat, add the butter, vegetables and garlic, lightly season, then cook until browned. Add the thyme and peppercorns and cook for another 2 minutes, then add the roasted bones and both stocks. Bring to the boil, reduce the heat and simmer for 2 hours, continuously skimming off any impurities that rise to the surface. Pass the stock through a fine chinois into a container over ice.

GROUSE SAUCE

grapeseed oil, for roasting
1.5 kg grouse bones and legs, chopped
1.5 kg duck bones, chopped
100 g butter
150 g shallots, thinly sliced
3 garlic cloves
10 g white peppercorns
750 g Madeira
750 g port
2 kg Veal stock (p. 244)
2 kg Chicken stock (p. 244)
4 sprigs thyme
1 bay leaf
salt, to taste

Preheat the oven to 180°C/350°F (fan). Heat an oven tray with a dash of grapeseed oil. Add the grouse bones and legs and duck bones, lightly season and cook until browned all over.

Heat the butter in a large saucepan over a medium heat, add the shallots and garlic, lightly season and cook until browned. Add the roasted bones and peppercorns, then pour in the Madeira and reduce it by three quarters. Add the port and reduce it to about 100 ml. Add both stocks and the aromatics and bring to the boil, then reduce the heat and simmer for 2 hours, continuously skimming off any impurities that rise to the surface. Pass the liquid through a fine chinois, then through a muslin cloth into a container over ice.

BRAISAGE

125 g butter
100 g shallots, thinly sliced
1 garlic clove, sliced
5 sprigs thyme
5 g fennel seeds
5 g coriander seeds
5 g white peppercorns
150 g button mushrooms, thinly sliced
200 g dry white vermouth
500 g Chicken stock (p. 244)

Melt half the butter in a medium saucepan over a medium heat, add the shallots, garlic, thyme and spices and sweat without letting the shallots take on any colour. Once the shallots have softened, add the mushrooms and cook until the water has evaporated, then add the dry white vermouth, chicken stock and the remaining butter. Stir and reduce the liquid by half, then pass it through a fine chinois into a container set over an ice bath.

BUTTERS, PURÉES AND BASICS

BEURRE NOISETTE

250 g unsalted butter, cut into 1-cm (½-inch) dice
salt, to taste

Place a medium saucepan over a high heat, add the diced butter and allow it to brown until there is a nutty aroma (be careful not to let it burn). Quickly remove the pan from the heat. Pass the beurre noisette through a fine chinois, season to taste and reserve.

PARSLEY BUTTER

grapeseed oil, for frying
2 garlic cloves, finely chopped
40 g shallots, finely chopped
60 g button mushrooms, finely chopped
200 g butter, diced, at room temperature
20 g flat-leaf parsley, finely chopped
30 g Dijon mustard

20 g Parma ham, finely chopped
10 g ground almonds
salt and pepper, to taste

Heat the grapeseed oil in a medium saucepan over a medium heat, add the garlic, shallots and button mushrooms and sweat down until completely soft and without colour. Set aside to cool. Once cool, put the garlic, shallot and mushroom mixture into a mixing bowl with all the remaining ingredients and mix well. Season to taste, then chill and reserve.

CONFIT SHALLOTS

250 g grapeseed oil
500 g shallots, brunoised
salt, to taste

Heat a spoonful of the oil in a medium saucepan over low heat, add the shallots and sweat without colour, seasoning with salt. Once they have softened, add the remaining oil to cover. Cover the pan with a cartouche and cook over a low heat for 45 minutes–1 hour, stirring regularly, until the shallots are completely soft. Check the seasoning.

EGG WASH

1 egg
20 g whole milk
10 g water

Combine all the ingredients in a small bowl and whisk.

ONION PURÉE

50 g butter
500 g white onions, sliced
3 sprigs thyme, wrapped in muslin cloth
100 g whole milk
salt, to taste

Melt the butter in a large saucepan over a low heat. Add the onions and thyme, season with salt, and sweat for 30 minutes, stirring frequently to prevent the onions from colouring. Add the milk and cook the onions until completely soft. Once the onions are cooked, remove the thyme, place the onions in a blender and blend on full power until smooth. Season to taste, pass the purée through a chinois into a container and reserve until required.

MUSHROOM PURÉE

grapeseed oil, for frying
120 g shallots, thinly sliced
100 g butter
1.2 kg portobello mushrooms, thinly sliced
350 g shiitake mushrooms, thinly sliced
2 garlic cloves, sliced
4 sprigs thyme, wrapped in muslin cloth
500 g double cream
salt, to taste

Heat the oil in a large saucepan over a medium heat, add the shallots, season with salt and sweat without colour. Add the butter, and when it foams add the portobello and shiitake mushrooms, season, and cook until soft and lightly browned. Add the garlic, thyme and cream and bring to the boil, then reduce the heat and simmer until the mushrooms are tender. Check the seasoning, strain the mushrooms and reserve the liquid. Remove the thyme, place the mushrooms in a blender and blend on full speed, adding as much of the reserved liquid as needed to create a smooth purée. Pass the purée through a chinois into a container and season to taste. Reserve until required.

SMOKED CHESTNUTS

500 g vacuum-packed chestnuts
apple wood chips, for smoking

Place the chestnuts in a perforated tray and spread them out in an even layer. Place the smoking chips in another tray and set them on fire with a blowtorch. Place the perforated tray on top and cover tightly with foil. Let it smoke for 1 hour. Remove from the tray and reserve until required.

LOBSTER BUTTER

grapeseed oil, for frying
500 g lobster shells, crushed
100 g carrots, diced
100 g onions, diced
100 g celery, diced
300 g butter, cut into 2-cm (¾-inch) dice
4 sprigs thyme
2 garlic cloves, sliced
20 g tomato purée (paste)

Heat the oil in a large saucepan over a high heat, add the crushed lobster shells and lightly brown all over, then add the diced vegetables to the pan and cook until light in colour. Add the butter, thyme and garlic and allow the butter to foam and take on a light colour. Add the tomato purée and cook for another 2 minutes, then reduce the heat and simmer for 30 minutes. Remove the pan from the heat and leave to infuse for 1 hour. Pass the lobster butter through a fine chinois lined with a muslin cloth. Discard the shells. Chill and reserve until required.

TOMATO FONDUE

10 large San Marzano tomatoes
50 g grapeseed oil
100 g shallots, brunoised
4 sprigs thyme
2 garlic cloves, crushed and wrapped in muslin cloth
50 g tomato purée (paste)
salt, to taste
caster sugar, to taste
Barolo vinegar, to taste
extra virgin olive oil, to taste

Peel and de-seed the tomatoes and reserve the juice. Finely dice the tomato petals.

Heat the oil in a large saucepan over a medium heat, add the shallots, lightly season with salt, and sweat down without colour. Add the diced tomatoes and

lightly season with salt and sugar, then add the thyme and garlic and cook out any remaining juices from the tomatoes. Add the tomato purée and stir frequently to prevent the tomatoes from colouring. Add the reserved tomato juice, reduce the heat and cover with a cartouche. Cook slowly for about 1 hour, until all the juice has been absorbed and the mixture has a rich, thick consistency. Remove the pan from the heat and finish by seasoning with salt, sugar, vinegar and olive oil to taste.

PICKLES, BRINES, OILS AND GELS

10% HERB BRINE

1.6 kg water
160 g salt
16 g rosemary
10 g thyme
1.6 g bay leaves
10 g garlic cloves
3 g black peppercorns

Combine the water and salt in a large saucepan and bring to the boil. Once all the salt has dissolved, remove the pan from the heat, set aside and cool to 40°C/100°F, then add the herbs and aromatics. When the brine is completely cool, pass it through a chinois and reserve in the fridge until required.

8% HERB BRINE

1 kg water
75 g salt
5 g pink salt
20 g juniper berries
10 g Tasmanian black peppercorns
15 g coriander seeds
10 g sprigs rosemary
20 g sprigs thyme
4 g bay leaves

Combine the water and both salts in a large saucepan and bring to the boil. Once the salt has dissolved, remove the pan from the heat, set aside and cool to 40°C/100°F. Lightly warm the spices in a pan to release their aroma, then add to the water along with the herbs. When the brine is completely cool, pass it through a chinois and reserve in the fridge until required.

15% HERB BRINE

1 kg water
150 g salt
8 g sprigs rosemary
8 g sprigs thyme
1 g bay leaves
8 g garlic cloves
3 g black peppercorns

Combine the water and salt in a large saucepan and bring to the boil. Once all the salt has dissolved,

remove the pan from the heat, set aside and cool to 40°C/100°F, then add the herbs and aromatics. When the brine is completely cool, pass it through a chinois and reserve in the fridge until required.

LOVAGE OIL

500 g picked lovage leaves
300 g grapeseed oil
5 g salt
5 g caster sugar

Wash the lovage leaves, then drain using a salad spinner to remove any excess water. Bring a medium saucepan of water to the boil over a high heat, then blanch the leaves in the boiling water for 10 seconds. Immediately refresh in ice water and squeeze dry. Transfer the blanched leaves to a blender with the oil, salt and sugar and blend for 10 minutes until the mixture resembles a split purée. Pass it through a fine chinois into a bowl set over an ice bath, then pour the oil into a sous vide bag, seal and hang it at an angle in the fridge for 24 hours to allow the water and the oil to separate. Once the water has drained to the bottom corner of the bag, cut a small hole in the bag to allow the water to slowly escape, leaving only the oil. Reserve the oil in the fridge in a squeeze bottle until required.

MINT OIL

250 g picked mint leaves
400 g grapeseed oil
2 g salt
2 g caster sugar

Wash the mint leaves, then drain using a salad spinner to remove any excess water. Bring a medium saucepan of water to the boil over a high heat, then blanch the mint leaves in the boiling water for 20 seconds. Immediately refresh in ice water and squeeze dry. Transfer the blanched leaves to a blender with the oil, salt and sugar and blend for 5 minutes until the mixture resembles a purée. Pass it through a fine chinois into a bowl set over an ice bath, then pour the oil into a sous vide bag, seal and hang it at an angle in the fridge for 24 hours to allow the water and the oil to separate. Once the water has drained to the bottom corner of the bag, cut a small hole in the bag to allow the water to slowly escape, leaving only the oil. Reserve the oil in the fridge in a squeeze bottle until required.

OYSTER LEAF OIL

200 g oyster leaves
50 g borage leaves
200 g grapeseed oil
4 g caster sugar
4 g salt

Place all the ingredients into a blender and blend for 5 minutes until the mix resembles a purée. Pass it through a fine chinois into a bowl set over an ice bath, then pour into a sous vide bag, seal and hang it at an angle in the fridge for 24 hours to allow the water and the oil to separate. Once the water has drained to the bottom corner of the bag, cut a small hole in the bag to allow the water to slowly escape, leaving only the oil. Reserve the oil in the fridge in a squeeze bottle until required.

NECTARINE AND HONEY GEL

270 g verjus
500 g honey
300 g white wine
600 g nectarine flesh
12 g Gellan F

Combine all the ingredients, except the Gellan F, in a temperature-controlled blender and bring the liquid to 90°C/200°F on a medium speed. Once it reaches 90°C/200°F add the Gellan F and blend on medium speed for 2½ minutes, then strain the liquid through a chinois into a container and leave to set in the fridge. Once it's fully set, break up the gel into small pieces, place in a blender and blend until smooth. Pour the mixture into a deep, square container, place in a sous vide machine and compress until it becomes clear. Place in a squeeze bottle in the fridge until required.

PICKLE LIQUOR

500 g water
400 g Chardonnay vinegar
10 g fennel seeds
10 g coriander seeds
4 g black peppercorns
4 medium shallots, sliced
15 g salt
150 g caster sugar

Combine all the ingredients in a saucepan over a medium heat and bring to the boil to dissolve the salt and sugar. Set aside to cool, then pass through a fine chinois and reserve until required.

PICKLED BUDDHA'S HAND

1 Buddha's hand
500 g water
400 g Chardonnay vinegar
10 g salt
150 g caster sugar

Cut the Buddha's hand lengthways into eight pieces and remove the pith. Cut the pieces to slices 2 mm (1/16 inch) thick and place in a container.

Combine the water, vinegar, salt and sugar in a saucepan over a medium heat and bring to the boil. Continue to boil until the salt and sugar have completely dissolved, then pour the pickle liquid over the sliced Buddha's hand and leave to cool. Place in the fridge until required.

BLACK TRUFFLE PUREÉ

250 g black truffle, finely chopped
10 g truffle juice
20 g black truffle oil

balsamic noir vinegar, to taste
Barolo vinegar, to taste
salt, to taste

Place the black truffle and truffle juice in a mortar and crush with a pestle to form a paste, then add the truffle oil in a steady stream while mixing continuously. Season to taste using both the vinegars and salt. Store in a container in the fridge.

PICKLED GINGER

250 g water
250 g Chardonnay vinegar
20 g salt
125 g caster sugar
3 g fennel seeds
3 g white peppercorns
3 g coriander seeds
250 g peeled ginger, brunoised

Combine the water, vinegar, salt and sugar in a saucepan over a medium heat and bring to the boil. Continue to boil until the salt and sugar have completely dissolved. Add the spices and ginger, then remove the pan from the heat. Set aside to cool, then place in the fridge until required.

MAYONNAISE

200 g egg yolks
2 cooked egg yolks (cooked for 12 minutes)
50 g Dijon mustard
20 g white wine vinegar
1 kg grapeseed oil
lemon juice, to taste
salt, to taste

Put both the raw and cooked egg yolks into the bowl of a stand mixer fitted with the whisk attachment. Add the mustard and vinegar and whisk until smooth, then gradually add the oil in a steady stream, whisking continuously, until emulsified. Season to taste with lemon juice and salt.

PICKLE GEL

550 g pickled cucumber brine
5 g salt
12 g Gellan F
90 g cornichons, brunoised

Put the pickled cucumber brine and salt into a temperature-controlled blender and bring the liquid to 90°C/200°F on a medium speed. Once it reaches 90°C/200°F add the Gellan F and blend on medium speed for 2 minutes. After 2 minutes, blend for an additional 30 seconds on full speed. Pour the mixture into a container and chill over an ice bath, then add it back to the blender and blend for 4 minutes. After 4 minutes, stop the blender, lift the lid and scrape down the sides of the jug. Continue to blend for 1 more minute until the mixture is smooth. Transfer the pickle gel to a shallow container, then place in a sous vide machine and set on programme 1. Close the lid. Allow the pickle gel to rise to the top of the container then press 'stop'. Repeat this process twice

more, or until the gel is clear. Pass through a fine chinois and mix in the brunoised cornichons. Place the gel into a piping bag fitted with a 5-mm (¼-inch) nozzle. Place in the fridge until required.

MOUSSE

CHICKEN MOUSSE

1 kg chicken breast
40 g salt
400 g double cream
salt, to taste

Place an empty blender jug into the freezer. Once chilled, place the chicken breast inside and blend on full speed for 30 seconds, then stop, scrape the mixture down from the edges of the jug and blend again for 30 seconds. Repeat this process once more. Scrape down the edges again, add the salt, and blend for another 30 seconds until smooth. Pass the purée through a fine tamis sieve into a bowl set over ice, then beat the purée using a spatula. Gradually add the cream, ensuring it is fully incorporated after each addition before adding more, then season to taste. Reserve in a container in the fridge.

PASTRY

CLEMENTINE PURÉE

800 g clementines
100 g caster sugar
9 g pectin
100 g clementine juice
salt, to taste
icing sugar, to taste

Blanch the whole clementines in a medium saucepan of boiling water three times, refreshing the water each time. Cut the clementines into quarters and transfer them to a blender with the sugar, pectin and clementine juice. Blend on full speed until smooth. Season to taste with salt and icing sugar, then pass the purée through a fine chinois and transfer to a piping bag fitted with a 5-mm (¼-inch) nozzle. Chill and reserve until required.

ELDERFLOWER CORDIAL

1 kg water
750 g caster sugar
20 elderflower heads (washed and green stems removed)
zest of 2 lemons
10 g citric acid

Combine the water and sugar in a medium saucepan and bring to the boil. Put the elderflower heads and lemon zest into a heatproof bowl, then pour over the boiling water and sugar mixture. Leave the elderflower to steep for 12 hours in a cool place.

Strain the liquid through a muslin cloth and discard the elderflower heads and zest. Add the citric acid. Store in the fridge.

GELATINE MASS

100 g water
24 g gelatine powder

Combine the water and gelatine in a bowl, whisk together and reserve in the fridge for 24 hours.

HONEY CRISPS

100 g isomalt
100 g liquid glucose
25 g honey powder
gold powder, for brushing

Combine the isomalt and glucose in a small saucepan over a high heat and heat until it reaches 158°C/316°F. Once it reaches that temperature, pour the mixture onto a silicone mat and allow to cool.

Preheat the oven to 160°C/325°F (no fan). Put the cooled isomalt and glucose mixture into a blender with the honey powder and blend to a fine powder. Place a 5 x 8-cm (2 x 3-inch) rectangle stencil that's 1 mm (scant 1/16 inch) thick onto a silicone mat and dust all the powder over the stencil using a fine chinois. Remove the stencil and place the mat in the oven for 4 minutes, then remove from the oven and allow to rest for 30 seconds. Once rested, peel the sugar away from the mat, then take each side, and pull in opposite directions then back in, to create a ruffled effect. Carefully place the honey crisps on a tray to set. Once set, brush with edible gold powder and reserve in an airtight container.

STOCK SYRUP

225 g caster sugar
25 g liquid glucose
200 g water

Combine all the ingredients in a saucepan over a medium heat and bring to the boil. Stir until the sugar has completely dissolved, then pour into a container and allow to cool.

WOODRUFF OIL

200 g woodruff leaves
300 g grapeseed oil

Wash the woodruff leaves, then drain using a salad spinner to remove any excess water. Heat the oil in a saucepan to 60°C/140°F. Place the leaves in a blender and blend, then slowly add the oil and blend for another 5 minutes. Transfer the liquid to a container and allow to infuse for 24 hours. Strain the oil through a muslin cloth, transfer to a sous vide bag and seal. Hang the bag at an angle in the fridge for 24 hours, to allow the water and the oil to separate. Once the water has drained to the bottom corner of the bag, cut a small hole to allow the water to slowly escape, leaving only the oil. Reserve the oil in the fridge in a squeeze bottle until required.

HAZELNUT PRALINE

350 g hazelnuts, blanched
100 g caster sugar
75 g water
50 g hazelnut oil
salt, to taste

Preheat the oven to 160°C/320°F (no fan). Spread out the hazelnuts evenly on a baking tray and roast in the oven for 15 minutes, tossing them every 5 minutes until golden.

Put the sugar, water and salt (to taste) into a medium saucepan over a high heat and heat until it reaches 155°C/310°F, to create a caramel. Add the toasted hazelnuts, then remove the pan from the heat and transfer the nuts and caramel onto a tray and allow to cool to room temperature. Put the caramelized hazelnuts into a blender with the oil and blend to a smooth paste, then season to taste.

BAKERY

MATURE RYE STARTER

DAY 1
100 g whole rye flour
100 g water, at room temperature

DAY 3 – TO REFRESH
200 g mix from above
100 g whole rye flour
100 g water, at room temperature

DAY 4 – TO REFRESH
200 g mix from above
100 g whole rye flour
100 g water, at room temperature

DAY 1
Combine all the ingredients in a mixing bowl and leave in a warm place to ferment for 48 hours.

DAY 3
Combine all the ingredients in a mixing bowl and leave in a warm place to ferment for 24 hours.

DAY 4
Combine all the ingredients in a mixing bowl, cover with cling film and leave the dough out at room temperature for 1–3 hours.

Place in the fridge for 12 hours.

Eat, sleep and repeat for a few years to give you a mature starter.

MATURE WHITE STARTER

DAY 1
150 g strong white flour
150 g water, at room temperature
15 g honey

DAY 3 – TO REFRESH
150 g mix from above
150 g strong white flour
150 g water, at room temperature

DAY 4 – TO REFRESH
150 g mix from above
150 g strong white flour
150 g water, at room temperature

DAY 5 – TO REFRESH
200 g mix from above
400 g strong white flour
180 g water, at room temperature

DAY 1
Combine all the ingredients in a mixing bowl and leave in a warm place to ferment for 48 hours.

DAY 3
Combine all the ingredients in a mixing bowl and leave in a warm place to ferment for 24 hours.

DAY 4
Combine all the ingredients in a mixing bowl and leave in a warm place to ferment for 24 hours.

DAY 5
Combine all the ingredients in a mixing bowl, cover with cling film and leave the dough out at room temperature for 1–3 hours.

Place in the fridge for 12 hours.

Eat, sleep and repeat for a few years to give you a mature starter.

COMING

FULL

CIRCLE

Undoubtedly, one of the greatest privileges we have had while at Core was catering the wedding reception for Prince Harry and Meghan Markle at Frogmore House in May 2018. We hadn't even been open for a full year, and to be chosen by the Royal couple was an immense honour. As the whole world saw, the day itself was a fairy tale, and we are proud of the part we played in such a momentous bit of British history. For me, however, the day was extra special, as I was able to cook alongside one of my dearest culinary heroes: the great Anton Mosimann.

Mosimann is a legend of classical French gastronomy. Once a Swiss prodigy, and in his time the youngest chef to earn the prestigious Diplôme de Cuisine, Mosimann has been at the top of his game for over fifty years. His restaurant in the Dorchester Hotel, which he took over at the tender age of twenty-eight, was the first hotel restaurant outside of France to earn two Michelin stars. He has cooked for kings, queens, prime ministers and presidents, and catered banquets all over the world.

He is also the author of *Cuisine à la Carte*, the first cookbook I bought, when I was fifteen; I had no clue about fine dining – at that point, as an artistically minded teenager, I just liked the look of his plates. But, as I read the book from cover to cover, over and over again, I fell in love with the gentle intricacy of the food he produced, and the glamorous world he lived in: chefs in tall white hats cooking beautiful food in grand hotel kitchens for the great and good. You didn't find restaurants like his in Bushmills – I was hooked, and from that moment on, I read everything I could about *haute cuisine*.

When we were offered the chance to cater for the Royal Wedding, I was told that I could pick any catering company of my choosing, to build the infrastructure and lay out the field kitchens we needed. Knowing that he had catered for Prince William and Kate, and that I may never get this opportunity again, I chose Mosimann, and as soon as he caught wind of us working together, he instantaneously snapped up a table at Core. When we met to start planning, the day after this dinner, he presented me with a detailed breakdown of everything we had served him: notes, drawings, the lot. He had already started tasking his team with reproducing them on the day.

When I worried that some dishes may be too intricate to replicate for that many people, he was quick to reassure me. 'Don't worry,' he said. 'I've held banquets on the sides of mountains. Right now, I have three whole kitchens sailing back from South Korea. Nothing is impossible if we put enough cooks behind it.'

We arrived at Windsor Castle bright and early on the day itself. The rest of the team were bussed in, but I drove through in a black Range Rover and was waved through by security – I think they mistook me for one of the Royals! Anton's entrance was as extravagant as anything I saw that day. Rolling across the tarmac in a vintage Jaguar E-Type – burgundy, of course. He parked up and stepped out to greet me, immaculately turned out, wearing his trademark bow tie. We were catering a Royal Wedding together, and his team were cooking my food, decades after I'd first tried to cook his. I had to pinch myself.

The service itself ticked along like a dream – Anton really was the consummate professional, moving around the kitchen as nimbly as ever, and his team were capable of anything. They supported us to perform at the very highest level, on the greatest stage we had ever been showcased on. It was a strange experience, in a way. Hundreds of millions of people all over the world watched Prince Harry and Meghan exchange vows, and we were only a few hundred yards away, with no TV, unable to see a second of it. And yet, unique as our experience of the day was, we had an unforgettable time, and it's a memory that we all still hold dear.

When our service was over, and the field kitchens were being packed up again, I went to go and find Anton. For twenty-five years, I had held onto my original copy of *Cuisine à la Carte*, and had brought it to the wedding for him to sign, which he did with delight. That same copy now sits on the shelf at Core, signed and dated by the great Anton Mosimann – a reminder of how far I've come since the moment his book caught my eye. It's always a risk to meet your heroes, but he was every bit the man I hoped he'd be.

INDEX

RECIPE NOTES

All butter is salted unless otherwise specified.

All salt is fine sea salt, unless otherwise specified.

All milk is whole (full-fat), unless otherwise specified.

All eggs are large (US extra large), unless otherwise specified.

Individual vegetables and fruits, such as carrots and apples, are assumed to be medium, unless otherwise specified.

Some of the recipes require advanced techniques, specialist equipment and professional experience to achieve good results.

Exercise a high level of caution when following recipes involving any potentially hazardous activity, including the use of high temperatures, open flames, liquid nitrogen and when deep-frying. In particular, when deep-frying add food carefully to avoid splashing, wear long sleeves and never leave the pan unattended.

Cooking times are for guidance only. If using a fan (convection) oven, follow the manufacturer's instructions concerning the oven temperatures.

Some recipes may include lightly cooked eggs, meat and fish and fermented products. These should be avoided by the elderly, infants, pregnant women, convalescents and anyone with an impaired immune system.

Exercise caution when making fermented products, ensuring all equipment is spotlessly clean, and seek expert advice if in any doubt.

Exercise caution and wear protective clothing when undertaking any butchering work.

All herbs, shoots, flowers, berries, seeds and vegetables should be picked fresh from a clean source. Exercise caution when foraging for ingredients. Any foraged ingredients should only be eaten if an expert has deemed them safe to eat.

When no quantity is specified, for example of oils, salts and herbs used for finishing dishes, quantities are discretionary and flexible.

All spoon measurements are level, unless otherwise stated. 1 teaspoon = 5 ml; 1 tablespoon = 15 ml. Australian standard tablespoons are 20 ml, so Australian readers are advised to use 3 teaspoons in place of 1 tablespoon when measuring small quantities.

Phaidon Press Limited
2 Cooperage Yard
London
E15 2QR

Phaidon Press Inc.
65 Bleecker Street
New York, NY 10012

phaidon.com

First published 2022
© 2022 Phaidon Press Limited

ISBN 978 1 83866 406 0 (trade edition)
ISBN 978 1 83866 523 4 (signed edition)

A CIP catalogue record for this book is available from the British Library and the Library of Congress.

Commissioning Editor: Emilia Terragni
Project Editor: Sophie Hodgkin
Production Controller: Sarah Kramer
Photography: Nathan Snoddon
Artworking: Rita Peres Pereira

The Publisher would like to thank Hilary Bird, Lucy Kingett, Laura Nickoll, Alexia Da Silva and Kate Slate for their contributions to the book.

Printed in China